The Great War
and the Missing Muse

The Great War and the Missing Muse

The Early Writings
of Robert Graves
and Siegfried Sassoon

Patrick J. Quinn

SUP

Selinsgrove: Susquehanna University Press
London and Toronto: Associated University Presses

Associated University Presses
440 Forsgate Drive
Cranbury, NJ 08512

Associated University Presses
25 Sicilian Avenue
London WC1A 2QH, England

Associated University Presses
P.O. Box 338, Port Credit
Mississauga, Ontario
Canada L5G 4L8

The paper used in this publication meets the requirements
of the American National Standard for Permanence of Paper
for Printed Library Materials Z39.48-1984

Library of Congress Cataloging-in-Publication Data

Quinn, Patrick J., 1946–
    The great war and the missing muse: the early writings of Robert Graves and Siegfried Sassoon / Patrick J. Quinn.
        p.   cm.
    Includes bibliographical references and index.
    ISBN 0-945636-49-0 (alk. paper)
    1. English poetry—20th century—History and criticism. 2. World War, 1914–1918—Great Britain—Literature and the war. 3. Graves, Robert, 1895–1985—Criticism and interpretation. 4. Sassoon, Siegfried, 1886–1967—Criticism and interpretation. 5. War poetry, English—History and criticism. I. Title.
    PR605.W65Q56   1994
    821'.91209358—dc20   92-56915
                                                                  CIP

PRINTED IN THE UNITED STATES OF AMERICA

To Richard: who put the idea into my head

To Trajan and Valens: for whom I hope to serve as a good example

And, of course, to Catherine, my wife:

> *Tender as early leaves on fragile boughs,*
> *Slender as Iris,*
> *Taut as supple metal—*
> *How shall you be praised?*

Contents

Preface

With the continuing proliferation of critical studies and biographies about World War I soldier-writers, the appearance of yet another book about war poets requires a statement of purpose in order to set it apart from purely critical works such as D. N. G. Carter's *Robert Graves: The Lasting Achievement* (1989) or largely biographical studies like Barry Webb's *Edmund Blunden* (1991) or R. P. Graves's latest installment of his uncle's life, *Robert Graves: The Years with Laura* (1990). In a sense, this book is a hybrid of both of the categories mentioned: it is neither a detached study of the poetry of Graves or Sassoon, nor is it a comprehensive history of both writers from their origins. But because the book examines both writers' autobiographical works, the details of their lives form a convenient developmental framework within which to scrutinize the transitions in their poetry from prewar jottings through postwar struggles to find their unique poetic voices.

This developmental approach also provides an opportunity to evaluate much of Graves's and Sassoon's poetry that has hitherto been largely ignored by critics who have felt that the decade of the 1920s in both writers' lives offered unfruitful pickings. Not surprisingly, a number of very effective poems do emerge from the pens of both writers, poems that often reflect and elucidate the personal struggles of both men. Graves's poetry of the 1920s, for example, mirrors his particular mode of escape from the reality of the moment: bucolic sentimentalism, dream analysis, or relativistic philosophy. And while Sassoon's range of intellectual diversion after the war was less encompassing than Graves's, his adherence to socialism, attacks on the Establishment, and rejection of twentieth-century values made his escape into a reflective Proustian past inevitable.

A further purpose of this book is to explain why the numerous volumes of poetry both men produced after the war failed to exorcise the memory of the Great War from their minds. Clearly, any study of these

writers must examine the tremendous impact the war had on their personalities and artistic consciousnesses, and to that end, this book does
examine representative war poems and discusses their poetic impulses and
levels of artistic success. Unfortunately, both poets failed to dissociate
themselves and their writings from the war experience for nearly a
decade, and this constant retention of war-related ordeals impeded their
return to normal civilian life (both men suffered from neurasthenic
reactions for years after the war) as well as their ability to discover new
subjects for their poetry. The search for subject matter commensurate to
the experience of the Great War, but not of the Great War, was to
dominate both writers' work through the 1920s. The relative failure of the
poetry of Graves and Sassoon during the period demonstrates how largely
unsuccessful they were in expatiating the war from their writings.

A comparative study of Graves and Sassoon is also important because
both writers in the final years of the 1920s turned to a form of autobiographical prose fiction to purge the war and its aftereffects from their
lives, and then proceeded to turn their backs on the offending world.
Graves wrote *Good-bye To All That* as a parting shot to all those people
who had cluttered up his life with hypocrisy and cant, who had forced
him to be an honorable schoolboy, a loyal Welch Fusilier, and a respectable husband. Under the guidance of his American lover and mentor,
Laura Riding, Graves was to free himself from the "goddawful" English
society and build a new world in Majorca where creativity and goodness
would prevail. In *Memoirs of a Fox-Hunting Man*, Sassoon also rejected
the postwar wasteland, but turned to the past to find solace in the halcyon
days of late Victorian England on the Kentish weald. By lovingly
recreating his childhood in the lightly fictionalized *Memoirs*, Sassoon
found an escape from the present, an escape so effective that it eventually
led to a self-imposed exile into rural Wiltshire where, for twenty years,
he would sift carefully through his own past.

Finally, during the period with which this study is concerned, Robert
Graves and Siegfried Sassoon were closely involved with each other
personally and poetically. Just a cursory glance at the correspondence
between the two in the Berg Collection at the New York Public Library
or the holdings at Southern Illinois University Library confirms the nature
of this friendship. A flow of literary analysis and constructive poetic
criticism (revisions, suggestions, allusions), which suggests a serious and
healthy cross-pollination of ideas about rhyme, meter, and word choice,
is juxtaposed with personal concerns about finances and literary person-

ages or academic careers (both writers returned to university after the war). Even as late as 1927, when both writers were clearly moving apart spiritually and physically, Graves complimented Sassoon by including him in *A Survey of Modernist Poetry*. There Sassoon was cited, along with John Crowe Ransom and e. e. cummings, as an "independent" poet —considerable praise from Graves and Riding, who attacked nearly every other modern poet. In a sense, then, this study is the study of two Englishmen whose initial friendship developed from a chance meeting in the Somme trenches to one of the more important soldier-poet friendships of the 1920s.

Anyone researching material in this area becomes aware of the large number of journal articles and critical books on World War I literature, and the surprising attention paid to Sassoon's *Counter-Attack*. Most critics of Sassoon, especially Arthur Lane in his *Adequate Response,* dismiss him largely as a writer of protest poetry and feel that if the war had not embroiled him, he would have continued to write gentle Georgian bucolics. As a result, Lane ignores virtually all the poems after 1917, and one feels as though Sassoon might somehow have met the same mortal end as Owen. The present study, although it offers some further thoughts on *Counter-Attack,* examines Sassoon's largely ignored postwar poetry, including his poetic experimentation with satiric verse and metaphysical lyrics. Sassoon's "overpoweringly dull" (Bergonzi 1980, 108) poetry of the 1920s has, to date, been examined only in Michael Thorpe's pioneering study, *Siegfried Sassoon* (1966), but that work lacks the advantage of Hart-Davis's recently published three volumes of Sassoon's diaries. Furthermore, Thorpe labored under the constrictions of not wishing to expose Sassoon's homosexuality in any of his poetic analyses.

Outside the strict genre of Great War literature, the only articles of critical importance about Sassoon are Joseph Cohen's "Three Roles of Siegfried Sassoon" (1957), which gives a generalized overview of his poetic development; L. Hugh Moore, Jr.'s "Siegfried Sassoon and Georgian Realism" (1969), which examines the prewar writings; and two articles on the Sherston trilogy by John Hildebidle and Thomas Mallon in *Modernism Reconsidered* (1983). The articles of Hildebidle and Mallon give careful scrutiny to the structure of Sassoon's *Memoirs* and autobiographical works; the critics offer insights into the poet's motivations for arrangement and choice of material, but neither article discusses the poetry of the period. A final book on Sassoon that should be mentioned is Felicitas Corrigan's selected letters and biographical study of Sassoon entitled *Siegfried Sassoon: Poet's Pilgrimage* (1967), a study of the inherently spiritual element in his poetry. Unfortunately, this study, with its Catholic bias, is very one-dimensional and narrow in its interpretations.

The publication since 1981 of the three segments of Sassoon's *Diaries*, covering the years from November 1915 to December 1925 (except for the omission of 1919, as yet unexplained), has contributed significantly to an explanation of the motivations and philosophy behind many of Sassoon's poems and autobiographical fiction. Unfortunately, Hart-Davis's scrupulous editing and Sassoon's deliberate omission of embarrassing incidents make supplementary biographical searching necessary. Paul O'Prey's *In Broken Images* contains nearly fifty letters, mostly from the Berg Collection (housed in the New York Public Library), that passed between Sassoon and Graves during their friendship from 1917 to 1933. The extensive holdings of unpublished Sassoon letters at the University of Texas's Humanities Research Center, especially those to Edmund Blunden, Lady Ottoline Morrell, H. M. Tomlinson, Henry Head, and Sydney Cockerell, have proved invaluable for biographical information, details of travel, and sources of poems. Furthermore, the large number of unpublished letters from Sassoon to Graves held in the rare book collection at the library of Southern Illinois fill in many of the gaps in the relationship between Graves and Sassoon that the published letters and diaries overlook. The frank comments on each other's poetic development suggest that each was aware of the strengths and shortcomings of the other's works, and that each took criticism from the other very seriously.

Graves's war poetry has been largely ignored or lightly passed over by critics. In fact, the poet himself deleted much of it from his later editions of collected poems. Except for Myron Simon's helpful article "The Georgian Infancy of Robert Graves" (1974), most critics have been content to select for analysis a few war poems and move on to his autobiography, *Good-bye To All That,* by which his reputation as a war poet is largely kept alive. The two major critical studies of Graves's poetry, Douglas Day's *Swifter Than Reason* (1963) and Michael Kirkham's *Poetry of Robert Graves* (1969), both have chapters on Graves's early poetry, but both were written before the appearance of the three major biographical studies of Graves: Martin Seymour-Smith's *Robert Graves: His Life and Works* (1982), and *The Assault Heroic* (1986) and *The Years with Laura* (1990) by Richard Perceval Graves, Graves's nephew. *The Assault Heroic* covers the first thirty-one years of Graves's life and is particularly illuminating on Graves's struggle during and after the Great War. Moreover, Day and Kirkham did not have access to O'Prey's two volumes of Graves's letters, which would have answered several of their queries concerning sequencing and sources of his poetry. Both writers relied very heavily on textual analysis, while trusting to the verisimilitude of *Good-bye* for the occasionally biographical confirmation of a detail; and while much of their criticism is exceedingly perceptive, their analyses of many of the immediate postwar volumes require updating and reevaluation. D. N. G. Carter's *Robert Graves: The Lasting Poetic Achievement* (1989) has made insightful contributions to the Graves critical canon, but its thematic approach offers little help in following Graves's development through the immediate postwar period.

The Humanities Research Center at the University of Texas holds a large number of Graves's letters which were also used in researching this book to supplement the already extensive biographical material available. Letters from Graves to H. E. Palmer, a fellow poet and teacher, and L. A. G. Strong, a critic and part of the Oxford literary circle of the twenties, are invaluable for their insight into Graves's method of poetic criticism and for personal information. The Southern Illinois University Library, as mentioned above, has a large number of letters to Graves which prove interesting reading, especially the 119 letters from Sassoon.

Most of the academic criticism of Graves is reviewed in James S. Mehoke's study of Graves entitled *Robert Graves: Peace Weaver* (1975). Amid a rather curious study of the White Goddess, Mehoke examines the critical reputation of Graves since World War II in his chapter "The Goddess and Her Critics" (1975, 13–35), beginning with Stephen Spender's article on Graves for *Horizon* in 1946. Nearly all the articles discussed overlook the early poetry but concentrate heavily on Graves's White Goddess and his evolving love poetry. The war poetry and the long, agonizing road to *Good-bye* have largely been forgotten in a period that saw in Graves only a mythic interpreter of the White Goddess's demands.

In summation, this book intends to survey the formative years of both writers to 1929 using a combined biographical and developmental approach to their lives and works. Its primary design is to examine the artistic styles that each of these largely dissimilar and strongly individualistic men explored in their attempts to assimilate the war and its psychological repercussions. The directions of their art and their lives were dictated by the Great War and its aftermath; however, it was not until

Graves and Sassoon were able to free themselves from the war's domination and to turn from poetry to autobiographical prose that they were able to move on to the next phases of their adulthood.

The transition from poetry to prose was neither smooth nor critically successful for Graves or Sassoon and the consensus of literary opinion regarding the quality of their postwar poetry is generally unfavorable. In many cases, however, this estimation deserves reconsideration. A further purpose of this book, then, is to demonstrate that a number of their poems have languished in dusty volumes too long. Admittedly, many of the poems examined here remain generally unread because they are experimental failures and reflect an uncertainty and lack of confidence—both men admit to this in their letters and memoirs. Moreover, because both writers failed to assimilate the stylistic and poetic techniques of the Modernist movement, their verse seems strangely hollow and insipid against the high Modernist mode of, say, Pound's "Hugh Selwyn Mauberley" or Marianne Moore's poems of the early twenties. Nevertheless, as far as the evolution of each as a writer is concerned, a study of the early poems is necessary to understand the various social, intellectual, and artistic factors that were eventually to lead to the decision to write prose memoirs. The success of his prose memoirs contributed greatly to each writer's self-esteem and literary prominence at a time when his reputation was in critical eclipse.

The success of their prose memoirs freed Graves and Sassoon to embark upon further literary explorations, but the writings of their respective "autobiographies" also forced them to reassess the course of their friendship from the perspective of ten years, with the result that both men realized how their lives had diverged and their priorities and artistic values had changed. Inevitably, neither man's autobiography was well-regarded by the other, and a rift ensued that effectively severed the two former Royal Welch Fusiliers. In part, this study chronicles the separate paths the two soldier-poets marched down after the war.

Acknowledgments

Permission to quote from Robert Graves's *Over the Brazier, Fairies and Fusiliers, The Treasure Box, Country Sentiment, The Pier Glass, On English Poetry, Whipperginny, The Feather Bed, Mock Beggar Hall, Welchman's Hose, Poems 1914–1926: The Collected Poems of Robert Graves,* and *Good-bye To All That* has been granted by A. P. Watt Ltd. on behalf of The Trustees of the Robert Graves Copyright Trust.

Permission to quote from *In Broken Images: Selected Letters of Robert Graves 1914–1946,* edited by Paul O'Prey, has been granted by A. P. Watt Ltd. on behalf of Paul O'Prey and The Trustees of the Robert Graves Copyright Trust.

Permission to quote from the works of Siegfried Sassoon has been granted by permission of George Sassoon.

Permission to use the photograph of Robert Graves by William Graves.

Permission to quote from Michael Thorpe's *Siegfried Sassoon: A Critical Study* has been granted by Universitaire Pers Leiden.

Permission to quote from Michael Kirkham's *The Poetry of Robert Graves* has been granted by the author.

Siegfried Sassoon's letters to Robert Graves are from The Robert Graves Papers, Special Collections, Morris Library, Southern Illinois University, and are reprinted by permission.

Permission to quote from a letter from Dame Edith Sitwell to Siegfried Sassoon has been granted by The Washington State University Library.

Permission to quote from Richard Perceval Graves's *Robert Graves: The Assault Heroic 1895–1926* has been granted by the publisher, Weidenfeld and Nicholson.

Robert Graves's letter to Gertrude Stein is from the Yale Collection of American Literature, Beinecke Rare Book and Manuscript Library, Yale University, and is reprinted by permission.

The Great War
and the Missing Muse

Introduction

In late July of the famous cloudless, hot summer of 1914, the nineteen-year-old Carthusian poet had finished his last quarter. As he made his way despondently toward London, the depressing thought of another three years of academic work at Oxford may have diverted his attention from the excitement that was mounting around him. When, however, a few days later news reached him that Austria and Serbia were at war and Russia was mobilizing, Robert Graves turned his back temporarily on the world of academia and set off to northern Wales to be with his family and to enlist in the infantry. His decision was based on two important considerations: that joining the army would postpone the prospect of Oxford for at least a year and, no less important, that enlisting was the patriotic thing to do. So by the morning of 12 August, the teenaged aspiring poet was on the road to Wrexham to join the Royal Welch Fusiliers at their regimental depot; he was in good spirits and waved to his family as long as possible as the train pulled away (Graves 1986, 111).

In late July of 1914, Siegfried Sassoon was playing cricket in a quiet rural village in Kent. During the match, several members of both teams quietly disappeared as they received notification of their recall to their military stations. As the twenty-eight-year-old poet stood in the slips, his mind must have been running over the purposelessness of his wanderings between Kent and London over the past year while he tried desperately to adopt "a steady professional attitude to the problem of poetic production" (*Weald*, 267). In fact, Sassoon was beginning to realize that while his entire twenty-eight years had been lived in comparative luxury and in near idyllic circumstances, he had little to show for his efforts other than some privately published verse and a couple of poems in magazines. The ominous prospect of war that was prophesied in the editorials of the *Times* struck a chord of conscience and gave a sense of purpose to the romantically inclined fox-hunter; the day after the cricket match, he bicycled over to Rye and enlisted in the yeomanry, where his skills as a horseman could be put to use. For Sassoon, just as for Graves, the prospect of military life would provide a respite from responsibility. In Sassoon's case it was the responsibility of having to choose between the leisured life of a fox-hunting man or the intellectually stimulating life of a man of letters.

Both men joined the Royal Welch Fusiliers (Sassoon decided to take a commission in the infantry after a riding injury), but over a year passed before they were to encounter one another. Both writers left a record of their first meeting near Béthune on 28 November 1915. In *Good-bye To All That,* Graves describes spotting a copy of the *Essays of Lionel Johnson* lying on the table during a visit to fellow officers in their dugouts. After glancing surreptitiously at the owner's name on the flyleaf, Graves sought out and then engaged in conversation Siegfried Sassoon, and he and his new companion wandered off into the town discussing poetry (a discussion that continued throughout the night). Graves was no doubt full of enthusiasm about his first book of poetry, *Over the Brazier,* which was about to be published, and showed several drafts of it to the newly arrived officer. The sensitive Sassoon found the poems too realistic and produced for Graves a copy of his idealized war poem "To Victory." The seasoned trench warrior rightly predicted that once Sassoon had seen the horrors of modern warfare, his poetic style would soon change (*Good-bye,* 224).

Sassoon's diary entry for 28 November is much less enthusiastic about a potential friendship with Graves. He describes Graves simply as "a young poet, captain in the Third Battalion and very much disliked. An interesting creature, overstrung and self-conscious, a defier of convention" (*Diaries 1915–1918,* 21). Later, in *Memoirs of an Infantry Officer,* Sassoon would admit to having been close friends with a "big and impulsive man," David Cromlech (Graves's fictional alter ego), when they met again just before the attack on Mametz Wood. Sassoon acknowledges having hitherto left him out of his story, but the description of their low-voiced colloquies as they spoke of all their joint aspirations for peacetime amid the gloom of sleeping soldiers and "pyramids of piled rifles" captures the essential nature of their wartime friendship: keeping each other's spirits high with talks of what great poetry they would write after the war.

For both poets, the war would prove to have profound effects on their lives and on the direction of their poetry. The well-documented psychological patterns of the Great War—the depression caused by the failure to achieve easy victory, followed by the frustrating and hazardous nature of trench warfare and the sense of hopelessness while waiting to be the next casualty (all for a few yards of worthless soil)—particularly touched both of these sensitive men. When the hopes of the Battle of the Somme had been significantly dashed, both poets largely rejected their Georgian poetic roots and attempted to write poetry about the war which showed its unseemly side as well as an awareness of the unrealistic attitude of the civilian population. Writing and editing their poetry together while recuperating in Harlech in northern Wales at Graves's family cottage—an exercise that would eventually spawn Sassoon's *Old Huntsman* and Graves's *Goliath and David*—the two writers began a tradition of mutual criticism that lasted for over ten years.

Both men's reputation as poets were enhanced by their connection with Edward Marsh's *Georgian Poetry (1916–1917)* and their own volumes of poetry, but without doubt the higher quality and greater impact belonged to Sassoon's works. Both poets had followed very closely the Georgian insistence on realistic detail and colloquial language in their writings, but Sassoon's terse, vituperative attacks on those institutions that wished to continue the agonies of war for financial gain or on individuals who wished to continue it for personal glory were full of an intense fervor that is absent from Graves's wartime verse. Sassoon had a knack for transforming the negative emotions of horror and disgust into accusatory verse. It gave his poetry not only a didactic flavor, but also an unmistakable taste of irony that was meant to shock his complacent, respectable readers into awareness of the actualities of the front. Before the war was over, Sassoon had engaged himself in a crusade against the military censors, jingoist press, civilian "patriotic" poets, and war profiteers; he relentlessly hammered at his English reading public with such direct and vivid poetic detail that his view of the war's futility came to be accepted by a large part of the English literary establishment.

Part of the cost of this protest was the averted court-martial incident which sealed the friendship of the two soldier-poets. In June of 1917, Sassoon was convalescing when he came under the influence of a pacifist group led by Bertrand Russell and Philip Morrell (the Liberal politician and husband of Ottoline). The group convinced Sassoon to write a letter protesting the conditions and continuance of the war to various journalists and politicians. When no response was forthcoming, Sassoon decided to overstay his leave and wrote to his company commander that "he [Sassoon] refused to perform any further military duties" (*Diaries 1915–1918*, 177). Sassoon also sent a copy of this pronouncement to Graves, who was himself recuperating in the Isle of Wight. Somehow, Graves mustered all his physical and mental resilience to pass the examination by a medical board. He made his way to Litherland Camp, where he found Sassoon refusing to come before the medical board and preparing for a long stay in prison. Although he was unable to argue Sassoon out of his proposed martyrdom, Graves convinced him that the military authorities planned to lock him in a lunatic asylum instead of granting him the privilege of a court-martial. Reluctantly, Sassoon agreed to attend the hearing by the medical board, at which Graves testified in support of the idea that his fellow officer had suffered a nervous breakdown.

The authorities duly sent Sassoon to Craiglockhart Hospital for treatment of his neurasthenia, while the exhausted Graves, "having got himself declared fit when he wasn't in order to extricate Sassoon from his own quixotism and the clutches of pacifists . . . had to take the consequences: dull duties at the repulsive, dirty . . . Litherland. . . . He should have been in Craiglockhart himself" (Seymour-Smith 1982, 59). Clearly, Graves had taken what he considered the proper course of action for his friend; and despite the hardships he had to endure to save Sassoon from certain court-martial and imprisonment, no evidence exists to suggest that he ever had doubts about supporting Sassoon.

Although he agreed with Sassoon's stance on the futility of war, Graves, unlike his fellow poet, seldom faced up to the ugliness of battle; instead, his artistic reaction was reminiscent of that of a child who is forced to study the conditions of his disordered room: he looks but he does not want "to see." Furthermore, there was a certain ambiguity about Graves's attitude toward warfare in that he never relinquished his pride in his regiment or let his romantic notion of soldiering wane. Despite the continuing specter of dissolution and waste, Graves tended to retreat into vague daydreams and a romantic whimsy. This is reflected throughout his war volumes in his reliance on traditional verse forms and eccentric rhyme patterns such as Skeltonics. The result of such divergent forces in Graves's war poetry was that critics, for the most part, acclaimed his work as buoyant and full of gallantry; but beside the profound sentiments of Wilfred Owen and the bitter polemics of Sassoon, his work appeared ineffectual and shallow.

With the onset of peace, both writers hoped to continue their friendship (despite Graves's rather sudden marriage to Nancy Nicholson and Sassoon's pique upon hearing the news of this union), and to improve their poetry through a symbiotic interchange of ideas. As might be expected, their ten years of intimate friendship were to see the development of widely divergent patterns of interest and behavior, but a number of curious parallels in their lives and works make a comparative study valuable. Both writers survived the Great War bodily intact, but suffered severely from a variety of nervous disorders that were conveniently diagnosed as neurasthenia. As a result of this disability, the adjustment to noncombatant status and civilian life was extremely difficult for both writers; writing poetry became a form of mental therapy to expiate the haunting memories of the front and the nagging guilt at having survived. Graves attempted to blot out the war by marrying and having a family as quickly as possible. His immediate postwar verses were largely escapist nursery rhymes and impressions of the peaceful country life around Oxford into which he had settled. Similarly, Sassoon attempted to find solace in his prewar contemplation of nature and to sublimate his homosexual leanings into slightly veiled love poetry. His frenetic desire to participate in London literary and intellectual life after the war was largely an attempt to disengage himself from dwelling on the events of the war.

Nevertheless, both men's attempts to forget the horrors of the war did not extend to obliterating the war itself from their minds. They realized that the sacrifices of their comrades required some tangible results, and for a brief period both Graves and Sassoon flirted with socialism in hopes that it would assist the working man to achieve a greater share of the national wealth. But the strain of postwar adjustment and of coping with several mental disabilities led Graves into a protracted study of psychology and dream analysis through which he tried, unsuccessfully, to sublimate his neuroses into poetry. Sassoon, trusting more in the medical assistance of the psychologist W. H. R. Rivers, was seemingly freed from his neurasthenia much earlier than Graves, but finding the emerging new world full of as much cant and hypocrisy as the world of the war years had been, he attempted to expose the pretentious postwar society's shortcomings with his satiric verse.

Much of Graves's poetry during the mid-twenties is a search for some belief or pattern of behavior that could unify his need for psychological wholeness and clarity of purpose. His ill-fated attempt to embrace the relativistic philosophy of Basanta Mallik and the intellectual skepticism that is apparent in *Mock Beggar Hall* demonstrate clearly that Graves's poetic impulse and his private life were as unproductive as Sassoon's. By 1925, with the publication of his *Satirical Poems*, Sassoon's inspiration had virtually dried up, and in fact he doubted whether he had the capability to write poetry at all. His desultory social life among his sporting companions was as unrewarding as his sophisticated life-style in the fashionable London circles; even Graves had begun to doubt Sassoon's poetic abilities.

It might be too convenient to say that 1926 was a watershed year for both Graves and Sassoon, but this certainly was the year in which both their works and lives began to coalesce into what was to become a recognizable pattern. This was the year that Graves met Laura Riding, who became the prototype of his muse figure, the White Goddess; and this was the year that Sassoon began the poetic inward voyage of self-examination of his past with his writing of *The Heart's Journey*, out of which came six prose works over the next twenty years. When Laura Riding appeared, Graves found the necessary catalyst to motivate him into escaping conventional bonds of subservience to a society and culture that had kept him in an unfulfilled marriage, made him fight a useless war, and forced him to endure with false equanimity the hypocrisy of the modern world. Similarly, with *The Heart's Journey*, Sassoon was able to recognize that the modern wasteland was only one dimension of existence; his discovery of the spiritual nature of life that resided just beyond mundane actuality filled him with a new confidence, which allowed him to investigate his own essential self through a scrupulous study of his development both as a poet and a human being.

The first fruit of this inward search for understanding was *Memoirs of a Fox-Hunting Man* (1928) in which, giving a simplified version of himself in a lightly fictionalized autobiography, Sassoon lavishly captured an idyllic late Victorian childhood in which continuity and sense of purpose were the operative values. But if the past was romanticized and praised by Sassoon in his inward search for the springboards of soul-making, Graves, like a Welsh bull in a china shop (the phrase is Blunden's), demolished any inclination of romanticizing the past in *Good-bye To All That* (1929). In his stagy prose autobiography, Graves lashed out at the outmoded values of his fellow Englishmen and announced that through the tutelage of his new mistress, he had been reborn: that together they would create a better world based not on the past, but on Riding's unique conception of the future. With that, Graves left his wife, his family, and friends and escaped to Majorca to a self-imposed exile with Laura Riding in order to start afresh. At about the same time, Sassoon and his artist lover, Stephen Tennant, left to spend time in Italy. Sassoon eventually returned to the quiet obscurity of Wiltshire, where he completed the Sherston trilogy, the first of two exploratory journeys into his self-development.

The publication of *Good-bye To All That* in November 1929 rent asunder what had already become a very unsteady friendship between Graves and Sassoon. Neither writer could fully grasp what the other writer was trying to achieve in his fictional autobiography. Graves saw *Memoirs of a Fox-Hunting Man* as a literary back number and justifiably criticized the book as a memorial to an idealized past by a man who was steadily becoming reclusive, who was retreating from the realities of the present world. For its part, *Good-bye* was written by a man clearly in confrontation with present conditions, and who blamed most of their "goddawfulness" on the dependence on past solutions. There is neither languid romanticizing nor lavish details of a prewar spring day in Graves's work; he is more interested in lashing out at the sham that continued to color English life after the war. He felt that if the feelings of individuals were trodden upon in the process, then they had to accept their requital in the cause of truth. And this rather overcandid attitude helped to bring about the end of the two poets' relationship.

Sassoon had been in Germany for most of the summer and early autumn of 1929 with his ailing lover Stephen Tennant. There he had been receiving continued reports about his mother's weakened state. When he returned to England, Edmund Blunden gave him an advance copy of *Good-bye* to read. According to Seymour-Smith, Blunden was—for some reason (envy is the motivation suggested on page 197)—primarily responsible for working Sassoon up to a frenzy about the inaccuracies and personal liberties taken by Graves in the book. Whatever the cause, the ploy worked exceedingly well. Sassoon burst into the offices of Jonathan Cape, Graves's publisher, and threatened to take "drastic legal action" unless Cape agreed to cancel certain pages. Cape concluded his resultant letter to Graves with the following explanation:

> I have only consented to do this because of the conviction that Sassoon was so wrought up about the whole thing I felt that he would not hesitate to take drastic steps and it was quite necessary to pacify him. I must look to you to endorse what I have done as being the only and best course. (Seymour-Smith 1982, 196)

Sassoon's main objections to the autobiography concerned a section relating to Graves's visit "to the house of a fellow officer [Sassoon] in Kent whose Mother having read Lodge's *Raymond* was endeavouring to communicate with her other son who had been killed" (Seymour-Smith 1982, 195). Not only was Sassoon upset at what his ailing mother might feel if she saw herself portrayed as foolish in Graves's book, but he was also worried about her reaction when she read his faithfully recorded remarks to Graves "that he thought his mother's behaviour pathetic, the dead boy, Siegfried's younger brother, not having been the person she thought he was, and that he feared for her sanity" (O'Prey 1982, 197). Sassoon voiced his own concern in a terse letter to Ottoline Morrell during the same week; there he admits that he had been horribly upset by Graves's book and comments that it contained things "which can't easily be forgiven" (Sassoon to Morrell, 12 November 1929).

Sassoon also felt that Graves had betrayed a trust by publishing without his permission a verse letter that he had written to Graves during his convalescence at Lancaster Gate Hospital in July of 1918. It was entitled "I'd Timed My Death in Action to the Minute." Sassoon had never published the poem because he was "shamed by its emotional exhibitionism" and had tried several times previously—unsuccessfully—to persuade Graves to give it back (O'Prey 1982, 206–7).

Cape eventually published *Good-bye* with the appropriate blanks and asterisks, but Sassoon continued to feel rancor even when he returned to Italy. He claimed that Graves's book attempted to finish off what remained of the friendship (Sassoon to H. F. Palmer, 10 December 1929). In fact, Sassoon was so upset by Graves's autobiography that it took him three months to find the equanimity to write to Graves about his feelings. The letters between the two men are enlightening for their bluntness and their common aim to wound each other (see O'Prey 1982, 197–209); but once the passion had been spent, the written content fringed on the trivial. Still, both men were much alive in each other's imagination in early 1930. Graves was drawing on his knowledge of Sassoon in his character-ization of David Casselis in *But It Still Goes On,* while Sassoon used Graves for his portrait of David Cromlech in *Memoirs of an Infantry Officer.*

The final spate of letters between the two appeared in May of 1933 when Graves rather presumptuously wrote to Sassoon to ask for £1000 to pay the builders of his and Riding's new house in Majorca. Predict-ably, the cautious Sassoon held back before sending Graves the money. At this point he was considering settling into a large country house in Wiltshire and contemplating marriage with Hester Gatty, so the outlay of his money required some hope of return. When Sassoon hesitated in sending the money, Graves saw this as an opportunity to renew his criticism of Sassoon's poetic "monument of his emotional shortcomings," *The Heart's Journey*. Sassoon countered this attack by claiming that Graves's recent poetry was deliberately incomprehensible (O'Prey 1982, 219–32).

Graves retorted that Sassoon's portrait of him as David Cromlech in *Infantry Officer* was abrasive and untidy. This portrait must indeed have been influenced to some extent by Sassoon's resentment of his fellow writer, but he wrote to Ottoline Morrell that although he was exasperated with Graves while writing the later part of the book, he tried with difficulty to concentrate on his memories of Graves prior to 1919 and to dismiss everything he had learned about him since then. Consequently, he felt that his treatment of Graves in the book was a fair one (Sassoon to Morrell, 2 April 1930). Graves, on the other hand, concurred with T. E. Lawrence that while "Siegfried Sassoon was the obvious hero of *Good-bye* . . . Cromlech had his face rubbed unnecessarily hard in the dirt" (O'Prey 1982, 225). In reality, the portrayal of Cromlech lies somewhere in between the two extremes; while Cromlech is portrayed as untidy, self-centered, and priggish, this is balanced, as Fussell points out, by his "intelligence and originality" (1975, 97). True, there is a rancorous delight in Sassoon's negative portrait of him, but instead of taking offence at superficial flaws in his fictional self, Graves should have complained that his potentially complex character was reduced to a stereotype. In any case, such contentiousness only furthered the rift between the two men.

Eventually, Graves found the money to complete his house without Sassoon's help (but not without a few barbed attacks on Sassoon's "lace-Valentine vulgarity" in *The Heart's Journey*). He became absorbed in his development of the Seizen Press and in his devotion to Laura Riding. Sassoon married Hester Gatty in December of 1933 and moved to Heytesbury the following month. The contact between both writers was then severed for twenty-seven years.

A reconciliation between Graves and Sassoon did not take place until October 1954, when the two men met accidentally while strolling beside King's College Chapel, Cambridge. Graves was in Cambridge to deliver a series of Clark Lectures on poetry, which Sassoon felt motivated enough to emerge from his reclusive sanctuary to attend. (This accidental reconciliation is somewhat defused by the recollection of Mr. R. O. Barber, assistant master of New House at Oundle School. He confirms that Sassoon and Graves met in the headmaster of New House's study after dropping their sons, George and William, off on the first day of the new term on 22 September 1954. I suspect it was here that Graves invited Sassoon to attend his Clark Lectures on poetry.) And while O'Prey assures us that by this time the two writers were personally reconciled and that their misunderstandings had melted away (1984, 233), the critical judgments of both remained as polarized as in the 1920s. In a letter to Edith Sitwell dated 10 January 1955, written after he had heard several of Graves's lectures, Sassoon said that their content was "interesting" but that he was troubled by Graves's disrespect for Wordsworth and Tennyson. He went on in a humorous, understated manner to say that Graves referred to "peculiar stuff" about Irish bards, and meters being derived from blacksmith's hammerings and people's rowing.

Shortly after the lectures, Sassoon sent Graves a copy of his latest book of poems, *The Tasking* (1954). Not surprisingly, Graves found it rather difficult. Graves's lack of sympathy with this type of inward-looking, soul-searching poetry had not changed, and, as Sassoon lamented in a letter to Blunden (16 February 1955), Graves managed to find only one readable poem in the whole book. Graves's criticism of "The Visitant," which he liked and paradoxically described as having "a certain controlled wildness," was dismissed by Sassoon as superficial and too scientific. Sassoon's feeling that Graves undervalued him as a serious poet is confirmed by Graves's rather caustic thumbnail sketch, written to the English poet and critic Derek Savage not long after this last meeting.

> Siegfried: yes too much money. But he didn't settle as a landed proprietor for some time after the War—lived in a Westminster flat and played piano, also godfather to destitute young actors. He was never really a rebel against society, only against British military stupidity . . . joined *The Daily Herald* merely because the Socialists had been anti-War; and for no other reason. . . . I met him the other day, and he was very glad to greet me; but he slipped away into furtive retreat. Besides his homosexual soul-scar, he has an Enoch Arden complex—or so he once told me—and a lot of self-protective dishonesty. (O'Prey 1984, 154)

These letters confirm that the two friends had gone in completely different directions in the interim and that little remained of what was once a vital and symbiotic relationship. Perhaps it is best to envision the two old soldiers meeting accidentally in the shadow of the imposing facade of King's College Chapel and reminiscing about the days when they were in Harlech recuperating from wounds and dreaming about

. . . doing wild, tremendous things
In free adventure, quest and fight
And God! what poetry we'll write!

"Letter to S. S."

1

Graves's War Poetry: *Over the Brazier,*
Goliath and David, and *Fairies and Fusiliers*

The sparse output of Graves's war poetry might appear puzzling at first glance, for here was a writer who had enlisted a few days after war with Germany was declared and who was not demobilized until three months after the armistice. Graves served gallantly as an infantry officer at the infamous Battle of Loos and at the Somme. A report circulated of his death at the Battle of the Somme; he was, in fact, not dead but severely wounded. This led to his being sent home for rehabilitation to the comparative luxury of England and Wales, where he was faced with a civilian population whose feelings about the war were both naïve and jingoistic. Graves could not fail to observe the disparity between the two predominant groups: the civilians with their "business as usual" and *pro patria mori* smugness, and the soldiers whose grim determination was solely to do their duty by their comrades. A victim of his loyalty to his fellow soldiers, Graves anxiously returned to the battlefront, but a bronchitis attack in February of 1917 took him back to the comparative safety of England for the duration of the war. While recovering at Oxford, Graves began to write poems that attempted to examine his experiences honestly and accurately. He avoided the sharply sardonic tones of his friend Sassoon, but no longer was he to mouth the empty platitudes and idealistic visions of his earlier war poetry. Graves was determined to make the best of the "damned days and nights" when he was forced to lie in the mud of Flanders and surrender his pride and natural inclinations to the machinery of war. Now, he hoped to alchemize this raw material into "lumps of gold" ("Assault Heroic").

Over the Brazier, published on 1 May 1916, was Graves's first attempt to synthesize his war experiences into these golden "lumps." And while it is true, as Douglas Day points out, that eleven of the poems from the collection were written while Graves was still a student at Charter-house (Day 1963, 4), close examination demonstrates that some of the poems, such as "Free Verse," "Oh, and Oh!" and "In the Wilderness," were written while Graves was in Wrexham and Lancaster for basic training during the early months of the war. In fact, only half of the twenty-six poems in the collection were actually written after the experiences of trench warfare on the western front.

The collection is passed over very abruptly by most students of war literature primarily because of the facile quaintness and mawkish Georgianism that celebrate the virtues of the English countryside and sing praises of rural values. "Jolly Yellow Moon" is often singled out by critics as an example of what Roy Campbell calls the "Merrie England" school of poetry to which Graves supposedly subscribed in 1916 (Day 1963, 4). Robert Canary sums up the attack on this kind of poetry when he writes:

> This poem ["Jolly Yellow Moon"] manages to combine some of the worst of the old with the worst of the new. The unmotivated syntactic inversion of the first two lines and the "doth" of the fourth line represent the kind of diction the better Georgians were reacting against; the adjective "jolly" comes from the pseudohearty diction that other Georgians sometimes fell into. (Canary 1980, 51)

In Graves's defense, most critics fail to note that this collection is full of his experimentation with many diverse influences. One can feel the young poet struggling to find his own voice in the Skeltonics of "Free Verse" and the lyrical sweetness of the Ralph Hodgson–influenced "Cherry Time." Furthermore, one cannot help hearing echoes of De la Mare in poems such as "Willaree" or "Ghost Music." But admittedly the poems lack the haunting mood imagery and lilting rhythms of their inspirer, as the stiff formalism of "Ghost Music" clearly demonstrates:

> Gloomy and bare the organ-loft,
> Bent-backed and blind the organist.
> From rafters looming shadowy,
> From the pipes' tuneful company,
> Drifting together drowsily,
> Innumerable, formless, dim,
> The ghosts of long dead memories,
> Of anthems, stately, thunderous,
> Of Kyries shrill and tremulous:

> In melancholy drowsy-sweet
> They huddled there in harmony,
> Like bats at noontide rafter-hung.

(This quotation and all subsequent quotations from Graves's poems are taken from original editions.)

The war poetry in *Over the Brazier* is uneven and sometimes banal, as in "On Finding Myself A Soldier," in which Graves compares his youth with a rose bud and his war experience with the opened bloom, its "Twelve flamy petals ringed around / A heart more red than blood." But even in the least successful of the poems from the volume, Graves was trying to convert the new impressions of the war experience into the fabric of poetry. And what makes the work readable is Graves's success in observing the changes in himself as he confronts the dichotomy between the "real" world and that "imagined" world of conservative public school consciousness and the Edwardian upper-middle-class values engendered by his family.

Graves's dual vision of life was quickly manifested during his military training in Lancaster in September of 1914. The lusty young Lancastrians, whose main thoughts were of desertion and seduction of the local women (*Good-bye,* 104–5), affronted Graves's puritanical vein with their loose moral standards. Thoroughly disgusted and upset by their open flaunting of sexual desire, Graves wrote "Oh, and Oh!" Although on the one hand the poem is a tribute to his platonic male lover, G. H. "Peter" Johnstone, its purpose is an examination of the "loutish" and "sluttish" Lancastrians he encountered on an evening stroll through the town. Out of this "loathly woof" of foul and ungainly ugliness, Graves is able to mint one positive response: his platonic lover is so far away from this industrial pit that the wantonness, filth, and sickness cannot affect their pristine relationship.

Graves's rather naïve attitude toward the sexual urge reminds us how much a public school boy he was when he joined the army at nineteen. His impression of the world was structured by comradeship, games, and getting on with things despite the imposition of the system. In *Good-bye To All That,* Graves discusses his public school life with both great relish and traditional loathing. Despite the hardships he had to confront at Charterhouse—the need to feign madness to be left alone or the constant harassment resulting from his German middle name and origins—Graves savored the schoolboy victories over injustice and blind tradition. His success in boxing and loyal friendships with loyal students (such as

Raymond Rodakowski) and tutors (such as George Mallory) all aided in his maturation process.

Among the effects of the Charterhouse legacy on Robert Graves was a loss of faith in the Church of England, whose values had been imposed upon the young Graves by his parents early in life. Indeed, one of the major themes of Richard Graves's biography of his uncle is the impact of Amy and Alfred Graves's heavy-handed morality upon their son. They taught that the virtues of prayer, Bible study, and self-sacrifice were the way to salvation, and that the personal worth of an individual could be judged only in terms of saintly behavior. This kind of idealistic vision was bound to flounder in the rather sordid atmosphere of a boys' dormitory where smutty talk was the norm. Graves confirmed this when he wrote, ". . . I was as prudishly innocent as my mother had planned I should be. I knew nothing about simple sex, let alone the many refinements of sex constantly referred to in school conversation. My immediate reaction was one of disgust. I wanted to run away" (*Good-bye,* 64).

Nevertheless, for the first few terms at Charterhouse, Graves kept his views of the other boys' behavior strictly to himself and awaited Confirmation exercises with great spiritual hope. When the ceremony itself proved to be empty of meaning for him, Graves felt let down and confused; he turned inward and began to write poetry "that was dissatisfied with itself" (68). Not long afterwards, he became aware of the healthy atheism of his friend Rodakowski and was troubled when he failed to find an adequate reply to Raymond's query: "What's the use of having a soul if you have a mind?" (76). Such questioning formed the beginnings of the slow erosion of Graves's belief in organized religion that was to reach its complete dissolution on the battlefields of France.

In an often overlooked poem from *Over the Brazier,* "Big Words," Graves captures the rapidly changing attitude of the soldier toward God as he perches in the trench before the attack is called. Images from his brief, but full, life run through the soldier's mind:

> I've whined of coming death, but now, no more!
> It's weak and most ungracious. For, say I,
> Though still a boy if years are counted, why!
> I've lived those years from roof to cellar floor,
> And feel, like grey-beards touching their fourscore,
> Ready, so soon as the need comes, to die:
>   And I'm satisfied.

The soldier reflects on finding God while rockclimbing in Wales before the war but subsequently losing his faith through the adoration of "false loves." Now in war, he has found faith "in the wisdom of God's way" once more; now he can accept death with equanimity and states:

> . . . I know I'll feel small sorrow,
> Confess no sins and make no weak delays
> If death ends all and I must die tomorrow

As the soldier is about to go over the top, he tells us that his talk of faith in God and blind acceptance of the Divine Will is but false bravado and idle speculation. God here is reduced to a psychological crutch. However, at the end of the poem, there is an abrupt couplet:

> But on the firestep, waiting to attack,
> He cursed, prayed, sweated, wished the proud words back.

Graves's stance throughout the major part of *Over the Brazier* is that something positive will come to fill the void of loss of faith and childhood innocence. In the initial stages of the war, it is the noble qualities engendered by the fighting men. In "A Renascence," for example, Graves eulogizes the military life-style as a Spartan cleansing of both the body and the soul; the loss of soldiers' lives in glory is the stuff of which good poetry is made. Similar in spirit to Isaac Rosenberg's "August 1914" or several of Rilke's early war poems, Graves's poetry conveys that the process of the sacrifice and death will regenerate the poetic impulse from the puerile world of "flabbiness" and effeminacy. But this "happy warrior" syndrome is short-lived in Graves. While it is true that he took great pride in being part of the tradition of the Royal Welch Fusiliers, his conventional upbringing in no way prepared him for the horrors of the western front.

Graves admits in his foreword to the *Collected Poems* of 1938 that the primary impulse behind his first main volumes of poetry was "a frank fear of physical death." Indeed, his poetry is in many ways an escape from a "realistic" confrontation with the slaughter around him and tends to over-refine the repulsiveness into traditional images of childhood or of Georgian poetry. "The Shadow of Death," for example, presents the nursery image of the bad fairy stealing the boy poet out of the cradle and transforming him into a soldier before he has sung his songs to humanity. In "Limbo," Graves contrasts life in the trenches with the comparatively bucolic life-style behind the lines. Criticized by some critics for its Georgian platitudes and the nature images that appear in the last four lines, the poems nevertheless manages to suggest the sense of relief and return to life that the soldier must have felt on leaving the half-life "of bursting shells, of blood and hideous cries / . . . where the reek / of death offends the living" to revisit ". . . the sunny cornland where / Babies like tickling, and where tall white horses / Draw the plough leisurely in quiet courses." This poem was written after Graves had been in the trenches at La Bassée and shows his inability to accept the war with the equanimity of a simple unquestioning warrior. Graves had to transform this startling experience into some kind of poetry.

The entire section of "Nursery Memories" is an attempt to link up the horrors of the front with the dark memories of childhood in order to put them in a knowable perspective. For a child, coming to terms with the mysteries of life and death is an exhaustive process of discovery and investigation, but from an adult perspective, these discoveries are self-evident. The war and its attendant confusion and disorientation put Graves back into a childhood situation of investigation and questioning; one way for him to make sense out of the chaos was to put events into a childhood framework in which he would have control of them.

The unsettling report in "The Adventure" that a machine–gun team has annihilated an "enemy wire party" and later discovers that all the bodies have disappeared is digested by Graves's transforming the experience into a childhood fantasy of killing tigers with stones. W. D. Thomas in his article "The Impact of World War I on the Early Poems of Robert Graves" sees this reversion to a nursery tone as "a symptom of his neurasthenia and his desire to put himself at a distance from an unpleasantness he is aware of, . . . while at the same time, denying the actuality of the event by treating it as a childhood occurrence" (121).

The remaining war poems in this volume all demonstrate Graves's need to escape the reality of the carnage and chaos around him. He was still desperately attempting to alchemize these experiences into lumps of gold, but the process may have had more of a therapeutic value than a poetic one for the young officer. In "The Dead Fox-hunter," where Graves commemorates the stoical death of Captain Samson at the Battle of Loos in September 1915, we can see his avoidance of reality. The poem opens with the discovery of Samson's body in front of his men, who "lay well aligned" behind him. They never reached their objective, "but they died well; / They charged in line, and in the same line fell." In gruesome fashion, Samson did not die cleanly when he was hit, but rather than scream out in pain and risk other men's lives to save him, "his fingers were tight clenched between his teeth." The first two stanzas provide the kind of pathos and detail that promise a comment on the futility of war or a lament for the suffering of the "little captain," but Graves avoids the issue and instead turns to insipid fantasy and sentimental platitudes:

> For those who live uprightly and die true
>   Heaven has no bars or locks,
> And serves all taste . . . Or what's for him to do
>   Up there, but hunt the fox?
> Angelic choirs? No, Justice must provide
> For one who rode straight and at hunting died.
>
> So if Heaven had no hunt before he came,
>   Why, it must find one now:
> If any shirk and doubt they know the game,
>   There's one to teach them how:
> And the whole host of the Seraphim complete
> Must jog in scarlet to his opening Meet.

Graves's letter to Eddie Marsh on 8 July 1917 gives Marsh permission to use any poem except "The Dead Fox-hunter" for entry into *Georgian Poetry 1916–17*. He says "some people in the regiment were very sick about it when it first came out, and only condoned it because *Brazier* was such an obscure production" (Seymour-Smith 1982, 9). One does not have to look too hard for the cause of their reaction.

In "1915," a poem written—according to Richard Graves—after Robert's faith in Peter Johnstone had been shaken when a letter from his cousin, Gerald, had suggested that Peter was "as bad as anyone could be" (Graves 1986, 127), Robert's love for Peter is expressed as a substitute for everything that was missing in the trenches. But the list of cultural and natural deprivations is little more than a traditional Georgian rhetorical device for evoking the pastoral. In this case the images of "pictures, books, / Music, the quiet of an English wood, / Beautiful comrade-looks, / The narrow, bouldered mountain-track, / The broad, full-bosomed ocean, green and black," seem labored and too prosaic to make good love poetry or nature poetry. What the poem does evoke, however, is a strong flavor of the need to escape "winter nights knee-deep in mud or snow" in La Bassée or Béthune and Graves's desire to be with his platonic lover once again.

This same nostalgic musing is also to be found in the title poem "Over the Brazier," in which the narrator retells a conversation that he and two comrades had several months before. The conversation centered on what the three companions would do after the war. The narrator surmises that after the war he will retire to a comfortable cottage in North Wales, full of books and complete with a flowering garden, where he will simply dream and write. His companions dream of the vast expanses of Canada and of a coral isle. The poem goes on to reveal that both have been killed and their dreams have vaporized with them. The narrator asks, "Mad War has now wrecked both, and what / Better hopes has my little cottage got?"

Over the Brazier is a volume that follows the accelerated maturation process of a schoolboy into a man. When Graves left Charterhouse, he was certain of his desire to become a poet and looked to *Georgian Poetry 1911–1912* for models to emulate. There he would have found in Brooke's verse the vitality and undergraduate bravado of youth ("The Old Vicarage, Grantchester"), the fancifulness of De la Mare's "The Listeners" or "The Sleeper," or Davies' celebration of pastoral English beauty in "Days Too Short." But the nature of the Georgian experiences could not stand up to the emotionally wracking traumas of the Great War, and Graves, like his fellow soldier-poets, strained to find a language and an approach to confront the horror of the slaughter. The faery world of myth and magic and the rural countryside of "Cherry-Time" seem worlds away from the rotting corpses stuck grotesquely on barbed wire. Graves's desire to keep a "stiff upper lip" amidst the madness may have been admirable from the point of view of military discipline and esprit de corps, but the cost in terms of mental and psychological damage was dear. By the time he published *Fairies and Fusiliers* in late 1917, the struggle to balance these opposite viewpoints had created an even larger rent both in Graves's poetry and in his philosophy.

In February of 1917, Graves's second book of poetry, *Goliath and David,* was privately printed by the Chiswick Press. The nine poems that appeared in the volume were edited by Siegfried Sassoon during the days the two men spent recuperating from wounds in Harlech in the late summer of 1916. At about the time the volume was released, Graves had been sent to Somerville College at Oxford to recover from a bout of bronchitis that would keep him from returning to the front. The private edition was passed around to Edmund Gosse as well as to John Drinkwater and Duncan Grant (Graves 1986, 172). In a letter to Sassoon dated 26 March 1917, Graves wrote that "the correspondence about *Goliath and*

David has been most exacting. Thanks awfully for all you did to edit the book. It has been a great success all around (O'Prey 1982, 66). All nine of the poems were reprinted in *Fairies and Fusiliers* later in the year, and upon examination give a fairly accurate picture of Graves's frame of mind during his second year at the front.

Of the nine poems in the volume, all but "Careers" and "A Pinch of Salt" seem to have been created out of Graves's war experiences. "Careers," a childish piece concerning sibling rivalry in the Graves household, is a distinctly odd choice for this collection, for it would appear to have been written before the war began. Robert Canary's suggestion that the poem demonstrates a greater positive identification between father and son than has been generally noticed (Canary 1980, 10) seems rather strained when one considers the mocking tone of the poem.

"A Pinch of Salt" can be linked thematically with two better poems in the collection, "The Bough of Nonsense" and "Babylon." All three of these poems are concerned with escaping on the wings of poesy from the unpleasant realities facing the sensitive poet. In "A Pinch of Salt," Graves equates poetry with the illusory quality of a dream which is almost as difficult to snare as catching a bird with a salt box. The formula for success is not to clutch at the dream, but rather to let it flow freely and aimlessly until the dream is completely in the poet's control, at which point he should tighten his grasp. "The Bough of Nonsense" presents two war-weary Fusiliers, S and R, who return home and "weave a nonsense hymn" in mock praise of the worship of nonsense over the world of sense. In fact the poem is an escape from the world of logic, sense, and order and an entry into Edward Lear's world of illogical, childish wonder, where "a row of bright pink birds, flapping their wings" suddenly appears over the barren Welsh landscape.

"Babylon," a Georgian-style poem praising childhood—and, by extension, rejecting the adult world of logic and conformity—was written on 26 June 1916, before Graves went into action on the Somme near Bazentin le Petit (O'Prey 1982, 53). Later Graves worked on this poem with Sassoon while both men were recovering from their wounds at Harlech. Graves presents childhood here as a period when every new discovery and impression is an exciting and awe-inspiring revelation. The spontaneity and sensitivity, however, are slowly crushed by the encroachment of adulthood, which obliterates the poetic vision and imagination of childhood; with this loss, the world becomes mundane and bland. Even the onset of a glorious spring, once an occasion for a resurgence of joy, has become for the twenty-one-year-old poet no more "than daisies to a munching cow; / Just a cheery pleasant season, / Daisy buds to live at ease on." The poem suggests the war has been partially responsible for having "made a breach and battered / Babylon to bits . . . "; all that remains for the poet are "a few ghosts of timorous heart, to linger on / Weeping for lost Babylon." The adult can no longer recapture the simplistic and spontaneous response to experience once he has been anaesthetized by the wisdom of adult sensibility. As Myron Simon writes: "In lamenting the lost world of childhood . . . Graves was not rehearsing a familiar sentimental fiction. He was, rather, invoking the sharp appetite for direct experience that so rarely survives in the coarsened sensibility produced by repletion and custom" (Simon 1974, 12). And the experience of war was so dehumanizing that contact with the "lost Lords of Faery" must have seemed gone forever.

The last five poems in *Goliath and David* are overtly antiwar. "The Lady Visitor in the Pauper Ward," set in the casualty ward of an English hospital, was probably written while Graves was recovering from his wounds from the Somme at Queen Alexandria's Hospital in London. It is important mostly for the testy attitude it expresses toward the lady visitor:

> Why do you break upon this old, cool peace,
> This painted peace of ours,
> With harsh dress hissing like a flock of geese,
> With garish flowers?
> Why do you church smooth waters rough again,
> Self old skin-and-bone?
> Leave us to quiet dreaming and slow pain,
> Leave us alone.

Although the lady herself may be seen to represent the war which has broken into a calm world of peacetime England, the poem is evidence that Graves was growing tired of the patriotic civilian response of his countrymen. The war, for most uncomprehending civilians, was a struggle against the mad Hun lusting after blood, who had to be destroyed before he raped England as he had raped Belgium; the realities of the Battle of the Somme had not yet pricked the English consciousness. Graves's awareness of the two different conceptions of war are made clear in the following excerpts from *Good-bye:*

England was strange to the returned soldier. He could not understand the war-madness that ran about everywhere looking for a pseudo-military outlet. Everyone talked a foreign language; it was newspaper language. I found serious conversation with my parents all but impossible. (283)

We [Graves and Sassoon] no longer saw it as a war between trade rivals; its continuance seemed merely a sacrifice of the idealistic younger generation to the stupidity and self-protective alarm of the elder. (288)

"The Last Post" is the first of Graves's poems in *Goliath and David* to convey the fear of death that belies the romantic image of the soldier. Using the hauntingly familiar image of the solitary bugler's romantic call for "lights out" on the deserted square, Graves lets us overhear a prayer whispered by the frightened bugler. Figuratively, he prays not to have his own "light" extinguished on the battlefield of France; he feels he is "too good to die." Once again, as in "Big Words," Graves tears at the facade of the fearless, dedicated British soldier to reveal behind it a fear-racked, cowering youth.

"A Dead Boche" moves the reader from the recruitment depots of Wales and Liverpool to the immediacy of the Somme battlefield. In *Good-bye* Graves writes of camping in bivouacs just outside Mametz Wood between 15 and 17 July amid the dead of the New Army battalions. At one point, he goes out to strip overcoats off the corpses of the Prussian Guards to keep his men warm on the chilly evenings. On several of these ghoulish journeys, he passes the same "corpse of a German with his back propped against a tree. He had a green face, spectacles, close shaven hair; black blood was dripping from nose and beard. He had been there for some days and was bloated and stinking" (*Good-bye*, 264). This description leaves little doubt as to where the inspiration for "A Dead Boche" originated.

The sheer horror of the descriptive detail in "A Dead Boche" has provoked several different critical reactions to the poem. Douglas Day, in *Swifter Than Reason,* sees the poem as an elaborate exploitation of the horrors of war which, in his opinion, fails because "the sole emotion expressed . . . and consequently aroused in the reader is one of disgust" (Day 1963, 12). Michael Kirkham, on the other hand, comments that "A Dead Boche" is the nearest Graves ever comes to rendering realistically the brutal impact of trench warfare, but feels that Graves has somehow recoiled from the subject (Kirkham 1969, 16–17). In contrast, G. S. Fraser finds that the poem contains the "roots of horror . . . a recurring theme in Graves's later poetry," but rejects the poem because the "dead Boche" is seen only as "a mere object" (Fraser 1959, 15). Interestingly, the critics here omit to mention the vital opening stanza where Graves clearly states his purpose:

> To you who'd read my songs of War
>   And only hear of blood and fame,
> I'll say (you've heard it said before)
>   "War's Hell!" and if you doubt the same,
> Today I found in Mametz Wood
> A certain cure for lust of blood:

The poem is addressed to Graves's complacent public that had read his earlier volume of poetry where he mouthed the naïve platitudes and heroic images of war. After the Battle of the Somme, Blunden would write in *The Mind's Eye*, "By the end of the day both sides had seen, in the sad scrawl of broken earth and murdered men, the answer to the question. . . . Neither race had won, nor could win, the War. The War had won, and would go on winning" (Fussell 1983, 13). Conditions had changed and the blood lust had to be cured. Here Graves is trying desperately to bring home to an uninitiated but belligerent public not so much a shock of horror, but a sting of reality that would rend the curtain of propriety and shed light on the true nature of war death. The details of the second stanza are realistic and immediate; if anything, they understate the case.

> Where, propped against a shattered trunk,
>   In a great mess of things unclean,
> Sat a dead Boche; he scowled and stunk
>   With clothes and face a sodden green,
> Big-bellied, spectacled, crop-haired,
> Dribbling black blood from nose and beard.

The civilian reader is left to meditate on this vestige of war and to ask if his hatred for the German race is satiated by the image of the mutilated corpse.

The last two poems of *Goliath and David* commemorate David Thomas, a good friend of both Sassoon and Graves who was killed at Fricourt on 18 March 1916 by a stray bullet. Graves reminisces in *Goodbye*, "I felt David's death worse than any other death since I had been in France. . . . It just made me feel empty and lost" (251). "Not Dead," an escapist pastoral, was written while Graves was recovering from his wounds in Harlech. During a convalescent walk through the woods on a hot day, as Graves painfully reviews the losses he has sustained in the war, he is suddenly aware of the presence of David around him in the guise of nature: "A brook goes bubbling by: the voice is his . . . / Over the whole wood in a little while / Breaks his slow smile." While Kirkham berates Graves for indulging in a regressive fantasy that omits to confront the real world of adult relationships (Kirkham 1969, 21–22), he fails to recognize that the poet is struggling to find a voice through which he can express the loss of a close friend. Graves's turning to the romantic, bucolic world of the pastoral to sooth his overstrung emotions is not a surprising choice.

"Goliath and David," the title poem of the volume which again commemorates David Thomas, is a powerful poetic assault on many of the institutions and myths that Graves had been observing since Thomas's death at Fricourt. This satiric attack is leveled not only at the traditional faith in God and country, but at those who write history in such a way as to suggest victory where none occurred. The poem is a bitter lament for the loss of innocence and the selfless sacrifice that young David made for his tribe: the same sacrifice that David Thomas had made a few months earlier.

But Graves gives a new twist to this "allegorical embodiment of the Old Testament story" (Kirkham 1969, 23–24): David, a brazen idealist who believes that with faith in God he can easily destroy the heathen on the field of battle, is slain by the giant Goliath with the ease of a knife cutting through butter; Goliath parries pebbles from David's sling and blows from the boy's wooden staff, and then, with "one cruel backhand sabre-cut," executes him. Not surprisingly, during the slaying "(God's eyes are dim, His ears are shut.)" After the boy has fallen, "spike-helmeted, grey, grim, / Goliath straddles over him." It is this sinister image of the spike-helmeted Goliath straddling over the rustic shepherd boy that lingers when the poem is over. The suggestion is that this uneven battle should never have been allowed to happen; that the woefully unprepared David should never have been permitted to enter into the skirmish without proper provision. David's God is uninterested in his sacrifice and his fellows in no way dissuade him from taking on the obviously superior Goliath. In a very real sense, David's death is due as much to the deceptions and false tribal values as to the swing of Goliath's saber.

Graves's realization of futile endeavor, shared with Sassoon during their joint recuperation, must have been mentally devastating for both of them. The marginal note that he made on his manuscript to "Goliath and David" at the time shows how he felt:

> War should be a sport for men above forty-five only, the Jesse's, not the David's. "Well, dear father, how proud I am of you serving your country as a very gallant gentleman prepared to make even the supreme sacrifice. I only wish I were your age: how willingly would I buckle on my armour and fight those unspeakable Philistines! As it is, of course, I can't be spared; I have to stay behind at the War Office and administrate for you lucky old men." "What sacrifices I have made," David would sigh when the old boys had gone off with a draft to the front singing *Tipperary*. (*Good-bye,* 288–89)

The results of Graves's documenting such experiences are best described in W. D. Thomas's article "The impact of World War I on the Early Poetry of Robert Graves":

> . . . while he was able to write about this death [Thomas's death], the actual act of contemplation and writing exacted a terrible price from Graves himself, for the act of concentration upon such an unpleasant topic in his weakened condition served to intensify the neurasthenia and his rapidly deteriorating mental condition. (17)

As the year continued, Graves's physical and mental deterioration resulted in a fainting fit during which he fell down a set of stairs and lacerated his head. During his recuperation at Somerville in June of 1917, Graves's rather delicate position was perhaps further aggravated by a brief, platonic love affair with Marjorie, a probationer nurse. R. P. Graves points out that this relationship "represented a major change in emotional direction" for Robert (Graves 1986, 173); indeed, the stress of the emotional involvement, together with a delayed attack of shell shock, was sufficient to force Graves into a convalescent home for officers at Osborne Palace in the Isle of Wight.

While Graves was convalescing amid Queen Victoria's serene, wooded walks at Quarr, he began working on his *Fairies and Fusiliers* collection. He later finished the work at Litherland Camp after he had been judged fit by the medical board and had helped in the celebrated rescue of Sassoon from court-martial (*Good-bye,* 312). Graves sent the proofs of *Fairies and Fusiliers* to Sassoon in mid-September of 1917 (Sassoon, *Diaries 1915-1918,* 186); by the time the book was released, he had transferred to garrison service near Rhyl in order to escape "mist coming up from the Mersey and hanging about the camp full of T.N.T. fumes" (*Good-bye,* 330).

Fairies and Fusiliers is thematically very similar to *Goliath and David.* Most of the poems fall either into the category of war meditations or into romantic idealizations and fancies that have their roots deep in the experimentation of poetic craft, and, more particularly, in the Georgianism favored by Eddie Marsh. But Graves, with a keen eye for irony, judges the situations around him objectively and independently in his verse, and, as Simon states, avoids the Victorian moralizing that is prevalent in much of the sentimental didactic verse of the period: "Graves maintained that it was the distinctive purpose of the artist to attend to reality at the level of experience, to look directly at the events themselves, and to allow neither self-indulgence nor public expectations to deflect and falsify his vision" (Simon 1974, 59).

Simon's remarks here are directed to Graves's work in general, but apply particularly well to the opening poem of *Fairies and Fusiliers,* "To an Ungentle Critic." Here Graves sets down a challenge to the critics of his poetry, using much the same tone that he will use to address his readers in "Reader Over Your Shoulder" some twelve years later: "I shall scrawl / Just what I fancy as I strike it, / Fairies and Fusiliers, and all." And he can still take a swipe at the older generation which fails to understand his work: "The holiest, cruellest pains I feel, / Die stillborn, because old men squeal / For something new." This belief in the poet's vocation as a ruthless quest for the simple truth, despite the cost to himself and to his audience, is a reaffirmation of the close relationship between the childish vision and the poetic apprehension of experience explored in "Babylon."

In "Faun," Graves presents again the trappings of a pastoral myth where King Faun leaped and danced freely in a safe and comfortable landscape. But in the second stanza, we gaze upon a hopeless King Faun:

> To-day against yon pine,
> Forlorn yet still divine,
>   King Faun leant weeping.
>   "They drank my holy brook
>   My strawberries they took.
>   My private path they trod."
>   Loud wept the desolate God,
>   Scorn upon scorn heaping,

"Faun, what is he,
Faun, what is he?"

Michael Kirkham, who tends to pass over Graves's early poetry rather abruptly, takes a long paragraph to analyze this poem. Kirkham sees it as a symbol of "the effect of a hostile world upon the poet's personality" (Kirkham 1969, 23). He further points out how the hostile world has despoiled the "innocent landscape" of the poet's personal feelings and the poet is left, like weeping Faun, "desolate." What Kirkham overlooks is that King Faun is not only left desolate, but he is also embittered by the realization that he has lost his innocence and inspiration (his "holy brook"). What is the poet without this inspiration and childish vision? What will become of the poet now that the basic necessities to make music are gone?

Graves attempts to answer that question in "Dead Cow Farm," a poem based on the myth that an Elemental Cow "began to lick cold stones and mud: / And so was Adam born, and Eve." This highly poetic act of divine creation is compared with Graves's mad world where chaos reigns. Once again there is an abundance of "primeval mud, cold stones and rain," but the completeness of the war's destruction ("Here flesh decays and blood drips red") has murdered any hope of ever again finding creative inspiration. The repetition of the judgment and the heaviness of the final line sound the death knell for poetic epiphany.

The previous three poems demonstrate the young Graves's attempts to find his way amidst the disconcerting impressions of the war. He was convinced that he wanted to write poetry, but the continuation of the war appeared to sap the aspiring Georgian of inspiration. The failure of the Somme offensive had obviously shaken his faith in the hopes of a decisive victory. As A. J. P. Taylor, the prominent British historian, writes:

> Idealism perished on the Somme. The enthusiastic volunteers were enthusiastic no longer. They had lost faith in their cause, in their leaders, in everything except loyalty to their fighting comrades. The war ceased to have a purpose. It went on for its own sake, as a contest in endurance. . . . After the Somme men decided that the war would go on for ever. (Taylor 1982, 120)

Recovering from his war wounds, sunk in the depths of depression concerning himself and his comrades, Graves wrote in *Good-bye* that after the Battle of the Somme, "Everyone was mad" (290). And this lunacy and expression were difficult to express in lyric or Skeltonic poetry, a problem Graves confronted in "The Assault Heroic."

Exhausted by five nights and days of waging war, the speaker in this verse falls into a fitful dream in which his world is transformed into the landscape of a Bunyan allegory. The soldier is locked in the "dungeon of Despair," surrounded by a looming "Desolate Sea." Voices from within the dungeon walls taunt the dreaming soldier with malicious battle cries:

> "Today we've killed your pride;
> To-day your ardour ends.
> We've murdered all your friends;
> We've undermined by stealth
> Your happiness and your health.
> We've taken away your hope;
> Now you may droop and mope
> To misery and to death."

But somehow in this psychologically devastating attack, the soldier finds a reserve of strength in his faith as a poet to turn the assault into victory.

> The stones they cast I caught
> And alchemized with thought
> Into such lumps of gold
> As dreaming misers hold.
> The boiling oil they threw
> Fell in a shower of dew,
> Refreshing me; the spears
> Flew harmless by my ears,
> Struck quivering in the sod;

The poet is able to rout the enemy and win back the castle keep from his persecutors. However, just as he is about to blow his horn in celebration of the victory, he is suddenly jarred back to consciousness by a sentry and forced to face yet another counterattack.

The poem, then, is a fantasy of what the soldier—and by extension Graves—hoped to achieve from the war. It expresses the desire to "alchemize" the war experience into an indubitable literary statement in the same manner as the medieval dream sequence was woven by the soldier's unconscious. But the constant interruption of reality makes this method of escape nearly impossible. While it is true that Graves would later decide that the gap between dream and poetics was not as remote as it appeared in 1916 (see, for example, his *Poetic Unreason,* 99–100); nevertheless, in *Fairies and Fusiliers* true alchemy of his war experiences into lumps of gold seldom occurs.

Kirkham's contention that the poem is a "burlesque description of strutting heroism, in which conflicts between nations are assimilated to the ridiculous antics of children" (1969, 15), seems strangely insensitive to the tone and movement of the poem. Further, Kohli's in-depth psychological probings into the subconscious of the writer and her confrontation with Graves's subpersonalities seem far too conjectural to have much concrete relevance to the understanding of the poem (Kohli 1975, 22). In fact, the poem is clearly Graves's attempt to sublimate his experience of five days on the battlefront into a dream fantasy in which the indomitable obstacles of death and destruction are warded off by the magic powers of poetry. The poet, though, is aware that such escapism is just temporary, and that he must return to the destructive world of the trenches once more.

The realization that soon he would be facing the German guns must have made the mystical land of Meirion with its "fairies and ghosts" seem exceedingly attractive to Graves and far preferable to the stark reality surrounding him. "Letter to S. S. From Mametz Wood," written on 16 July 1916 just before Graves was seriously wounded on the Somme, is a poem-letter describing the area in Wales where Sassoon and he would meet "après-la-guerre." Once safely settled in the mystical Welsh hills around Harlech, ". . . we'll rest awhile / We'll dress our wounds and learn to smile / With easier lips." Then the two soldiers will visit the Caucasus, Persia, and China "doing wild, tremendous things / In free adventure, quest and fight, / And God! what poetry we'll write." Graves created this blithe, fanciful poem in response to a discussion a few nights earlier when he and Sassoon had agreed to get away from all memories of the war and write together about new experiences and places (Sassoon, *Diaries 1915–1918,* 93–94). Considering the hellish conditions that were waiting for Graves when he moved up to the front, such happy escapism might have been the only prophylactic possible. Surely, only a limited number of poetic responses could have been available to Graves to help him face what lay ahead.

There [at the front] the big guns had done their work, and the Fusiliers entered a scene of terrible desolation. Corpses lay all around, and there were also numbers of dead horses and mules. The ground was thickly pitted with shell-holes, and the mist was heavy with shell-fumes. They bivouacked on the edge of Mametz wood, which was full of the dead, and in which there was not a single tree unbroken. (Graves 1986, 151)

Of course, Graves did manage to evade death on the Somme and celebrated his survival in the poem "Escape," a mythological reenactment of his reaction to being wounded and of his semiconscious dreamlike battle to avoid physical sacrifice. And while, admittedly, the poem itself makes poor use of Skeltonic rhyme and is peopled with an unlikely combination of characters ("Of demons, heroes, and policeman-ghosts"), it is important as an insight into Graves's maturation. The very fact that he should choose to write about the incident in a mythological framework has caused several critics to judge the act of writing the poem as evidence of his escape from reality. W. D. Thomas contends that in "Escape," "we see Graves distancing himself from even his own death by resorting to classical imagery and allusion. The language . . . is scholarly and aloof, giving the impression that the author does not want to be part of the event he is recording" (1975, 116–17), while Kirkham claims that Graves's natural optimism is symptomatic of "his inability to face either the objective horror of war or his deepest feelings about it" (1969, 16). Generally, there appears to be a critical consensus that Graves was incapable of writing realistic verse; indeed, Graves's letter to Edward Marsh on 7 August 1916 (less than three weeks after he had been reported dead), shows that he had already turned the incident of his being missing in action into a lighthearted myth. Graves plays down his wounds and his suffering here, and even compares the pain favorably with his nose operation of the previous year. In both letter and poem, the mood is jocular and "fantastic" because Graves has escaped; his imagination has been freed from the grizzly, hellish realities of battle. Graves has fought the final battle and has emerged as the victor: "'Life! life! I can't be dead! I won't be dead! / Damned if I'll die for anyone!' I said . . ." With the aid of Proserpine (who may be one of the earliest manifestations of the mythological goddesses who were to assist him) and by his own improvisation, Graves outwits the three-headed Cerberus by slipping him a morphia-filled ration biscuit and crawls over his "hairy carcase" to the sunlight.

Graves's metamorphosing his escape from death at the front into mythic terms is hardly surprising. Having rejected Christianity by this time, he could interpret his own resurrection only in familiar Latin and Greek myths learned at school. This reaction is not evidence of Graves's "avoiding any deep commitment of his feelings to the war" as Kirkham suggests (1969, 15), but rather of his finding the proper vehicle by which to convey these extraordinary happenings. As Fussell points out: "The problem for the writer trying to describe elements of the Great War was its utter incredibility, and thus its incommunicability in its own terms" (1975, 139). Graves may be accused of lack of inventiveness, but not of a lack of commitment of feelings.

Graves felt a very strong commitment toward his comrades in arms and his regiment, and in fact this allegiance is made very clear in several of the poems in *Fairies and Fusiliers.* In "Two Fusiliers," he claims that the experiences of war are what will forever bind friendships after the war.

> By wire and wood and stake we're bound,
> By Fricourt and by Festubert,
> By whipping rain, by the sun's glare,
> By all the misery and loud sound,
> By a Spring day
> By Picard clay.

And in the lively "To Lucasta on Going to the Wars—for the Fourth Time," Graves's soldierly pride is more important than the statesmen's rhetorical and pious blustering about laws and treaties. The pride in the company of men with whom he serves is all that counts, once the initial excitement of going to war diminishes.

Graves's commitment to his men is also made evident throughout much of *Good-bye.* In one case, Graves recalls that he had argued with the brigade headquarters concerning a proposed attack on a German salient; his argument that the attack would prove futile eventually resulted in its being called off, much to the relief of his fellow officers and men (*Good-bye,* 300). In a second instance, when Graves tried to talk Sassoon into consenting to appear before a medical board instead of refusing to perform military duties at Litherland, his main avenue of attack was an appeal to Sassoon's sense of loyalty to the regiment.

> I reminded him [Sassoon] of the regiment; what did he think that the First and Second Battalions would think of him? How could they be expected tounderstand his point of view? They would say he was ratting, that he had cold feet, and was letting the regiment down by not acting like a gentleman. . . . The army could . . . only understand it as cowardice, or at best a lapse from good form. (*Good-bye,* 324)

In the words of Daniel Hoffman: "He [Graves] entered into the clannish martial spirit of the regiment and has never relinquished the sense of specialness, of earned privilege, of having won his right under fire to be a captain in an outfit of such manly and historic virtue" (Hoffman 1967, 153).

But by 1917, Graves's pride in the military tradition had been buffeted by the realities of modern warfare; he was fully cognizant that the impersonality of the war had made the tradition of individual heroic valor in warfare largely obsolete. In fact, "The Next War" warns the young boys of England who play at being Royal Welch Fusiliers that their turn will come soon enough:

> Another War soon gets begun,
> A dirtier, a more glorious one;
> Then, boys, you'll have to play, all in;
> It's the cruellest team will win.
> So hold your nose against the stink
> And never stop too long to think.

Against the traditional children's playground values of loyalty and courage is set the adult world of motivations: "pomp and greed and rage." Graves clearly regards the sacrifice of young idealistic values to corrupt adult selfishness as being the whole truth about the cause and continuation of modern warfare.

> Wars don't change except in name;
> The next one must go just the same,
> And new foul tricks unguessed before
> Will win and justify this War.
> Kaisers and Czars will strut the stage
> Once more with pomp and greed and rage;
> Courtly ministers will stop
> At home and fight to the last drop;
> By the million men will die
> In some new horrible agony;

In spite of his pride in the regiment and concern for his men, Graves had become intellectually and emotionally satiated with the war and its tensions; it had wrought a change in his view of Christianity and in the rest of his traditional values; it had shaken his confidence in the judgment of his parents and the whole civilian and noncombatant staff. Furthermore, the death of his friends in battle and loss of respect for his platonic lover, Peter Johnstone, through the discovery of his suspected homosexual liaison with a Canadian soldier, had left the physically weary Graves with a strong sense of isolation—an isolation that was aggravated by his being back on the home front while his men were still in France, and by his having to face a civilian contingent that neither understood nor sympathized with his preoccupation with the war.

2

Love, Escape, and
Country Sentiment

According to Graves's own account of the later months of 1917 in *Good-bye,* he was training young officers from cadet battalions at Rhyl when he "remembered Nancy Nicholson" (331). In fact, the statement is not quite accurate; Graves was still at Litherland when he decided to take weekend leave in Wales with his parents, and, while there, he decided to visit the girl in the black velvet dress who had haunted his memory since he had met her in January of 1917.

The weekend is well described in R. P. Graves's biography (182–83), but the book never really analyzes the motivations for the speed with which Graves decided to marry Nicholson less than four months later. Seymour-Smith suggests Graves's fear of discovering latent homosexuality and need to prove his heterosexuality as explanations for the rapid courtship; in other words, the need to be sure that he could love a woman was Graves's prime motivation for this marriage (Seymour-Smith 1982, 74–75). Thus, Seymour-Smith asserts that Graves was caught in a moral dilemma: that the poet needed to confirm his heterosexuality in an act which his strict moral background allowed only within the marital sacrament. In fact, the critic echoes Sassoon's remark that at this time Graves was somewhat of a prig about sexual matters and that he was a virgin on his marriage night. However, neither of his biographers really reflects on Graves's relationship with Marjorie during his convalescence, a relationship that demonstrates that his tendency toward heterosexual relationships was previously established to at least some degree.

Graves recognized in the very boyish and independent-minded Nancy Nicholson a kindred spirit. They were both fond of what Graves called "child sentiment"; in fact, their first correspondence deals partially with "some children's rhymes of [Graves's] which she was going to illustrate" (*Good-bye,* 332). As I have already pointed out, Graves's tendency to escape into his childhood past when life at the front became too unpleasant to bear often betrays itself in his poetry. Instances are poems like "Cherry Time" and "The Caterpillar," which both appeared in *Fairies and Fusiliers* and which seem little more than nursery doggerel. For her part, Nancy, at the time of Robert's courtship, was engaged in a series of illustrations for Stevenson's *Child's Garden of Verses.* Their mutual interests amid a world gone mad with war must have proved quite a relief for the battle-weary Graves.

The love that sprang up between the two is analyzed very carefully in Richard Graves's biography. In a careful reconstruction of a particular visit that Graves paid to Nancy at Hilton in Huntingdonshire (Nancy was involved in a land work as part of the war effort), the biography attempts to capture the elusive quality of attraction that Graves felt in Nancy.

> Robert was already in love with Nancy, and he listened to what she had to say with growing admiration. His deep attachment to his mother had predisposed him to think well of women with strong convictions; as a follower of Samuel Butler he applauded Nancy's spirited attacks upon convention; and as a romantic Robert wished to adopt Nancy's ideals as his own. (Graves 1986, 188)

But these intellectual speculations, as valid as they might be, tell only half the story. Graves's love of a woman was not only an insurance against his latent homosexuality, but it was also the release of a poetic impulse that was an affirmation of life itself; loving a woman brought Graves, for the first time, the possibility of fathering children. His love for children is well documented throughout *Good-bye* and letters of the period. In fact, at this time Graves was looking after the battalion colonel's children and seemingly enjoying himself with "tea and tiddlywinks" (O'Prey 1982, 86). In short, for the first time in his adult life, Graves felt in his relationship with Nancy the overwhelming expansiveness of a socially legitimate outlet for his romantic feelings.

In December of 1917, Graves proposed marriage and was accepted by Nancy on the condition that he see a doctor to ascertain whether he would be capable of any further active war service. When medical opinion confirmed that Graves's shattered nerves were enough to keep him from active duty, the wedding was set for 23 January in London. Despite problems over the wording of the marriage service (which Nancy felt was demeaning), and Nancy's refusal to take Graves's name, the ceremony was carried out successfully.

In a poem entitled "Morning Phoenix" that appeared the following year in the privately printed *Treasure Box,* Graves writes of his passionate love for his new wife in almost manic images. The love he bears for Nancy is so intense that he longs for some kind of cool relief to lessen the scorching flame "that burns me all the day." The potency of this new feeling of desire in the repressed soldier is both welcomed and feared. In a manner reminiscent of the way he dealt with his war experiences, Graves wants to transform this unwieldy and virtually incomprehensible experience into something cooler and more serene so that his "calcined heart and shrivelled skin" can recover some sense of objectivity.

In "The Kiss," from the same volume, Graves frames his verse with a general chronology of the lovemaking process. The opening stanza of the poem mirrors the almost trancelike ritual of love's spoken endearments to set the stage for the physical intimacies that will follow. The verbal precoital phase is reminiscent of the initial platonic and romantic stage when the awareness of love between two people is first conceived.

> Are you shaken, are you stirred
>   By a whisper of love,
> Spellbound to a word
>   Does Time cease to move,
> Till her calm grey eye
>   Expands to a sky
> And the clouds of her hair
>   Like storms go by?

But when the relationship moves onto the physical plane, here symbolized by the kiss, the entire fabric of the verbal creation is somehow transmuted into a selfish, obsessive concentration of consuming fire ("the First Power moves / Over void and dearth"). The final stanza reflects the postcoital state. Troubled by his surrendering to the sensual act, the lover realizes that his submission to sexual passion is ultimately a sundering from the loved one, for instead of spiritual unity he has experienced the isolation of death. When lovemaking is reduced to a purely physical exercise, "A passion, a shout, / The deep in-breath, / The breath roaring out," the end result can only be disillusionment.

R. P. Graves, however, presents a fairly idyllic picture of the initial days of the Graves's marriage when they lived in Rhyl and points out that at this time nursery rhymes began to flow from Robert's pen. Surely poems like "The Treasure Box" and the rather fawningly gentle "Fox's

Dingle," as well as the "Four Rhymes from the Penny Fiddle," are among those he is thinking of. It was not long, though, before the idyllic world of the Graves's was shattered by the deaths in quick succession of Nancy's mother and brother (events that both biographers pass over rather hastily, but which may be relevant to Nancy's uncompromising hatred of war and men in general). The wounding of Sassoon, the death of the literary critic Robbie Ross—on whose decease Graves wrote to Sassoon that "there'll never be another Robbie, cynical, kind-hearted, witty, champion of lost causes, feeder of the fatherless and widowed and oppressed" (Graves 1986, 199)—and the serious illness of Robert's brother no doubt added further tension to an already death-weary family. Added to these external problems was Robert's shell shock, which kept his nerves on end and made him liable to break into tears at any time, but especially so when he pondered the lives that he had taken in the war. The next concern was to be for Nancy's health, when it was discovered that she was pregnant.

The pregnancy had consequences that bothered the Graves's marital equanimity as well. Nancy began to feel that Robert's desire to have children was somehow tied in with a sense of male lust; Robert's naïve puritanism, coupled with his ignorance of the reproductive functions, caused him to feel guilty and somewhat confused, as is evidenced by "The Kiss" and "Morning Phoenix." Seymour-Smith, whose dislike of Nancy is more candid than that of R. P. Graves, sums up the situation succinctly:

> At the age of twenty one he [Graves] was confused by his feeling of friendship. Clearly there was a "huge tug" between him and Nancy, even if both were embarrassed by it. Simply being married and begetting a child, as he so soon did, meant a great deal to Graves, but alienated Nancy by what seemed, to her, his clumsy sexual urgency. She became increasingly unsociable, and often complained of feeling unwell—so that she would neither have to go to bed with him nor greet his friends. (Seymour-Smith 1982, 75)

Nancy's behavior at this time shocked the idealistic Graves, who even at this early stage must have begun to worry about the future of their marriage. When the war ended, Graves was at Rhyl and about to depart for Limerick, but he overstayed his leave to be with Nancy at the birth of their first child. The suggestiveness of Graves's note in *Good-bye*, when he writes about the birth of "Nancy's Baby" on 6 January 1919, is not lost on the reader. Writing of the physical effects of childbirth, Graves states that "Nancy had no foreknowledge of the experience—I assumed that she knew—and it took her years to recover from it" (343). In the 1957 edition of *Good-bye,* Graves amends the ambiguous clause between the dashes to read "I assumed she must have been given some sort of warning" (228). The point is that the birth was not a pleasant experience for Nancy, and that the pain and ill-preparation were a further arrow in the quiver of grievances that she was to collect against her husband.

There appears to be little doubt that Graves attempted to mollify his high-strung wife in the early years of their marriage. Within two months of the war's end, he resigned his commission, and, after a serious bout of influenza in Hove, Graves and his new family took up residence in the house of his artist father-in-law, William Nicholson, in Harlech. It was during this time at Harlech that some of the more subtle wounds of the war—the nightmares and nervous tics that haunted Graves for ten years—became manifest. He explains:

> I was still mentally and nervously organized for war; shells used to come bursting on my bed at midnight even when Nancy was sharing it with me; strangers in day-time would assume the faces of friends who had been killed. . . .

> I was very thin, very nervous, and had about four years' loss of sleep to make up. I found that I was suffering from a large sort of intestinal worm which came from drinking bad water in France. . . . I knew that it would be years before I was fit for anything besides a quiet country life. . . . My disabilities were many; I could not use a telephone, I was sick every time I travelled in a train, and if I saw more than two new people in a single day it prevented me from sleeping. (*Good-bye,* 353–54)

Ironically, Graves felt his reactions to be unfortunate not because they caused him irrevocable suffering, but because they brought Nancy discomfort. And while one would expect some sympathy from a loving wife, even the apologetic R. P. Graves admits that her attitude was capricious (Graves 1986, 208). Capricious or not, Nancy harbored a hostility toward her husband that went beyond fairness or reason. That Nancy believed in "the judicial equality of the sexes" and that "all the wrong in the world was caused by male domination and narrowness" was perhaps a legitimate complaint of any thinking woman of her age, but to ignore her husband's suffering and to include him as part of her universal condemnation of men wounded the young poet greatly (*Good-bye,* 355).

In "Lost Love," perhaps the most sensitive and incisive poem in the *Treasure Box* volume, Graves attempts to analyze how the loss of love and idealism in his marriage affected his emotional state; by this point, Graves had fully realized that his concept of the perfect marriage was in serious jeopardy of being unfulfilled.

"Lost Love" reflects the heightened sensitivity and vulnerability one feels when steeped in the grief caused by the loss of love. Here the lover's senses are enhanced to such a level that he is capable of super-human actions: "He can watch a grass or leaf / Every instant grow; he can / Clearly through a flint wall see, / Or watch the startled spirit flee / From the throat of a dead man." This heightened awareness only makes the suffering more acute, and the lover wanders aimlessly about, seeking some type of respite from his melancholy. The only compensation for the suffering is the lover's ability to turn the experience into poetry.

Day exaggerates when he claims that "while a strong love is to be feared, the poet should desire it, for it enhances his powers of vision—especially when the love is a hopeless one" (Day 1963, 32). This might be an acceptable contention for later in Graves's career, but at this stage the sadness is accepted as it is; the poem is an epitaph to the drifting away of something once grasped, but that is now gone. It is another poetic plaint for the loss of innocence.

Throughout 1919, the financial affairs of the Graves family continued downhill as they lived well above their means. In order to secure a safe income, Graves rather reluctantly agreed to use his government grant and go up to St. John's College, Oxford. On 10 October 1919, Graves moved into a small three-bedroom cottage at the foot of John Masefield's garden in Boar's Hill and began to read for a degree in English (*Good-bye*, 357–60). During his first term at Oxford, he worked on the final proofs of *Country Sentiment*, which was to be published in the early spring of the following year.

Country Sentiment, as Graves states in the preface to *Whipperginny*, was written with "the desire to escape from a painful war neurosis into an Arcadia of amatory fancy . . ." In *Good-bye* he writes, "Instead of children as a way of forgetting the war, I used Nancy. *Country Sentiment*, dedicated to her, was a collection of romantic poems and ballads. At the end was a group of pacifist war-poems" (342). Many of the poems in the volume were written in Harlech during Graves's second year of marriage and reflect very strongly the poet's attempt to blot out the remnants of the war by escaping into the innocent worlds of nature and childhood. Further, as Douglas Day points out:

He was seeking at this time . . . to create poems which would have a therapeutic value for him—which would allow him to exorcise the turbulent and potentially self-destructive emotions aroused in him by his wartime experiences. Graves's "anodynic" phase, then, consists for the most part of deliberately childlike and fanciful poems, by which he hoped to restore to himself some measure of emotional tranquillity. (Day 1963, 23)

Kirkham agrees that the atmosphere of childhood pervades *Country Sentiment* (Kirkham 1969, 29), but careful investigation reveals that while childhood is the single most dominant impression in the book, there are many subthemes which, when placed together, demonstrate that the overall tone of the volume is not as bucolic as Graves or his critics would have one believe. The thematic structure of the poems in the book can be divided into five particular areas: nursery rhymes and folk ballads; poems of social commentary; verses describing the role of the poet; Graves's attempts to deal with his wartime neuroses; and finally, his laments on the failure of love. And while, admittedly, a poem like "Ghost Raddled" might occasionally fall inconveniently into two categories, the poems may generally be categorized into one of the five groups. Ironically, in "A First Review" Graves anticipated that his readers would criticize the rather untidy grouping of subject matter in the volume.

> Love, Fear and Hate and Childish Toys
> Are here discreetly blent;
> Admire, you ladies, read, you boys,
> My Country Sentiment
>
> But Kate says, "Cut that anger and fear,
> True love's the stuff we need!
> With laughing children and the running deer
> That makes a book indeed."
>
> Then Tom, a hard and bloody chap,
> Though much beloved by me,
> "Robert, have done with nursery pap,
> Write like a man," says he.
>
> Hate and Fear are not wanted here,
> Nor Toys nor Country Lovers,
> Everything they took from my new poem book
> But the flyleaf and the covers.

Graves, who must have perceived potential problems with his reading public, reaffirms here that he must write about what concerns him. This staunch individualism in a poetic stance demonstrates that his poetic inspiration came out of everyday experiences and was closely tied to his own response to life; what he wrote was what he felt, and the need to work out his problems through poetry was considered a legitimate vehicle for stating his eclectic opinions. The fact that Graves published *Country Sentiment* knowing full well that he would fail to please his critics and readers anticipates "The Reader over My Shoulder," in which he was rudely and completely to disregard his audience. But here, Graves's attitude is more a resigned expectation, a shrug of the poetic shoulders and a sigh, along with a forlorn What can they expect of me?

The nursery rhymes in *Country Sentiment* are sweetly entertaining and obviously escapist both in flavor and purpose. To dismiss them simply as childish sentiments, however, would be to misunderstand Graves's purpose; indeed, the opportunity to write nursery rhymes and ballads may be seen as an emancipation from didactic restraints forced upon the poet by his critics and audience. In nursery rhymes, the poet is able to allow the spontaneity of his emotions (both rational and irrational) to flow unhindered through the simplistic verse form. In "To E. M. — A Ballad of Nursery Rhyme" (written for his friend, the critic Edward Marsh), Graves likens the unsophisticated form of the nursery rhyme to the sweet, wild strawberry which grows "beside the trickling stream" and contrasts it favorably with the cultivated strawberry, grown in the well-manicured English garden. The wild berries are tastier and more pungent than their bland cousins; they will, Graves suggests, continue to grow long after the garden variety has wasted away.

At the heart of the poem is the contention that "pure poetry" is part of a long tradition of creative daydreams that have been buffeted into a simple rhyming pattern and language until the lines themselves grow "smooth and round / Like pebbles in Tom's brook." Such stories continue to be remembered and passed on because they contain elements of truth; as such, they stand in contrast to the cultivated academic poetry written to please an audience or to serve a particular philosophical stance. This contrast between the nursery rhyme and "academic" poetry is well stated in Simon's summation of the poem.

Graves is actually contrasting "pure" poetry, i.e., the direct expression of quintessential human experiences (like love and lust and terror) through unmannered language and insistent rhythms, with "philosophical" or "academic" poetry, i.e., the attempt to disguise doctrine as poetry. The former is held to be rooted in the essential experience of men, so that it exercises a timeless fascination upon those who would only ask of poetry what it is uniquely able to provide. The latter fades on the page with the decline and disappearance of its extrinsic value. (Simon 1974, 62)

The most successful of the nursery rhymes in *Country Sentiment* is undoubtedly "Allie." In this lilting song, Graves crystallizes an idyllic moment of his childhood as he observes the almost hypnotic effect of Allie's voice on all the creatures of the field and river. Eventually her song calls even the "children from the green" and envelops them in the trancelike world of play where time is unknown. The song, therefore, has the ability to transport the poet from his mundane world into the experience of childlike wonder. There is little doubt, as Devindra Kohli points out, that "the traumatized Graves found the poetic value of nursery rhymes in their communal intonation, hypnotic rhythms and condensed thought and symbolism" (Kohli 1975, 76). In fact, mesmerizing sounds, childhood symbolism, the consolations of country sentiment, and amatory fancy all meet in "A Song For Two Children," which Graves wrote while waiting for demobilization in Limerick. He explains in *Good-bye* how he was beginning to realize at this point that his true loyalties lay not with the regiment, but with his family in England; and this poem presents the same conflict in dramatic terms.

At that moment some companies of the battalion returned to barracks from a route-march; the drums and fifes drew up under my window, making the panes rattle with "The British Grenadiers." The insistent repetition of the tune and the hoarse words of command as the parade formed up in the square . . . challenged Banbury Cross and Babylon [Graves's nursery images in the preceding stanzas]. The British Grenadiers succeeded for a moment in forcing their way into the poem:

> Some speak of Alexander,
>   And some of Hercules,
> but were driven out:
>   But where are there any like Nancy and Jenny,
>   Where are there any like these?
> I had ceased to be a British grenadier. (*Good-bye*, 344–45)

Here he quotes the second and third stanzas of the poem, which use the simple language of nursery rhyme to express his love for his wife and new daughter and to escape from the militaristic system; moreover, the lilting rhythms of nursery rhyme—"Balow lalow or Hey derry down"—drown out the formal cadences of the drill field, a victory for the childish world over the grim reality of wartime. He conveys the same fanciful vision in other poems in the collection such as "Baloo Loo For Jenny" and the folkish "Hawk and Buckle."

The ballads are, by definition, more serious than the lullabies and nursery rhymes; moreover, they seem to suggest that Graves was examining the concept of love very carefully. The folk ballad that opens *Country Sentiment*, "A Frosty Night," involves an interesting dialogue between a concerned and inquisitive mother and an unsettled, secretive daughter. When the mother asks her child why she looks so shaken, the daughter, glowing with the thrill of a furtive love tryst, claims that all is well and asks to be left alone. The mother senses that something monumental has taken place:

> Ay, the night was frosty,
>   Coldly gaped the moon,
> Yet the birds seemed twittering
>   Through green boughs of June.
>
> Soft and thick the snow lay,
>   Stars danced in the sky.
> Not all the lambs of May-day
>   Skip so bold and high.

The use of the pathetic fallacy here suggests that the mother has truly sensed the equivocal nature of her daughter's experience, but when the mother confronts the daughter with "Who was it said, 'I love you'?" the daughter becomes defensive. Kirkham sees this rather traditional ballad as a very important expression of Graves's literary and intellectual development, for it is the first of his poems to frame a concept of love fundamental to his poetic thought (1969, 38). Kirkham appears to understand Graves's vision of love here as both baleful and benevolent—as represented in the line spoken by the mother when she describes the daughter's appearance, viz., "You looked a ghost or angel." Kirkham claims that the seed of the White Goddess myth is sown in this line. Admittedly, Kirkham's theory is attractive, for the depiction of the dual character of nature is evident in the ballad; the frosty winter night metaphorically embraces "green boughs of June," and, despite the heavy

snowfall, frisky stars "danced in the sky" as in celebration of May Day.
But the emphasis of the poem is on the daughter, who bears no resemblance whatsoever to Graves's demanding mistress. On the contrary, her
evasive replies to her mother's questioning and her dogged determination
to keep her own counsel where her new love affair is concerned seem far
more relevant to the interpretation of the ballad itself than Kirkham's
ruminations. The drama in the poem centers on the daughter's desire to
fathom her own emotional responses rather than to share them with her
suspicious and unsympathetic mother.

This poem is similar in theme to a much better poem in the collection
entitled "Apples and Water," which also depicts a mother-daughter
relationship. Here, the mother and daughter watch a troop of tired and
parched soldiers march by their country cottage. The daughter's generous
impulse is to assist the soldiers by giving them apples and water. But the
cautious mother holds the daughter back and cries bitterly,

> "Ah, sweet, had I but know at first
>   Their throats are always dry."

> "There is no water can supply them
>   In western streams that flow,
> There is no fruit can satisfy them
>   On orchard trees that grow."

> "Once in my youth I gave, poor fool,
>   A soldier apples and water,
> So may I die before you cool
>   So Your father's drouth, my daughter."

Once again, the mother figure suppresses the natural spontaneity of the
daughter's impulse out of fear that her daughter will become the victim
of love's changeability. While Seymour-Smith's suggestion (1982, 69)
that Graves wrote this poem out of self-reproach (for making Nancy
pregnant a second time) appears somewhat dubious, the idea of male lust
is very much in evidence. In fact, in both of these poems the question of
the fickleness of love seems to be an issue; both of the mothers appear
to have been betrayed and discarded by their men. As a result of their
own negative experiences, they try to impose a shield around their
daughters to stave off the onset of love, but their caution and vigilance
have little effect. Love, in all its seductiveness, will overcome all impedi-
ments, as witnessed by the daughter's experience in "A Frosty Night."

Graves's own insecurity about the permanence of love led him to the ballad form as a safe outlet for examining his own ambiguous feelings toward the nature of love. But, as he states in *The English Ballad,* the ballad form was stylistically limiting where its subject matter was concerned:

> The specialization in [the ballad] form is matched by a specialization in treatment of subject. . . . It is . . . sometimes allegorical: the ballad-proper does not moralize or preach or express any strong partisan bias. The song and the story alone are considered. The singers identify themselves with the characters, and the only comment on the story is the tone in which each character speaks. (21)

The ballad, then, for Graves had become a dead end, for its form restricted his internal searching. The sonorous rhyming and romantic stances of the nursery rhymes and ballads were no longer capable of sustaining the complexities of Graves's neurosis or his continuing awareness of the failure of his marriage. Kirkham concurs here when he writes:

> In submitting to the influence of the folk-ballad, folk-song and nursery rhyme Graves was seeking to dissolve personal conflict in a traditional, generalizing situation. The situation is implicit in the form of these poems . . . as well as in their themes, and so the influence necessitated close, in some instances servile, imitation. His experiments in this mode produced some successes . . . but it is difficult to see where they could have led if he had continued with them. (Kirkham 1969, 39)

Despite Graves's comments to Edmund Blunden in July 1919 that "war-poetry is played out I'm afraid, commercially, for another five or ten years. . . . Rotten thing for us, but it's no good blinking at it" (O'Prey 1982, 113), he still included a small selection of war poems in the *Country Sentiment* collection. This group of ten poems stands apart at the end of the volume in a section entitled "Retrospect." Perhaps this reflects Graves's intention of putting the war behind him and moving on to new subjects and poetic experiments.

"Haunted," the opening poem of the "Retrospect" section, examines the guilt Graves felt for surviving the war intact. In *Good-bye,* Graves states that as he walked down the streets of Harlech after the war, strangers would assume faces of friends who had been killed (352); here, he uses the same disconcerting experience to weave a poem of culpability.

The key word appears to be "ashamed" in the penultimate line of the last stanza:

> Gulp down your wine, old friends of mine,
> Roar through the darkness, stamp and sing
> And lay ghost hands on everything,
> But leave the noonday's warm sunshine
> To living lads for mirth and wine.
>
> I met you suddenly down the street,
> Strangers assume your phantom faces,
> You grin at me from daylight places,
> Dead, long dead, I'm ashamed to greet
> Dead men down the morning street.

While the poem is strictly personal in tone, the message is more general in its intent. The ghosts of the dead soldiers are given free rein in the realm of darkness where they have been sentenced to be forgotten; clearly, they are ordered to "leave the noonday's warm sunshine / To living lads for mirth and wine." But the dead no longer obey the commands of the living, and they "grin" out even in the morning sunshine. The guilt of the living is emphasized in the shame of their enjoying the sun and the sensual elements of life, a pleasure denied their fallen comrades. The poem anticipates the frightening neuroses that were to haunt Graves throughout the decade before the publication of *Good-bye.*

In "Here They Lie," a neat four-line epitaph to his fellow soldiers who died in battle, Graves attempts to find some merit in their heroic sacrifice. The conclusion that they died "by free will" and "had pride," however, rings rather hollow considering the holocaust that was World War I. About all that can be said of this existential view of fallen soldiers is that Graves chooses to see nobility in the individual action of giving up one's life in a heroic manner. The poem appears strained and as full of traditional tombstone clichés as those verses used later by Kipling's War Graves Commission.

"Sospan Fach (The Little Saucepan)" is a poem in which the evocative power of the song of four Welsh colliers caught under a tree in a hailstorm thrusts the poet-listener back to Mametz Woods. He remembers the same song being sung there under much different circumstances.

Fierce burned the sun, yet cheeks were pale,
For ice hail they had leaden hail;
In that fine forest, green and big,
There stayed unbroken not one twig.

They sang, they swore, they plunged in haste,
Stumbling and shouting through the waste;
The little "Saucepan" flamed on high,
Emblem of hope and ease gone by.

Rough pit-boys from the coaly South,
They sang, even in the cannon's mouth;

The song reminds the narrator of the mindless slaughter of the brave Royal Welch Fusiliers with whom he had served quite recently. The reminiscence grows so strong that he is physically relieved when the choir breaks up as the sun shines through; as he says, "Another note would break my heart!" Yet again, Graves is made to reflect and relive the battles on the Somme, and once more, the only positive aspect of the whole experience for him is the bravery that the soldiers showed in the face of death: "They sang, even in the cannon's mouth." Graves was always sensitive to the sheer waste of human lives that governments deemed necessary to solve international crimes, but this very realization placed a huge moral responsibility on a man whose commission obliged him to order his troops into the midst of the German machine guns.

Of all the poems in the "Retrospect" section, "The Leveller" has probably been given most critical scrutiny because of Graves's attempt in it to parody the style of Sassoon. In a letter written to Sassoon on 16 July 1918 (just three days after Sassoon was accidentally shot in the head by one of his own sergeants), Graves writes:

I wrote a trench poem the other day to show you I could write just like you, about two men I knew killed by the same shell, one a sodden Anglo-Argentine and t'other a boy of 18, very young looking: the first called out "mother, mother" and the other cursed God and died. The last verse is pure Sassons [sic], as your parody was once pure Masefield. (O'Prey 1982, 98)

The use of situational irony in the poem demonstrates convincingly Graves's ability to distance himself from the particulars of war and write very successful verse in the detached method of his fellow poet. Sergeant

Smith's letter to the womenfolk of the dead men in the last stanza reinforces the hypocrisy of the war and the continued attempts of the higher powers to keep the reality of the battlefield from the noncombatants:

> Old Sergeant Smith, kindest of men,
> Wrote out two copies there and then
> Of his accustomed funeral speech
> To cheer the womenfolk of each.

A final poem of two stanzas, "Give us rain"—one that does not appear in "Retrospect"—deserves a brief investigation for its social commentary:

> "Give us Rain, Rain," said the bean and the pea,
>   "Not so much Sun,
>   Not so much Sun."
> But the sun smiles bravely and encouragingly,
> And no rain falls and no waters run.
>
> "Give us Peace, Peace," said the peoples oppressed,
>   "Not so many Flags,
>   Not so many Flags."
> But the Flags fly and the Drums beat, denying rest,
> And the children starve, they shiver in rags.

The opening stanza is a narrative metaphor for what will be explained in the second stanza. The bean and the pea, both plants that require moist soil for growth, implore the sun for respite from its parching heat, but the sun shines on relentlessly and ignores the needs of the plants. In a like manner, after the war the oppressed peoples beg for relief from their misery, but all they hear are the pompous ravings and nationalistic promises of the four powers at the Versailles peace conference. And while these powerful nations play with the political spoils of war, starving, freezing children continue to suffer the physical deprivations it effects. In part, the poem is Graves's reflection on the deterioration of the British people's idealism in the war and on the inability of political action to address the war's continuing legacy. Later, in *Good-bye*, Graves returns to this theme when he states: "The Versailles Treaty shocked me; it seemed to lead certainly to another war and yet nobody cared . . . I began to hear news, too, of my mother's relatives in Germany and the penury to which they had been reduced. . . . Nancy and I took all this to heart; we now called ourselves socialists" (354).

Although the war poems are given a separate identity in *Country Sentiment* by their position at the end of the volume, they are probably its least interesting section. Here, Graves achieves no new insights about the nature of the war; in fact, his musings on guilt and the irony of war seem stale and redundant. This he sensed in a letter to Blunden, and yet he allowed these poems to be printed in order to fill out the volume. Like Sassoon's, his social crusade appears to have been of short duration; and in fact Graves's sister Rosaleen, who according to R. P. Graves was both Nancy's and Robert's closest confidante after the war, recollects that she "never once heard [Robert] talking about politics or socialism of any sort" (Graves 1986, 215).

If Graves was not overly concerned with politics, he initially showed an enthusiastic interest in the study of English literature at Oxford. Furthermore, the development of his relationship with Edmund Blunden, his fellow poet at Oxford, and with Siegfried Sassoon further strengthened Graves's commitment to the craft of poetry. Three poems in the *Country Sentiment* volume demonstrate his preoccupation with both the role of poet and the essence of poetry itself.

"The God Called Poetry" was written just before Graves's marriage to Nancy. In a letter to Sassoon written on 11 January 1918, Graves boasts that Robbie Ross thinks the poem a masterpiece, and he himself is of the opinion that "it's rather a hit" (O'Prey 1982, 91). Sassoon confirms Graves's estimate in his own journal by rating the poem "very fine" (*Diaries 1915–1918*, 203). In his first critical study of poetry, *On English Poetry*, Graves again uses the poem to demonstrate the "thought machinery" that produces poetry. He explains that in his vision, the God of Poetry has "two heads like Janus, one savage, scowling and horrible, the face of Blackbeard the Pirate, the other mild and gracious, that of John the Evangelist" (62). The inspiration for the poem came from an experience at a camp near Liverpool where Graves was watching a guard of honor drilling under the aegis of a keen young officer whose parade ground manner reminded Graves of the personality of Christopher Marlowe. Graves furthers his literary approach to the scenario by wondering how Shakespeare would have handled the drill. Would he have laughed or missed the parade completely, as was Sassoon's custom? The combination of two apparently contradictory approaches to the drill and two different poetic personalities—the roaring genius of Marlowe and the passive, receptive genius of Shakespeare—forms the catalyst for the creation of the Janus-like god of poetry.

The poem is curious for its simplistic philosophy of contraries. For Graves, poetry has both a destructive and a healing nature, but the poet who serves the God of Poetry must dedicate himself to fusing the contradictory elements of the universe in order to create a sense of balance in his work. The poet's view of the world must be one that straddles the conventional distinctions of positive and negative, one that recognizes that life is amoral and philosophically neutral where human affairs are concerned. The poet must follow the lead of his contradictory, "glorious fearful" god, who tells him:

> "I am YES and I am NO,
> Black as pitch and white as snow,
> Love me, hate me, reconcile
> Hate with love, perfect with vile,
> So equal justice shall be done
> And life shared between moon and sun,
> Nature for you shall curse or smile:
> A poet you shall be, my son."

This was written at a time when Graves was trying to reconcile the horrors of war with the positive expectations of marriage with Nancy, but Kirkham's argument that the poem is simply a pleading for the restoration of positive values that might rescue Graves from moral uncertainty seems to ignore the nature of the duality presented in the poem (Kirkham 1969, 57). Rather, it is an acceptance of the two-faced Janus as an emblem for the dualistic, even Manichaean vision of the universe. Out of the conflict between the powers of good and evil comes the energy from which the poet will derive his inspiration.

"The Voice of Beauty Drowned" is an important poem in that Graves compares his poetry to that of his contemporaries. Graves likens his poetry to the voice of a "slight and small" bird attempting to sing from his heart in the midst of a thicket. His plaintive song awakens the other birds, but they tell him to "tune [his] melody to [their] note" or not to sing at all. In spite of this, the bird's need to sing causes the song to flow out again, but now his song is drowned out by the jangling notes of the woodland choir. Graves says of his own "song":

> Lovelier could no music be,
> Clearer than water, soft as curd,
> Fresh as the blossomed cherry tree.

His lonely song, however, cannot be heard amidst the cacophony of the birds around him; hence, it goes unnoticed.

Evidently, the poem attacks the new style of poetry, which Graves sees as lacking both in emotional and lyrical sensitivity. The animosity toward his fellow poets, of course, continued through Graves's life. It surfaced again in his *Contemporary Techniques of Poetry,* where the only poets to receive his praise were those independent of, and safely outside of, the three poetic factions that he was to label the Conservatives, the Liberals, and the Left-wingers (5).

"Ghost Raddled," which has been more appropriately renamed "A Haunted House" in recent editions, may—except for "Rocky Acres"—be the most elusive poem in *Country Sentiment.* Attempts to analyze it have led to rather diverse results. Graves himself obviously felt the poem was significant, because he placed it at the front of his 1938 edition of *Collected Poems;* and it has remained largely unchanged in form in the latest edition of Graves's collected poems.

The poem, reminiscent of A. E. Housman's "Terence, This Is Stupid Stuff" but without the wit, presents a conversation between an audience, which demands to be entertained with a pleasant song, and a "surly" poet, who can only sing from "clouded tales of wrong / and terror." A strong suggestion of the reading public's desire to forget the horrors of the war and to be titillated by sweetly sentimental songs of romance is evident, but the churlish poet will have none of it. His repertoire of poems consists of "spirits in the web hung room," demons that clang unseen bells, and of "lust frightful, past belief." Graves creates an analogy between a haunted house and the condition of England after the war. This image of English society as a dilapidated house haunted by frightening demons and guilt also comes to reflect the "haunted" mind of the poet himself. How can the poet, amid the residue of war guilt and shell shock, manage to find within his troubled mind the material to weave love songs and "country sentiment"?

> A song? What laughter or what song
> Can this house remember?
> Do flowers and butterflies belong
> To a blind December?

The image of a "blind December" is particularly effective here because the shortness of December days and chilly night winds—not to mention the fact that most vegetation is dead or dormant—work together to capture accurately the atmosphere of desolation and foreboding that the poet feels.

In "Ghost Raddled," Graves makes no attempt to conceal his own neurasthenic symptoms and physical debilities which, as R. P. Graves points out, were very severe during the period 1920–21.

> But despite the enjoyment which Robert took both in his work and in his circle of friends . . . ill health and financial worries constantly overshadow the period. Robert had still not recovered from his wartime experiences, and he and Nancy tended to live beyond their means. (Graves 1986, 223)

Financial considerations aside, Graves was suffering more and more from the neurasthenia that compelled him to relive in his imagination the battles he had fought in northern France as long as five years before. In W. D. Thomas's article on the impact of the war on Graves, the author quotes from *Clinical Psychiatry* by Mayer-Gross to demonstrate how many of the characteristics of neurasthenia Graves manifested. In summary:

> [Neurasthenics] are often . . . restless in an aimless, fidgety manner, over-sensitive to noise and light, and easily irritated by the presence of others. They avoid company, live a solitary, carefully regulated life, and are incapable of following any regular occupation. (Thomas 1975, 118)

Perhaps the most important conclusion of "Ghost Raddled" is that "honest men" are the ones to suffer from the nightmarish afflictions of neurasthenia. Furthermore, from the poet's viewpoint, society is sadly unconcerned with its victims, and there appears to be little hope for reconciliation between the two groups. "Honest men" are wakened alone in the dark of night "with glaring eyes / Bone-chilled, flesh creeping"; the neurasthenic must suffer alone.

The very struggle of the neurasthenic can be glimpsed in Graves's dark poem "Outlaws," where the rational mind fights to keep from complete submergence in the irrational manifestations brought about by the subconscious. The elusive forces that are generated by the coming of nightfall are symbolized in the poem as "the pagan gods no longer worshipped, banished from consciousness, but still leading a subterranean existence" (Kirkham 1969, 43).

> Old gods almost dead, malign,
> 　Starved of their ancient dues,

> Incense and fruit, fire, blood and wine
> 　　And an unclean muse.
>
> Banished to woods and a sickly moon,
> 　　Shrunk to mere bogey things,
> Who spoke with thunder once at noon
> 　　To prostrate kings.

Graves finds no resolution in this poem. His upbringing and religious background, his education, his culture and society—nothing has prepared him for the glimpse into the void that the war has created. His inability to cope with his own irrational responses leads him to fear that he will be dragged into the darkness where the malignant primitive gods—closely associated with power and lust—reign. By extension, then, Graves reflects in this poem on his own fears of not being able to keep control of his rational self. The intensity and duration of his nightmares and the uncontrollable physical responses to the slightest noise or unknown person must have tormented the poet and made him wonder about his sanity. At this time, the only solutions for Graves were either to procure psychological help (which he at first rejected) or somehow to learn to accommodate the neurasthenia in his life and work. Graves tried to turn this inward journey through the "moving sea of black" into poetic exploration in "Rocky Acres."

The physical landscape of "Rocky Acres" is often seen by critics to represent Harlech, where Graves went to recover from his wounds during his sick leaves and where the poet found a quiet spot for reflection and meditation.

> This is a wild land, country of my choice,
> 　　With harsh craggy mountain, moor ample and
> 　　bare.
> Seldom in these acres is heard any voice
> 　　But voice of cold water that runs here and there
> 　　Through rocks and lank heather growing without
> 　　care.
> No mice in the heath run, nor no birds cry
> For fear of the dark speck that floats in the sky.
>
> He soars and he hovers rocking on his wings,
> 　　He scans his wide parish with a sharp eye,
> He catches the trembling of small hidden things,

> He tears them in pieces, dropping from the sky:
>   Tenderness and pity the land will deny,
> Where life is but nourished from water and rock
> A hardy adventure, full of fear and shock.

The land described in the first two stanzas is harsh and brutal, lacking the civilizing qualities of tenderness and love. It is, however, the country of the poet's choice, and he stands ready, like an Arthurian hero about to set off on a quest, to explore the unknown terrain. Thus the physical landscape mirrors the psychological landscape of Graves's mind at this time. Graves appears to have accepted his untrammeled unconsciousness as an uncompromising world where beneficent nature and logic have no relevance; his purpose is to experiment in order to discover what close examination might yield to assist his poetic development.

> Time has never journeyed to this lost land,
>   Crakeberries and heather bloom out of date,
> The rocks jut, the streams flow singing on either hand,
>   Careless if the season be early or late.
>   The skies wander overhead, now blue, now slate:
> Winter would be known by his cold cutting snow
> If June did not borrow his armour also.

In the confused world of neurasthenic nightmares, all references to time and passing of the seasons are gratuitous. No predictability is found in the land of mental anarchy—everything is foreign to the mind accustomed to the order and structure of the waking world. But in spite of its bleakness, the stark, primordial landscape has an attraction in its indifference to the poet's expectations.

> Yet this is my country beloved by me best
>   The first land that rose from Chaos and the Flood,
> Nursing no fat valleys for comfort and rest,
> Trampled by no hard hooves, stained with no blood,
> Bold immortal country whose hilltops have stood
> Strongholds for the proud gods when on earth they go,
> Terror for fat burghers in far plains below.

Graves seems to claim here that those irrational impulses pervading his subconscious have their origins in the earliest impulses of man. These forces "whose atavistic power Graves cannot and would not control with consciousness" (Hoffman 1967, 165) represent a new and powerful impulse for his poetic vision. The clean vision, yet uncorrupted by the false values of "fat burghers" in society, offers him an opportunity not only to be inspired by the constant tension between the primitive vision and modern effete society, but also to help cure himself of his neurasthenia by confronting and thereby diffusing the cause of his fears, much in the way the mother transforms the child's nightmare in "Dicky" into a logical and sensible occurrence.

Like many of his fellow veterans, Graves craved during his rehabilitation the attentiveness, sympathy, and care of a devoted wife to help combat the physical results of the war. According to Graves's biographers, however, Nancy Nicholson seems to have been lacking in all three qualities and to have made Graves's reentry into civilian life difficult. The two biographies of Graves, however, present contradictory portraits of her. Seymour-Smith refers to her as "scatty" and "difficult," and even quotes a diary entry by Constance Masefield (wife of John and landlady of the house the Graves were renting) that refers to Nancy as "mulish" (Seymour-Smith 1982, 82). R. P. Graves is much more sympathetic in his depiction of her:

> Fortunately Nancy, however difficult she was at times, remained extremely sympathetic to Robert's mental suffering; and sometimes, when she proposed a sudden "burst for freedom," it was not just to satisfy a private whim, but to distract Robert from one of his gloomy moods by providing a change of scenery. (Graves 1986, 232)

In *Assault Heroic,* Nancy is depicted as naïve and somewhat spoiled, but her love for Graves appears genuine, and R. P. Graves quotes a number of letters to show how well she was accepted by his family.

In contrast, *Good-bye,* admittedly written from a less-than-objective point of view, suggests that Nancy's sympathies for Graves were somewhat negated by her views on the role of women in history. Rather than looking at each particular relationship on its own merits, Nancy seemed to generalize too freely.

> The most important thing to her was the judicial equality of the sexes; she held that all the wrong in the world was caused by male domination and narrowness. She refused to see my experiences in the war as in any way

comparable with the sufferings that millions of married women of the working class went through. . . . Male stupidity and callousness became an obsession with her and she found it difficult not to include me in her universal condemnation of men. (*Good-bye,* 355)

Graves sent the first draft of his poem "Vain and Careless" to his sister Rosaleen only three weeks after his marriage to Nancy (Graves 1986, 355). In the poem, the lovely lady is so negligent that she gives her child to a beggar, the man so vain that he walks on stilts to be seen. The poem's message is wittily put: vain or careless people have no capacity to love. Kirkham's rather restrained opinion is valid that while the poem's "connection with the poet's personal situation is tenuous, [and] an appreciation of the poem does not depend on knowing it . . . it seems to refer to conflict in his marriage between the poet's pride and his wife's coolness" (1969, 35). The final stanza demonstrates that the lilting musicality of the early verses has given way to serious considerations.

> This gentle-born couple
> Lived and died apart.
> Water will not mix with oil,
> Nor vain with careless heart.

The lady's carelessness here is said to result specifically from her affections toward the man; their inability to commit themselves to an intimate understanding of each other's needs because of their inward concerns will eventually lead to estrangement from each other. Graves was evidently scrutinizing the marital problems he would have to work out with his wife.

"The Beacon" is a far more enigmatic and disturbing poem. Superficially a pleasant pastoral of classical tradition, the shepherd and his mistress exchange "love / Under dim boughs," but a glowworm interrupts their covert lovemaking with its flare; its refusal to turn out its light irritates the shepherd. The glowworm's explanation closes the poem and creates its ambiguity:

> "I also am a lover;
> The lamp I display
> Is beacon for my true love
> Wandering astray.

> "Through the thick bushes
>   And the grass comes she
> With a heartload of longing
>   And love for me.
>
> "Sir, enjoy your fancy,
>   But spare me harm,
> A lover is a lover,
>   Though but a worm."

The poet implies that the glowworm's love for its mate is somehow founded on an intimacy which dwarfs that of the human lovers. The implication is reinforced by the primary symbol in the poem: the glowworm's beacon. The shepherd and his mistress exchange their mysteries "under dim boughs," in the darkness when "the Sun's to bed." The atmosphere of their lovemaking is somewhat murky and furtive, whereas the love of the glowworm (the customary creature of the night) shines bright both literally and metaphorically. Apparent in the worm's love is a sense of hope and faith and a patience for the fulfillment of love's promise. Hence, the last two ambiguous lines in the poem can be read to mean that the true lover is the worm, which enjoys more than just the physicality of love.

The suggestion of the poem is that men are interested solely in sensualism and the fulfillment of physical desire, whereas the glowworm's love represents a complete fulfillment of love in an all-encompassing sense. In life the puritanical Graves was often made to feel by his wife that his desire for sexual fulfillment—his lust—was in some way an imposition on her. And perhaps Graves is lamenting here that his only joy in a somewhat loveless marriage lay only in its physical consummation. Clearly, he and Nancy were out of sympathy with each other just before the publication of *Country Sentiment;* in fact, in *Good-bye,* Graves records, "[Nancy] began to regret our marriage, as I did also. We wanted somehow to be dis-married—not by divorce, which was as bad as marriage—and able to live together without any legal or religious obligation to live together" (368). Ironically, as Seymour-Smith points out, Graves attributed the regret to Nancy alone in the 1957 edition of *Good-bye.*

> He did not want to be "dis-married" at all, and was appalled when Nancy suddenly announced that she did. But in 1929 he was still too proud to admit it.

What really happened is revealing. Nancy told him that she regretted their marriage. As is his want when confronted with bad news, he made the best of it. (*Good-bye,* 83–84)

So, making the best of a bad situation, Graves turned to his poetry and berated himself for his insensitivity to his wife. Nevertheless, when one reads "The Beacon," one wonders how many times the epithet "worm" was used to describe members of the male gender in Nancy's frequent tirades.

One last poem in *Country Sentiment* deserves attention for its reflection of the early disintegration of the Graves-Nicholson marriage. "Song: One Hard Look" is a poem of ever-growing disillusionment with love. The poem shows how a string of seemingly insignificant events can become extremely critical, depending upon the contexts in which they appear.

> A straw will crack
> The camel's back,
> To die we need but sip,
> So little sand
> As fills the hand
> Can stop a steaming ship.

In the final stanza, Graves explains the point of his illustrative examples.

> One smile relieves
> A heart that grieves
> Though deadly sad it be,
> And one hard look
> Can close the book
> That lovers love to see—

The rather insignificant gesture of a smile between lovers can act positively to help heal a serious rift and to make reconciliation possible. But under the same circumstances, an inability to express sympathy and understanding can dry up any hope of reconciliation between lovers. The tone of the poem—the matter-of-factness with which the last two lines are written—suggests that the poet has been the recipient of "one hard look" very recently. He appears to be urging, almost pleading, with his lover to heed the consequences of her harshness before all hope of sharing love disappears.

Graves saw the disintegration of his marriage as a reflection of his own faults, of faults that could be corrected. The love poems in the *Country Sentiment* volume exhibit a belief that much can be accomplished by sensitivity to the lover's needs and confrontation of the various problems with a positive attitude. But Nancy Nicholson was not the soul mate that Graves needed at that time. Her lack of understanding of Graves's neurasthenia and postwar problems of adjustment, combined with her aversion to men, determined that the idealism Graves felt at the outset of the marriage was bound to be eroded as their marriage continued.

Country Sentiment, in many ways, is a pivotal work in understanding the origin of many of the circumstances that led to the writing of *Good-bye* some nine years later. In the collection Graves reveals the various frustrations and disappointments with which he was faced in postwar England. As he states in his preface to *Whipperginny,* the book was primarily escapist and exploratory in nature. His efforts to escape from the violence of his war memories through the simplicity of fairy tales and the ballad form proved to be largely unsuccessful, but at least Graves was able to break away from the conventional restrictions and prejudices of the traditional Victorian poetry that the Georgians were trying so hard to displace.

Within a short time, Graves fell out of sympathy with his fellow Georgians and began to examine the place of the poet in the postwar world of Modernism. His response was eccentric, but his examination helped to justify and objectify the mounting tension in his personal life and, in turn, induced him to continue with his poetic explorations. He was already viewing Georgian poetics as outmoded in the newly fragmented world, but also began to reject the new Modernism in favor of his own particular brand of poetry. The Georgian themes of "nature and love and leisure and old age and children and animals and sleep" (*Modernist Poetry,* 119) were relics of a time long past. Graves's search for themes that spoke for the age were to lead him into an examination of his disappointment in love and his war-induced neuroses.

3

Inward Explorations: *The Pier Glass, Whipperginny,* and *The Featherbed*

Graves's dissatisfaction with his marriage, together with the financial burden of a growing family and the pressures of reading for a degree at Oxford, must have pushed his already strained nerves to the breaking point. Making the best of a bad situation, the poet turned away from his marital problems and delved deeply into the causes of his war neuroses and nightmares to produce the impetus for his next volume of poetry, *The Pier Glass.*

Except for the six poems that had appeared earlier in *The Treasure Box,* almost all the poems in *The Pier Glass* were written in 1920, when Graves's mental condition was once again unstable. On 7 October 1920, just after Secker had accepted the poems for publication, Graves wrote the following lines to Eddie Marsh:

> I never seem to see anybody these days and when I do they excite my shell-shock so that I am useless for days after. I am worn-out from much work, chiefly in the last few weeks, helping Nancy with her shop that she has sportingly started up here. (O'Prey 1982, 119–120)

The volume was published in late February of 1921, and in a letter to Edmund Blunden thanking him for a favorable review in the *Nation and Athenaeum,* Graves explained carefully how the poems should be interpreted.

> You can see it [*Pier Glass*] better if you think of it as half a reaction against shell shock by indulging in a sort of dementia praecox . . . of fantastic daydreams, cf. "Troll's Nosegay," "Hills of May," etc., half as an attempt to stand up to the damned disease and write an account of it (hence, "Incubus," "Gnat," "Down," "Pier Glass," "Reproach," and so on), the obscurity of which is not so obscure as the original. (O'Prey 1982, 123–24)

In fact, Graves's division of poems is very helpful when one attempts to analyze the contents of the volume. The majority of poems, forming the first half of the collection, deal with his efforts to understand and diagnose his neurasthenia through the medium of poetry, and the second section continues to examine Graves's preoccupation with love. Kirkham, who agrees that the poems fall into two distinct categories, comments in his criticism that "neither of the themes, war neurosis and love, is explored; the former is regarded merely as an appalling and apparently causeless fact, the latter is hailed simply as a panacea for all ills" (1969, 47). Kirkham, however, overlooks Graves's extended attempts to confront and overcome his nervous disorder through poetry and downplays the concern Graves had of losing his poetic fount of inspiration in the process of seeking out a cure. Indeed, Kirkham's judgment that Graves passively accepted his illness is as questionable as his suggestion that the love poetry in this volume is simply escapist. On the contrary, of all the love poetry written for this volume, only "The Patchwork Bonnet" suffers from the cloying elements of sentimental escapism.

The opening poem of *The Pier Glass* attempts to put the problem of Graves's guilt-laden unconsciousness to rest. "The Stake" is, on the surface, an argument between two towns over the guilt or innocence of a person buried under a crossroads with "a stake through his heart." During the spring, the stake begins to throw out shoots, ostensibly gaining life from the decomposition of the body below. An argument then commences over the nature of its shoots.

> Naseboro' says "A Upas Tree";
> "A Rose," says Crowther;
> But April's here to declare it
> Neither one nor the other.

Both townsmen are wrong in their speculations; the new life springing from the stake is neither the sweet-smelling romantic rose nor the saplings from the poisonous Upas tree, but rather, as might be expected, the shoots from an honest English oak.

> A green-tufted oak-tree
> On the green wold,
> Careless as the dead heart,
> That the roots enfold.

"Careless" is the key word here, for the tree is depicted as continuing to grow without effort and completely oblivious to the dead body below.

The poem, then, is Graves's positive attempt to atone for the deaths that he caused in the war; he makes an intellectual affirmation that his current sufferings and feelings of remorse have no relevance to those now dead. To try to justify the deaths of the soldiers with romantic allusions (the rose) or staunch military rhetoric (the Upas tree) is both false and insincere; rather, Graves must learn simply to accept the reality of life and death as part of the natural course of existence and to remember that in nature, nothing truly dies—new life continually springs forth from the old. His argument is convincing from a logical point of view, but his discounting of the emotional response makes the poem incomplete.

"Reproach," Graves's attempt at atonement for having played his part in the slaughter on the battlefields of France, demonstrates quite convincingly that the poet is still haunted by his actions. A figure with a "grieving moonlight face" stares down and reproaches the speaker, who tries to dispel the image with his own rational verbal formula:

> I am not guilty in my mind
> Of aught would make you weep.

The image charges Graves with being untrue and unkind. Such blatantly understated terms scald the poet's "heart with shame" as he recognizes his complicity in the killing of fellow soldiers during the war. And through the use of pathetic fallacy in the final stanza, the shame and bewilderment at this heinous crime bear witness to Graves's own recognition of his "ancestral sin."

> The black trees shudder, dropping snow,
> The stars tumble and spin.
> Speak, speak, or how may a child know
> His ancestral sin?

The ancestral sin here is not "original sin," as Day postulates (1963, 32); it is the sin against humanity that is apparent in all war—the sin of pride that sets men to fighting together against other men. The nagging spirit of the night will not let Graves extricate himself from the responsibility for his role in the bloodshed; a payment must be extracted for his complicity, and that payment is the guilt-ridden neurasthenia that haunts his vision.

In "Down," a poem very carefully analyzed by Graves's critics, the poet allows the reader to journey with him figuratively to the "no man's land" of his neurasthenic mind. Lying in bed when the clock strikes two on a windy summer night, a sick man is disturbed by the crowing of a hen-roost "three hours from dawn." In order to distract himself from dwelling on his guilt, he tries in vain to concentrate on the answerless riddles of his childhood. Eventually, the guilt sinks deeply into his thoughts, and, as Kohli puts it, in a "claustrophobic dream structure" (1975, 95), the sick man begins to drown in his own conscience.

> Mouth open, he was lying, this sick man,
> And sinking all the while; how had he come
> To sink? On better nights his dream went flying,
> Dipping, sailing, the pasture of his sleep,
> But now, since clock and cock, had sunk him down
> Through mattress, bed, floor, floors beneath, stairs, cellars,
> Through deep foundations of the manse, still sinking
> Through unturned earth.

The sick man sinks into the ground where he feels he belongs: the place he has cheated before, and the place where the bones of his comrades rest. Suddenly the image of his comrades falling down during an attack is depicted in a funereal tableau: "weeping, down, drowned, lost!"—lost in the bowels of the earth forever. Graves's guilt, then, haunts him not only for having killed Germans; it haunts him for having survived. Later, in one of his *Crane Bag* essays entitled "What Was That War Like, Sir?" Graves points out that nearly fifty years after the war he is still haunted by the nightmare of visiting the trenches. He reflects here on the deaths of his comrades which occurred with a macabre regularity.

> Death lurked around every traverse, killing our best friends with monotonous spite. We had been spared, but why? Certainly not because of our virtues. (*Crane Bag,* 59)

In the second half of "Down," the speaker tries to remember the simplicity of childhood when one could lose control of one's spirit and delve into an imaginative reverie, having the spirit return fuller and richer than when it left. This recoupling of the spirit and the body in joyous harmony is now lost as the guilt-laden world of experience sunders any communication between the waking body and the seething unconsciousness. The poet's mind continues to fall further and further into madness—perhaps into death—in the final stanza.

> Falling, falling! Light closed up behind him,
> Now stunned by the violent subterrene flow
> Of rivers, whirling down to hiss below
> On the flame-axis of this terrible world;
> Toppling upon their water wall, O spirit . . .

The poem characterizes the nature of Graves's mental anguish and demonstrates clearly that the poet derived little positive inspiration from his nightmares. The mythical geography that maps the landscape of the poet's mind very accurately also sketches the utter hopelessness he feels; in no way does he indicate that his mental suffering is likely to be curable.

"Incubus" is a less successful poem than "Down," but it attempts to display the helplessness that Graves felt when the long nights of semisleep turned into the brooding exploration of his unconscious. The evil spirit traps the body as it lies "arms in supplication spread" and whispers its horrors into the ear of its victim. The second stanza describes in graphic detail his helplessness as nightmarish thoughts flash through his dreaming mind.

> Through the darkness here come I,
> Softly fold about the prey;
> Body moaning must obey,
> Must not question who or why,
> Must accept me, come what may,
> Dumbly must obey.

The final stanza is something of an aubade that forces the grim, dark powers of the night away and ushers in the welcome daylight. The "morning scent and treetop song, / Slow-rising smoke and nothing wrong" help establish again a sense of normality, but the reader cannot forget that "half-Death's" dispersal is only temporary, and that the incubus will be back with a vengeance in the coming night.

The title poem of the volume, "The Pier Glass," which Donald Davie claims is "almost entirely parasitical on early Tennyson" (1962, 41), was originally inscribed to "T. E. Lawrence, who helped me with it." Indeed, in *Good-bye,* Graves mentions that T. E. Lawrence "made a number of suggestions for improving these poems [*Pier Glass*] and [Graves] adopted most of them" (371). This poem enjoys the rare distinction of having been fully analyzed by both of Graves's biographers. It has also attracted countless interpretations from a host of Gravesian critics; most agree that the poem is in some way a metaphor for Graves's neurasthenic state.

"The Pier Glass" is divided into four distinct stages, but these stages do not fall smoothly into four stanza divisions. The poem opens with a servant woman roaming through a lost manor in an involuntary reverie that comes upon her at night and on "sultry afternoons." Her route is always the same, for she is "drawn by a thread of time-sunk memory." The second division recounts her thoughts as, entering the empty bedroom, she is confronted by the sight of the bed. Here her virginity was cruelly violated when her master, intent on expressing his *droit de seigneur,* summoned her from "attic glooms above"; here, too, she avenged herself by murdering him. She gazes into a cracked pier glass and sees a ghost of her former self reflected. The act of killing another human being, no matter how justifiable, has sucked the life out of her. This very lifelessness is emphasized in the third stanza, in which the empty room and the woman's life are synthesized to mirror the same reflection.

> Is there no life, nothing but the thin shadow
> And blank foreboding, never a wainscote rat
> Rasping a crust? Or at the window pane
> No fly, no bluebottle, no starveling spider?
> The windows frame a prospect of cold skies
> Half merged with sea, as at the first creation,
> Abstract, confusing welter. Face about,
> Peer rather in the glass once more, take note
> Of self, the grey lips and long hair dishevelled,
> Sleep-staring eyes.

Overwhelmed by this unnatural reverie, the servant woman prays to Christ to show her that life still exists outside her paralyzing neurasthenic phantasma. Surprisingly, her reflections are answered by the appearance of a swarm of bees between the pier glass and the outside wall; they are busy returning with honey for the survival of the hive. Their purposeful or purposive activity leads the woman "home at last / From labyrinthine wandering." The final section of the poem echoes her deliberations as she recollects her past violence in the room. With a renewed effort, she

decides to confront the cause of her disorder, contemplating whether she
can find it in her heart to forgive the injustice done to her. Her judgment
is evident from the last four lines:

> Kill or forgive? Still does the bed ooze blood?
> Let it drip down till every floor-plank rot!
> Yet shall I answer, challenging the judgment:—
> "Kill, strike the blow again, spite what shall come."
> "Kill, strike, again, again," the bees in chorus hum.

Admittedly, the last stanza of the poem, which has been the subject of
much criticism, is ambiguous. In fact, Graves himself omitted this stanza
from all of his later collections. Seymour-Smith gives the following
explanation for its weakness:

> Graves wrote the first part of the poem more or less as we know it and
> showed it to [T. E.] Lawrence for his approval. Lawrence could not
> understand it, but was fascinated by it; he suggested to Graves that he keep
> it cryptic, but add a few tantalizing clues. So Graves "manufactured" an
> ending giving such clues, became interested in the section on its own
> account, and therefore did no more than confusedly adumbrate the White
> Goddess. (Seymour-Smith 1982, 93)

While the connection between the White Goddess and the ghostly
woman in "Pier Glass" is more credible than Seymour-Smith would have
his readers believe, an explanation for Graves's choosing a female figure
as evidence of his own mental instability is not particularly difficult to
provide; the woman's wretched condition is brought about as a reaction
to the violent deed enacted in revenge. She is a victim, as so many of
Nancy's women were victims, of a man's lust and dominance. Graves,
too, is a victim of his own conscience which recognizes the duality of his
condition; he felt justified in performing his war service, but he became
the victim of a nightmarish disorder in recompense for his actions. The
victimization of the woman who has been forcibly raped by her master
acts as a simplified allegory of Graves's state of mind whenever he
involuntarily returned to examine his war experience. The inability of the
woman—or Graves, for that matter—to forgive her enemy affirms the
belief in the rightness of the initial deed.

The four poems analyzed here are indicative of Graves's concerns
about his deteriorating mental condition and its effect on his poetic
output. But the poem that is truly emblematic of his illness is "The

Gnat," a strange tale about a poor shepherd who fears he will die when a gnat lodged in his skull begins to grow. As the shepherd imagines the gnat swelling inside his head, he kills his loyal dog because he is afraid that after his death no one will treat the dog as well as he. Ironically, after the dog is killed, the gnat flies harmlessly out of the shepherd's mouth, and the shepherd is left a despondent laborer without the companionship of his trusty animal. Graves explains the meaning of this bizarre poem in *The Meaning of Dreams* (159–65), the crux of which is synthesized by Canary:

> Graves said that he originally knew only that he felt an odd sympathy with the shepherd but that he now sees the gnat as an emblem of his own shell shock. The shepherd has hesitated about going to the minister with his problem, as Graves had hesitated about going to psychologists, for to be rid of his madness might mean to kill that which he loved best, his sheep dog (poetry): "The last line of the poem probably refers to psycho-analysis; meaning that all that will be left for me when I have ceased to be a poet will be scraping among the buried and unfruitful memories of the past." (Canary 1980, 165)

If Graves was afraid that psychoanalysis would dry up his inspiration as it cured his neurasthenia, he certainly seemed willing to accept the therapeutic power of love both as a hope for inspiration and as remedy for his shell-shocked mind. In the preface to *Whipperginny,* he claims that he wrote a number of verses for *The Pier Glass* with "the desire to escape from a painful war neurosis into an Arcadia of amatory fancy." Graves must have had in mind here such poems as "The Patchwork Bonnet," with its images of domestic bliss, and the lyrical ballad "Black Horse Lane," with its study of aged passion; both are examples of wish fulfillment on the part of the ailing poet. In "The Finding of Love," the poet offers a hopeful scenario in which all his mental troubles are dissolved by the analeptic powers of newfound love. The poem is purely escapist in nature; it is unabashedly romantic and full of nursery sentiments and Georgian images. The opening lines present the lover's emotional state before the onset of new love:

> Before this generous time
> Of love in morning prime,
> He had long season stood
> Bound in nightmare mood
> Of dense murk, rarely lit

> By Jack-o'-Lanthorn's flit
> And straightaway smothered spark
> Of beasts' eyes in the dark,
> Mourning with sense adrift,
> Tears rolling swift.

Slowly the lover is freed from his distressing "clouded vision" by the onset of "an unknown gradual flame" which magically absorbs the confusion of his life and releases him from his affliction.

> No more, no more,
> Forget that went before!
> Not a wrack remains
> Of all his former pains.
> Here's Love a drench of light,
> A Sun dazzling the sight,
> Well started on his race
> Toward the Zenith space
> Where fixed and sure
> He shall endure,
> Holding peace secure.

The curious aspect of this poem is not so much "the amount of self-deception in the falsely triumphant conclusion, in which the poet assures himself that desire has become actuality . . ." as Kirkham states (1969, 46), but the culminating description of love as "steadfast" in the last line. Graves voices the hope here that somehow his love for Nancy will suddenly dissolve his problems and transform them into joys. His plea is simply for Nancy to be consistent in her feelings for him; he requests her not to add to his insecurities but to give him a firm basis in their relationship and so assist him through the mental anguish of his neurasthenia. As Seymour-Smith points out, however, Graves was discovering some unpleasant facts about Nancy and his marriage at the time of writing *The Pier Glass:*

There was a certain moral capriciousness, a lack of firmness, about Nancy which made her unsuitable as a Muse; he [Graves] was painfully and reluctantly realizing that he could never learn to love her. The young and war-stricken Graves of 1917 and 1918 had yearned for a loving, devoted wife and a long life of pastoralized bliss blessed by scores of children. But not even Nancy's feminism was convincing. His fate, as he now secretly admitted to himself and to Lawrence, was to be misunderstood—to be subjected to the whims of a scatterbrain. (Seymour-Smith 1982, 94)

Several poems in *The Pier Glass* suggest that Graves's concept of love was becoming somewhat jaded at this time. In "Kit Logan and Lady Helen," he examines the consequences of love betrayed; and in a similarly negative vein, the "Hills of May" describes a lady so egotistical that she ignores man completely and moves on to another sphere of existence. But the poem that accurately captures the emotional flavor of Graves's early years of marriage is a capricious study of women, "The Troll's Nosegay."

> A simple nosegay! was that much to ask?
>   (Winter still gloomed, with scarce a bud yet
>   showing.)
> He loved her ill, if he resigned the task.
>   "Somewhere," she cried, there must be
>   blossom blowing.
> It seems my lady weeps and the troll swore
>   By Heaven he hated tears: he'd cure her spleen;
> Where she had begged one flower, he'd shower
>   fourscore,
> A haystack bunch to amaze a China Queen.
>
> Cold fog-drawn Lily, pale mist-magic Rose
>   He conjured, and in a glassy cauldron set
>   With elvish unsubstantial Mignonette
> And such vague bloom as wandering dreams
>   enclose.
> But she?
>   Awed,
>   Charmed to tears,
>   Distracted,
>   Yet—
> Even yet, perhaps, a trifle piqued—who knows?

R. P. Graves points out that Graves was working on this poem as early as February 1919, during his recovery from pneumonia, and that the poem passed through some thirty-five drafts before it was completed (1986, 207). Oddly, the poem is not criticized by Day or Kirkham, yet it seems to anticipate the whimsical demands of the White Goddess and the poet's dogged devotion to her unpredictable nature much more closely than their suggestions of her origins. Its content clearly derives from a need somehow to satisfy Nancy's unreasonable request for something as unobtainable as a bunch of fragrant flowers in the dead of winter. The devoted Graves is determined that he will do everything possible to fulfill her quirky request and "cure her spleen."

To satisfy his wife, Graves conjures up from his imagination an aromatic bouquet of lilies, roses, and fragrant grey-green Mignonettes and places his poetic offering before his lover, much in the same way that he will later pay homage to his White Goddess. The reaction to this offering is mixed at best; the woman merely accepts the prize without clearly indicating her gratitude. Somehow the gift of the poetic nosegay is not enough. The poet can only shrug his shoulders and wait for the next demand, a scenario that closely parallels Graves's attitude toward Nancy during the early years of their marriage.

In summary, *The Pier Glass* is primarily Graves's poetic investigation into the sources and manifestations of his neurasthenia with the hopeful aim of being able to understand and overcome the affliction through the therapeutic nature of poetry. In order to accomplish this task, Graves had to examine and bring to light the dark side of his unconscious and hope that once exposed, it could be rationally understood. Furthermore, *The Pier Glass* continues to expose Graves's ruminations on love and its manifestations, but the volume clearly demonstrates that the escapist elements of *Country Sentiment* were in the process of being replaced by a more pessimistic and negative view of the love relationship. And clearly, at this point, Graves seems to have realized that he had reached a dead end as far as his poetry was concerned; he could not continue indefinitely to write about the psychological aberrations of his unconscious and his awareness of disintegrating love. In the preface to *Whipperginny,* he points out that while several poems in this volume continue the "aggressive and disciplinary" mood of *The Pier Glass,* "in most of the later pieces will be found evidences of greater detachment in the poet and the appearance of a new series of problems in religion, psychology, and philosophy" (*Whipperginny*, v).

After the publication of *The Pier Glass,* a volume which met with no particular critical acclaim, Graves was under great financial and psychological pressure. However, because of timely financial assistance from T. E. Lawrence and William Nicholson as well as from Robert's mother's shrewd house-buying scheme, the financial burden was lifted by 1 June 1921, and Graves was able to complete a revised draft of *On English*

Poetry and send it off to Sassoon for evaluation. The book, which R. P. Graves calls "a highly autobiographical tract about the poetic life" (1986, 247), is partly an attempt to work out a theory of poetry using the new psychological theories of Freud as translated by Drs. W. H. R. Rivers and Henry Head.

Graves met Rivers through Sassoon while the latter was convalescing at Craiglockhart after his "mental collapse." He was attracted to Rivers's theories of the actual thinking process and the close linking of the dream state to the poetic trance, and read Rivers's two studies, *Instinct and the Unconscious* and *Conflict and Dream.* In the preface to *The Common Asphodel,* Graves discusses the influence of Rivers's theories on him:

> It was easy to identify myself closely with convalescent and reconstructive humanity. Still in a neurasthenic state from my own war experiences, I was starting life again, at the age of twenty-three, free of pre-War commitments. My hope was to help the recovery of public health of mind, as well as my own, by the writing of "therapeutic" poems; and to increase their efficacy by a study of the nature of poetry "from subjective evidence."

> As a neurasthenic, I was interested in the newly expounded Freudian theory: when presented with English reserve and common sense by W. H. R. Rivers, who did not regard sex as the sole impulse in dream-making or assume that dream-symbols are constant, it appealed to me as reasonable. I applied this case-history method of accounting for emotional dreams to the understanding of romantic poems, my own and others', and found it apt enough. (vii)

On English Poetry is a difficult book to criticize because there appears to be no system or logical organization in the presentation of material; subject matter flows backwards and forwards much like the movements of a waiter in a large restaurant. In chapter 1, for example, Graves gives the reader two definitions of poetry to which he returns later in chapter 52, only to apologize for his previous definitions.

Practically all of Graves's critics—Hoffman, Stade, Kirkham, Day, Canary, and Seymour-Smith—point out the essentially Romantic quality of *On English Poetry;* in fact, echoes of Shelley's "Defence of Poetry," Coleridge's *Biographia Literaria,* and Wordsworth's "Preface to the *Lyrical Ballads*" can be found without much searching. What is unique to this book is the linking of nineteenth-century Romantic criticism with early twentieth-century psychological theory as presented by Rivers in his two major works: *Conflict and Dream* and *Instinct and the Unconscious.*

In *On English Poetry,* Graves presents three major contentions that are indicative of Rivers's influence on him. The first is that the true poet, because of his heightened awareness, is somehow different from ordinary men; the second is that some mental conflict is necessary in the poet in order for him to create poetry; and the third is that the process of writing poetry is closely related to the dream state.

Graves's initial premise concerning the poet's heightened awareness derives directly from Rivers's findings in *Instinct and the Unconscious.* In his unpublished doctoral dissertation, "Robert Graves on Poetry: 1916–1929," George Stade devotes nearly thirty pages to Rivers's theories and their implications. The main purport of his findings is as follows. In *Instinct and the Unconscious,* Rivers gives a biological view of the various psychoses and neuroses that he treats. Much of his work centers on the healing processes of divided nerves as they recover sensitivity. Initially, the patient's nerves develop a protopathic sensibility where sensitivity to pain is extreme and unlocatable. The pain pervades the entire organism with violent intensity. However, at a certain stage in the healing process, the nerve begins to develop "normal"—or epicritic— discriminative sensibility. (Epicritic sensitivity occurs when one feels a jab of pain with a proportional sense of its intensity; the area of pain can generally be located with reasonable accuracy.) Rivers writes that these two kinds of sensibility—protopathic and epicritic—evolved during the phylogenesis of the human species, the protopathic response having preceded the epicritic response in the evolutionary process. In a healthy man, epicritic sensibility inhibits the protopathic reaction until injury occurs, whereupon the latter reasserts its archaic prerogative. This turn- about is the paradigm for the war neurosis that afflicted Graves (Stade 1965, 26–57).

At the time of writing *On English Poetry,* Graves was in an extreme- ly uncomfortable mental state. He was irritable, hyperemotional, solitary, and acutely sensitive to any change from the norm. As Richard Graves points out in his biography, Graves tried to cure himself through self- knowledge, self-reliance, and the imaginary confrontation of his demons in poetry, but eventually he came to believe that his nervous affliction in some way set him apart from others. His neurasthenia, he implied, was designed to help him observe clearly and sensitively the degenerating condition of the postwar world and to be much more open to an intuitive awareness that was necessary for the creation of true poetry. Somehow, through the regression of his mind to a prerational state (analogous to the protopathic state in a nerve disorder), Graves came to believe that he was closer to the basic instinct of poetry than other writers.

To cement his unique position as poet further, Graves suggests in *On English Poetry* the theory that poetry is "the unforeseen fusion in his [the poet's] mind of apparently contradictory emotional ideas" (13). The conflict that develops around these contradictions is the catalyst that sets the poet off into his creative trance, to which he is easily propelled because of the protopathic-like state in which the "irrational" poet finds himself. Poetic inspiration, according to Graves, works as follows: the poet collects and stores a number of incompatible ideas until some "outside shock" puts the ideas at odds with one another. When the conscious mind cannot hold or reconcile these internal conflicts, the true poet utilizes self-hypnosis and falls into a trancelike stage, taking on some unconscious identity to the extent that he loses his own ego. The poet then writes spontaneous poetry and lets his unconscious mind solve the problem that has caused the disturbance in the first place. Once the poet's problems are solved, the trancelike state diminishes. Thus, the poet must be careful to avoid solving all of his conflicts, or his inspiration will dry up. The true poet, and especially one who suffers from a nervous disorder, is so full of contradictions and contrasts that the chances of his inspiration dissipating are negligible indeed.

The relationship between the poetic trance and sleep-dreaming is very close; in fact, in one section of *Conflict and Dream,* Rivers calls a dream a "miniature psycho-neurosis" (143). He points out that any conflict that disturbs the tenor of a man's life can be the material for a dream, and that the dream can often be an attempted solution to the problem (150). The process of dream interpretation mirrors the process the poet faces when he emerges from his trance with the inspired but disorganized rough draft of his trance poem in front of him. The poet must now place the words in a logical and metrical pattern so that they will be understood and appreciated without difficulty by the reader. Finally, the poetry itself may become a form of psychotherapy for both poet and reader. When this result is achieved, the poem, like the interpreted dream, becomes a symbolic presentation and resolution of the individual's emotional conflicts. The resolution has engaged both the intuitive and critical faculties of the mind; the result is true poetry, which Graves defines as "both the controlled and the uncontrolled parts of the art taken together, because each is helpless without the other" (*On English Poetry,* 17). The poet must now await another conflict before another poem can emerge by means of the same process.

The three concepts discussed in *On English Poetry* had already become very much a part of Graves's poetic philosophy when he was writing his next volume of poetry, *Whipperginny*. The new collection shows a marked shift from *The Pier Glass* in attitude and tone, and, as Graves wrote in *Good-bye, Whipperginny* (published in 1923) showed the first signs of his "new psychological studies" (402). The volume also shows indications of a developing cerebral aloofness and downright hostility that Graves felt toward his reading public and critics. In the preface to *Whipperginny*, for example, Graves tells those readers that demand "unceasing emotional stress in poetry at whatever cost to the poet" that he has a Chinese parable for them:

> The petulant protests of all the lords and ladies of the Imperial Court will weigh little with the whale when, recovering from his painful excretory condition, he need no longer supply the Guild of Honourable Perfumers with their accustomed weight of ambergris. (v–vi)

The intensity of this attack shows convincingly that Graves believed his own vision of true poetry, heightened by his neurasthenic sensibilities, was a rare and unappreciated discovery.

Although Graves admits in the preface that some of the poems in the book are "bankrupt stock of 1918" and that still others are escapist in nature, many of the newer poems display quite clearly some type of conflict that is resolved by careful reflection of the problem; unfortunately, they also show more concern for intellectual facility than for the craft of poetry. Further, many of the resolutions in the volume are of a detached and purely objective mode—the new Graves was no longer to lay open his neurasthenic wounds or his love struggles for all to see. Instead, the reader is put in the position of a learned psychiatrist who, in the process of observing an emotionally fraught scene, suddenly exposes his presence and passes an objective intellectual judgment on the situation. Graves strove in this volume for balance; he was working toward bidding farewell to the neurasthenic theme, endeavoring to say good-bye to the aspirations of romantic love, good-bye to emotional engagement with his readers—in short, good-bye to anything that put him in a defenseless position with regard to his emotions. Indeed, it would take a confrontation with Laura Riding for these emotions to appear again.

The eponymous poem that opens *Whipperginny* is an interesting example of Graves in transition from his amatory, escapist self to his new emotional detachment. The poem explains that people play card games to get through difficult times: to escape the realities of love and war.

> To cards we have recourse
> When Time in cruelty runs,
> To courtly Bridge for stress of love,
> To Nap for noise of guns.

Through card games, the players escape into a fairy world where conquests of love and power are acted out in a realm of fancy.

> Then read the antique word
> That hangs above this page
> As type of mirth-abstracted joy,
> Calm terror, noiseless rage,
>
> A realm of ideal thought,
> Obscured by veils of Time
> Cipher remote enough to stand
> As namesake for my rhyme,
>
> A game to play apart
> When all but crushed with care;
> Let right and left, your jealous hands,
> The lists of love prepare.

Graves, in fact, sees his poetry as providing a similar flight of fancy, for inside the pages of his book, the reader can escape into a world of theoretic conflict and play out the results in mock reality. But Graves tells us in the epigraph that Whipperginny is an "obsolete" card game; and this is the relevant point. For Graves, the purpose of poetry is no longer simply flight from the actual world; that simplistic concept, like the card game, is complete obsolete. The travails of the world must be realized, confronted, and reconciled before significant progress can be made.

In *Whipperginny* are also several love poems that belong to Graves's old vein of amatory fancy. Their optimistic longings for recapturing the past anticipate the futile attempts of Fitzgerald's Gatsby to obscure the present in the mists of yesterday. In the self-incriminatory "Sullen Moods," Graves blames himself for marital discord and asks his partner to remember that his occasional gruffness is a reflection of his dissatisfaction with himself, not with her. Since, however, she has become a part of him in the marriage, he often rebukes her for his own shortcomings. The solution to this quandary of identification and transference is to escape back to the past when they were both completely separate entities:

"Remind me, rather, to disjoin / Your emanation from my own." Once they have accomplished this reaffirmation of their previous selves, they can recapture the "promise of glory" that has been dimmed by the rigors of domestic life.

In the rather unusual mental landscape of "The Red Ribbon Dream," the poet tells us that he followed a disembodied voice to "the place where I longed to be . . . where Love went before me." Love is presented in the guise of a beautiful girl who wears a "thin red ribbon on her calm brow." The perplexed and timorous man of the earlier sections of the poem is transformed into "a hero and a bold boy" who dares to embrace Love with an impulsive audacity. The red ribbon, symbolizing the awakening of love and sensual desire, twists in the hero's hair, "so I laughed for joy." But suddenly, with his laugh for joy, the lover is thrust back into the present where the doors of the past are locked:

> I stand by the stair-head in the upper hall;
> The rooms to the left and right are locked as before.
> Once I found entrance, but now never more,
> And Time leans forward with his glassy wall.

The conclusion of the poem does not, as Kirkham suggests, symbolize "the inevitable betrayal that follows the ecstasy of romantic love" (1969, 60), but rather stresses the inevitability of being unable to subjugate time to our whims. Time is the antagonist, not love, and in this poem Graves still professes a belief that if only he could go back to the past and relive those joyous moments, all would be well.

These romantic longings and unobtainable fancies are not sustained in the second half of *Whipperginny*. In "A False Report," a poem that acts as a bridge between the old romantic Graves and the new antisentimentalist, Graves examines in an extremely belligerent manner the biblical story of Samson and the Philistines. The "Philistines and dullards" criticize Samson for his weak, effeminate romanticism: "Samson the proud is pillow-smothered." But the crowd has misjudged its man, for out of this deprecated image emerges the jawbone-swinging avenger. Graves's identification with Samson is evident: out of his mildly sentimental poetry will emerge a new and stronger poetic vision with as much force and renewed vitality as the restored Samson (Graves to Marsh, 17 December 1921).

Graves announces in "A False Report" (called "Angry Samson" in later volumes) his intention to write of love from an impersonal and objective point of view, and "The Lord Chamberlain Tells of a Famous Meeting" demonstrates this theory in practice. The 130-line poem tells of the meeting of two princes of East and West during a spying mission at a hostile military camp. The tale of this confrontation is recounted without embellishment by the lord chamberlain, who cautions the listeners not to be swayed by "credulous annalists," "vagabond dramatists," or "allegorical painters" who try to create out of this portentous meeting something more than the actual events. The creative distortions of verity are what Graves wants to eliminate from his own poetry, and Kirkham's claim that the poem "allegorizes a self-admonition—to put off the various romantic disguises in which hitherto Graves had decked out his conflicts" (1969, 68) rings true. The two princes, despite the momentousness of their meeting, demonstrate the restraint and nobility that the poet should emulate in his writing.

> That was the noblest, East encountering West
> Their silent understanding and restraint,
> Meeting and parting like the Kings they were
> With plain indifference to all circumstances;
> Saying no good-bye, no handclasp and no tears;

Graves also uses this new attitude of restraint and dispassionate objectivity in the metaphorically religious conflict between the imprisoned rabbi and friar in "The Bowl and Rim." The surface conflict here is between the incompatible teachings of the Roman Catholic church and Judaism. The two opposing views of Christ's divinity (a seemingly insurmountable tenet that separates the two faiths) are brought together by the representatives of each faith as they suffer persecution "linked by their ankles in one cell." Discovering inconsistencies in their dogmas, they become reconciled by the realization of love inherent in both faiths. Together, from the dankness of their prison cell, the rabbi and friar sing out:

> Man-like he lived, but God-like he died,
>   All hatred from His thought removed,
> Imperfect until crucified,
>   In crucifixion well-beloved.

The extended metaphor here mirrors Graves's own realization that he must slowly begin to examine and confront his psychological concerns with objectivity and dispassionate rationality. The outcome of this intellectual probing was not only to be good inspiration for poetry, but also a more honest and open conception of living.

Four remaining poems in *Whipperginny* deserve attention and summary analysis because they deal with Graves's attempts to relate his intellectual approach to his major emotional conflict: his ambiguous feelings of love for Nancy. Perhaps the most elusive of the four is "The Lands of Whipperginny," which is brief enough to be quoted in full:

> Come closer yet, sweet honeysuckle, my coney, O my Jinny
>   With a low sun gliding the bloom of the wood.
> Be this heaven, be it Hell, or Lands of Whipperginny,
>   It lies in a fairy lustre, it savours most good.
>
> Then stern proud psalms from the chapel on the moors
>   Waver in the night wind, their firm rhythm broken,
> Lugubriously twisted to a howling of whores
>   Or lent an airy glory too strange to be spoken.

The first two lines create the impression that what is to follow will be a traditional bucolic pastoral, but the *carpe diem* theme in the two following lines suddenly introduces a new side to Graves: whether love is good or bad, the poet is going to enjoy it for what it is. The light Marlovian refrain is replaced by the strictly puritanical tones in the second stanza, where stern chapel music is twisted into the howling of whores and nightmarish cries. What is the nature of love, the poet asks: bucolic serenity or a lusty, nightmarish, passionate encounter? In this poem, the only clue given to the reader is in the epigraph from Thomas Nashe's novel of adventure, *Jack Wilton:* "Heaven or Hell or the Lands of Whipperginny." Perhaps the nature of love is a synthesis of all three states? In this poem, Graves comes to no such conclusion; for now, the awareness that love contains the beautiful, ugly, and fanciful is enough.

Graves studies the curious nature of love once more, but now with distance and objectivity, in "The Ridge-Top," wisely renamed "Love in Barrenness" in later collections. The poem has elicited a number of widely divergent interpretations. Thomas Blackburn calls it simply a "romantic exercise, a set piece whose object is itself, not a woman" (1961, 76). Hoffman suggests that the last two lines—"O wingless Victory, loved of men, / Who could withstand your triumph then?"—echo the "ancient goddess who rewards her idolater with the indifference of marble" (1967,

187). Hoffman, it seems, sees an ur-White Goddess figure in the making wherever a marmoreal female figure in classical garb appears.

"The Ridge-Top" opens with a description of a barren landscape where "even the long dividing plain / Showed no wealth of sheep or grain." This is the metaphorical landscape of Graves's marriage gauged from the stern, uncompromising eye of observation. Here is no warmth, no companion—just a world where the only sign of life is "the lost curlew / Mourning out of sight below." The two lovers stand surveying the emptiness and desolation. Suddenly, the north wind, symbolic of the poet's passionate desire, rises and presses "with lusty force" against the woman's dress. Repelled by this physical contact, the woman's frigid body turns to stone, her "body's inward grace" transformed into marble. But the transformation of the woman from living flesh to marble (the opposite of the Pygmalion and Galatea myth) is neither condemned nor romanticized; the final rhetorical question that concludes the poem (quoted above) is easily answered: the woman's triumph is an empty triumph—a victory of barrenness over love consummated. The loss of love, however, is not lamented; it is simply stated. Thus, Graves remains true to his newfound objectivity.

In "Song of Contrariety," Graves examines the problem of love's expectations (as opposed to love's actualities) in a purely intellectual, philosophical manner. The question Graves asks is why love at a distance seems much more alive and vibrant than when it is actually achieved. When the lover envisages the woman of his fantasies in the dark night of his passion, "She could not disobey, / But slid close down beside you there / And complaisant lay." But when the two are finally coupled in flesh and blood, the roseate glow of the dreams disappears. Instead of the delight of an imagined union, "joy and passion both are spent / Fading clean away." Rather than finding relief from his despair when the love becomes manifest, the lover experiences even greater frustration because his partner cannot live up to his dream.

> That Love, lent substance by despair,
> Wanes, and leaves you lonely there
> On the bridal day?

The careful study of love as an abstract issue makes the poem ultimately unsuccessful. The speculations are presented without conviction or engagement, and while the reader is in sympathy with the metaphysical notions, Graves fails to persuade the reader in the manner, for example, of John Donne.

Finally, in "Children of Darkness," Graves takes his theory of opposites in conflict and presents a pessimistic view of the offspring of lovers that is based on T. E. Lawrence's odd notions of procreation (Graves 1986, 237). The poem adumbrates a conflict between the spirit of the unborn child, who attempts to spur his reticent parents on to coupling, and the parents themselves. There is conflict between the passion of the night and the cool recollection of that passion by daylight; there is conflict in the womb between the darkness of the "pent place" and the ample space of the light outside; and the conflicts are extended because once the child is born, there will be opposition between the child and parents. The poem, therefore, is built on a system of contraries and conflicts.

On the most simple level, the poem addresses the problems of lovers being sure of each other in the enveloping darkness of passion, but whose nighttime abandon cannot easily be sustained in the cool objectivity of daylight; it stresses the importance of balancing light with darkness—of facing up to the fact that what passes for love at night is little more than carnal release when examined objectively during the day. For Graves, lovemaking is a covenant of trust between two people, but this covenant by its very nature is full of doubt and uncertainty in the light of day. This uncertainty is contrasted with the certainty of the unborn child, who waits eagerly to be born from the dark womb; but the child, too, will soon learn of the precariousness of life. With "unveiled eyes" he will learn to "loathe to gaze upon the sun."

This breaking of the covenant of love is carefully analyzed in *The Feather Bed,* a five-hundred-line poem that Graves had initially planned to be included in the *Whipperginny* collection, but that was published separately on the advice of Eddie Marsh. The volume was the first of five small books and pamphlets published by Leonard and Virginia Woolf at the Hogarth Press and contains a long, explanatory letter to the American poet John Crowe Ransom, with whom Graves felt a poetic sympathy, partially because both had published poems on the rather obscure biblical Judith of Bethulia. Finally published in July of 1923, the poem had been on Graves's mind for several years beforehand, as we can see from his defense of it in a letter to Eddie Marsh as early as December of 1921:

> You acknowledge that there is passion and spirit in my new writing; but you can't catch the drift—it isn't, be assured, that your brain is ossifying but that mine is liquefying and *Feather Bed* represents a particular variety of liquefaction suited to the problem proposed. . . .

You say my style is a wonderful instrument but that I am not, you think, putting it to its best use. The best use is *surely* to write the necessary poems, and I assure you I haven't a moment to waste on the unnecessary. (O'Prey 1982, 130–31)

One can indeed sympathize with Marsh about "catching the drift" of *The Feather Bed,* because the poem is not only full of sexual implications and images but, by the time of publication, had been further complicated by the influence of philosophical speculations induced by Graves's new friendship with Basanta Mallik, an Indian graduate student and political advisor to the maharajah of Nepal.

The origins of this poem are suggested by R. P. Graves in a sentence at the end of his chapter on *Whipperginny:* "*The Feather Bed* is a curious fantasy which may contain an echo of Robert's warm feelings for Barbara Morrison, who had left his household to work in a convent before departing for Canada . . . it suggests that Robert faced a serious personal problem trying to reconcile his sexual desires with traditional ideas of virtue" (Graves 1986, 267). Since R. P. Graves's biography maintains a sympathetic concern for continued loyalty in the relationship between Robert and Nancy, this sentence is very evocative. Further, the virulent attack on Rachel's decision in the poem to turn away from physical love in favor of the cloistered sterility of the convent only serves to emphasize Graves's own suspicion of self-denial as a virtue. Thus, the agony of the protagonist in the poem might conceivably have its roots in the poet's own frustration about losing his beloved "Old Barbaree" to "the bloody nuns" (Graves 1986, 226). But whatever the poem's genesis, the overall tone and purport of its movement echo the sentiments of the later poems in *Whipperginny.* The poem is full of disillusionment with romantic undertakings and seems to suggest that the only sensible attitude toward life is one based on aloofness and what Day calls "cynical and uncommitted restraint" (1963, 60).

As Graves points out in his "Introductory Letter to John Ransome" [*sic*], the poem is "a study of a fatigued mind in a fatigued body and under the stress of an abnormal conflict" (15). The neurotic hero-narrator is seen in the poetic prologue wandering aimlessly in a Bunyanesque landscape where "three times he had struck / The same sedged pool of steaming desolation" and tripped over "falls of scree, moss-mantled slippery rock / Wet bracken, drunken gurgling watercourses." Eventually, the weary traveler comes down out of the hills to find a road sign pointing the long way home with a dead snake "twined on the pointing

finger." Kirkham interprets the dead snake as a symbol of dead desire in
the lover (1969, 76), but this explanation fails to take into account the
lust-dominated interior monologue that follows in the body of the poem.
The protagonist's desire for his lover is not dead at this point in the
poem; in fact, the frenzied journey home is an attempt to wear down the
body in order to put the mind to sleep.

The main part of the poem, an interior monologue during which the
fatigued speaker drifts in and out of consciousness, opens with the protagonist resting upon a feather bed in an old inn "leg-chafed and footsore
with [his] mind in a blaze" as he contemplates a recent letter from his
lover, Rachel, announcing her decision to enter a nunnery. His contemplation concerns the course of action he should take to win his lover back:

> To beat Love down with ridicule or instead
> To disregard new soundings and still keep
> The old course by the uncorrected chart,
> (The faithful lover, his unchanging heart)

In a dreamlike state, the protagonist calls for Rachel's image to explain
to him her past feelings. The image replies, "If I thought I loved, no man
would doubt it." But haunted by uncertainty and fearing that the image's
reply is influenced by his own pride, the hero-narrator reflects how much
he had once been influenced by Rachel's physical beauty, and he laments
his failure to consummate their love. Suddenly jolted from his unconscious ramblings, the grieving lover tosses tormented in the mouldy inn,

> Lying sleepless and alone in double beds,
> Shaken in mind, harassed with hot blood fancies.

The fancies grow more bizarre as the night goes on; a parade of religious
characters walks past his best until "a red-haired beaky-nosed burly nun
/ Called Sister Agatha" points out the postmark on the envelope in which
Rachel's letter and gift (a book called *The Wisest Course of Love*) have
been sent.

> Now she lays
> A manicured finger on the office post-mark,
> Leering down in my face.
> I see it now,
> You ugly she-bear. Wisest Course of Love
> Is Maidenhead?

This cruel irony sends the lover into a somber and bitter reflection on what life in the sterile convent will be like for Rachel. "The carnal maidenhead / Untaken, but the maidenhead of spirit / Stolen away." Rachel will be corrupted by the pride and exclusiveness of the mother superior, and all her lover's secrets will be made public knowledge. She will eventually deny the power of love, her beauty and sweetness withering like dried flowers: "Rachel forfeits there all power to love."

The conflict of the poem is between the two concepts of love: that of Rachel, who sees herself in the service of God by denying any sexual pollution of her being, and that of her ardent lover, who feels that his desire for fleshly satisfaction far outweighs any hypocritical abnegation of physical intimacy. The untenability of Rachel's belief is made clear when the mother superior herself, in need of sexual fulfillment, slips furtively into the bedroom of "the fine young man, / The hot young man whose kisses tasted sweet / To our new postulant!" to practice "the wiles of the Earthbound." In a strange reversal of roles, the consummation of the act leads the protagonist to realize the self-satisfied nature of the lust that he has forced upon Rachel; in his new awareness, he acknowledges that he has never truly loved, and he sinks into the abysmal darkness of unfulfillment with regrets reminiscent of Hamlet's laments.

> For me? Love's Sacrifice? It was not love.
> The Broken Heart? Not mine. I'll say no more
> Than mere goodbye. Go, get you to a nunnery,
> And out the candle! Absolute darkness
> Surrounds me, sleepy mother of good children
> Who drowse and drowse and cry not for the sun,
> Content and wisest of their generation.

Because the poem ends quite unsatisfactorily, the reader is forced into a careful scrutiny of the introductory letter to Ransom and of the epilogue for some guidance as to Graves's meaning. In the letter, Graves divulges that the poem was influenced by his reactions to his recent readings of the Old and New Testaments concerning "the progressive understanding of God throughout the ages by the Jews." Graves's conception of the Jewish god here is of a deity that has evolved through three distinct stages, the first two of which are represented by the two main characters of the poem.

The characteristics of the male protagonist reflect the self-seeking instincts of man in his most primitive state, of the animal whose single concern is self-gratification; the god of this race of man is Saturn. Rachel, in contrast, represents the civilized being, as embodied in the god Jehovah, who values an imposed social order over individual animal instincts. For Graves, Jehovah—the god of the present—is "predominantly male, violent, blundering, deceitful, with great insistence on uniformity of rites, duties and taboos, at whatever cost to the individual." The conflict between Rachel and the male protagonist manifests the contrast between these two deities. Neither Rachel nor her "lover" achieves any satisfaction—Jehovah and Saturn are never to resolve their ancient differences—and so Graves is forced to introduce the *deus ex machina* character of Lucifer, the third deity, the god of the future, who represents the rejection of both communal dictates and of individualism. Lucifer, "the hope of eventual adjustment between ancient habits and present needs," fulfills the role of reconciler and as such makes obsolete "the negative virtue of Good fighting with Evil, and proposes Absolute Good which we can now conceive as Peace" (*Feather Bed*, 6–7).

In the epilogue of the poem, the morning star, Lucifer, tries to comfort the spurned lover by telling him that there will come a day when the conflicts between lovers, between good and evil, between passion and intellect, will be peacefully resolved:

> I am the star of morning poised between
> The dead night and the coming of the sun,
> Yet neither relic of the dark nor pointing
> The angry day to come. . . .
>
> Lucifer, Lucifer am I, millstone-crushed
> Between conflicting powers of doubleness,
> By envious Night lost in her myriad more
> Counterfeit glints, in day-time quite overwhelmed
> By tyrant blazing of the warrior sun. . . .
>
> Gaze up and far above them see me shining
> Me, single natured, without gender, one
> The only spark of Godhead unresolved.

But the lover is too far lost in his own self-pity and sexual frustration to hear Lucifer's redeeming words.

For Graves, the poem demonstrates a faith in the process of synthesis and his hesitancy to assign absolute values to any situation. Furthermore, from a psychological standpoint, Canary's observation that the poem reads as though the protagonist's ego is "crushed between the dark night of the id and the tyrant demands of the superego, unable to achieve a single nature" (1980, 67) appears valid. However, the very existence of Lucifer offers alternatives to the spiritual suicide inherent in the worship of Jehovah and the lustful emptiness of the devotees of Saturn. The single unifying nature of Lucifer's vision has not been grasped, but the poet senses its presence.

The synthesizing nature of Lucifer derives clearly from the psychological studies and self-analysis that Graves was putting himself through at the time of writing. The added dimension of the personification of this integrating force called Lucifer also demonstrates that Graves had been seeking answers to his own search for a unifying figure in both biblical and philosophical spheres. The resulting figure stands in vivid juxtaposition to the bellicosity of Saturn and Jehovah. The genderless Lucifer symbolizes the harmony possible in sexual relations. Guiltless, he stands for the negation of absolute standards of morality in the less-than-perfect world; and Lucifer embodies the promise of relief from worry in a world filled with chaos and uncertainty. Lucifer, then, is the hope that is left at the bottom of Pandora's box; but as Graves surely realizes, Lucifer's time has not yet come.

The poet also restates several of Graves's antipathies: the institutional nature of religion, the worship of and desire for discarnate love, the bullying and domination of the male, and the smugness of social definitions of right and wrong. But in *The Feather Bed* much of the philosophical speculation is mere suggestion. The poem is more of an attack on Graves's old demons with a hope for the future tacked on than a reasoned philosophical argument. In his next volume, *Mock Beggar Hall,* written much more under the influence of Basanta Mallik than *The Feather Bed,* Graves began to sharpen his metaphysical disputations into his own esoteric version of Mallik's Eastern wisdom.

4

Philosophical Speculations: *Mock Beggar Hall,* *Welchman's Hose,* and *The Poetic Unreason*

In *Good-bye,* Graves admits that discussions between Mallik, Sam Haines (a young Balliol scholar and friend), and himself were so intense that "metaphysics soon made psychology of secondary interest for me: it threatened almost to displace poetry" (403). Rather surprisingly, the passage is omitted in the 1957 edition, and all allusions to Mallik are expunged. Nevertheless, the following passage from the original edition regarding Mallik's philosophy could, without much effort, be said to echo the essential concerns of Graves's next volume of poetry, *Mock Beggar Hall:*

> Basanta's philosophy was a development of formal metaphysics, but with characteristically Indian insistence on ethics. He believed in no hierarchy of ultimate values or the possibility of any unifying religion or ideology. But at the same time he insisted on the necessity of strict self-discipline in the individual in meeting every possible demand made on him from whatever quarter, and he recommended constant self-watchfulness against either dominating or being dominated by any other individual. This view of strict personal morality consistent with scepticism of social morality agreed very well with my practice. (*Good-bye,* 403–4)

R. P. Graves points out that while Robert Graves was writing many of the poems in *Mock Beggar Hall* in 1923, he had once again "embark[ed] on a course of psychoanalysis . . . which raised a host of sleeping demons" in his poetry (Graves 1986, 278–79). Graves's nephew claims that the new poems, reflecting his psychological purging, have a "haunted air," and substantiates his claim by pointing out that Mock-beggar Hall is the name of a former leper house that Graves had dreamed was full of quarreling ghosts. However, upon close investigation of this collection, which was eventually published by Hogarth Press in March of

1924, this "haunted air" is not easily discernible. On the contrary, the poems bristle with too much light—too much deftness of intellectual argument. Almost all of the poems in the collection are philosophically slick and cerebrally poignant to the point of being didactic. In this volume, Graves fails to recollect his own warning from *On English Poetry* that a true poet who has solved his own emotional problems and transmuted them "into a calmer state of meditation on philosophical paradox" (36) has no inspiration left for poetry. The philosophical concerns are too grossly intellectual for the delicacy of the poetic plane. The "matter" of *Mock Beggar Hall* is summed up deftly by George Stade in his doctoral dissertation when he states:

> These poems are about "remembered conflicts of an earlier heat" (*Whipperginny*, p. 43). He considers problems, questions, uncertainties, contentions, arguments, antinomies, imperfections; hesitatingly offers hypotheses, theses, syntheses, and counter-arguments; but ends up with incertitudes, irreconcilabilities, contrarieties, "thought amazements," conundrums, equivocations, paradoxes, riddles, "verbal quags," and a new cause for dispute. He poses idealists against materialists, nuns against agnostics, priests against atheists, dialecticians against dullards, colonists against colonials. . . . and decides that "wherever there is conflict, all sides are wrong." (Stade 1965, 139)

Under the influence of Mallik and his new philosophical direction, Graves became preoccupied with the contrariety manifested in human experience and with the need to find a synthesis. Sometimes these contradictions are resolved in familiar antimaterialist, antirationalist, and relativist attitudes echoed in the theories of Einstein (Pcttct 1941, 217), but in many cases the posing of the problems acts simply as an intellectual puzzle which must have aided Graves to escape from his continuing psychological and marital difficulties. The most typical poem in the volume, "Antinomies," makes this point clear.

"Antinomies," a title that suggests a conflict between points of view, opens with the poet's muse in the guise of a grasshopper bidding him to sing. The lethargic poet, "lying in long grass one hot afternoon," hears the church bells ringing for evensong and thinks of the puritanical rector pouring forth from the pulpit "the text about the flesh warring with Spirit / Spirit with flesh." This evanescent thought is given form when the poet observes two eighteenth-century garden statues, *Furor Poeticus* and *Phryne Judged,* that stand one on either side of him. The poet, now inspired, imagines the psychosexual conflict between Praxiteles, the master sculptor, and his model. The woman, Phryne, sees in the admiration of the sculptor nothing that resembles the sensuous or physical. "He lets love-splendour pass / In thoughts of line and mass." For her, Praxiteles' failure to see beyond the surface contours of her body is foolish and tragic. Praxiteles, on the other hand, is disturbed by his mistress's sensuality. Initially, he had felt they were united together on the spiritual quest for perfection in art ("She came as my true friend / This art our common end"), but Phryne's needs of fleshly satisfaction corrupt the artist's spiritual concentration:

> Flesh was her all-in-all;
> O fell, and in this fall
> Here, woman, you shall view
> This marble ruined too,
> My mind in terms of you,
> On either part the same,
> Scorned beauty, passion, shame.

The poet's muse berates him for this kind of balanced argument in verse: "Cunningly balanced; rather too precise / A clear antinomy, purporting no more / Where does it lead us? Mutual ruination, / Deadlock, but have you nothing to suggest?" But the poet answers his dissatisfied muse that "no conflict ends / Except in ruin of opposing views." The poet claims, then, that taking sides in any argument is ridiculous because right and wrong do not exist, because absolutism is ridiculous. Therefore, all the poet can do is present both sides of the argument and wait for truth (much as one must wait for Lucifer, the morning star, to appear) "to knock the swords aside." Until then, the poet's only constructive action is to find the counterbalance of every argument and present it, hoping that a solution of compromise will make itself evident from a study of both sides.

The poem closes with an example from Aesop's fables: that of the Man and the Satyr. In Graves's version the paradox of blowing on one's hands to warm the fingers and blowing on one's food to cool the porridge may never be clearly understood, but at the least the reason for doing it can be grasped by the Satyr—and that is something, after all.

This is the philosophical stance behind nearly all the poems in the volume. Every truth is relative to another truth; what one man sees as justification for an action, another sees as unjust. Even in a poem as seemingly uncomplicated as "Northward from Oxford: An Architectural

Progress," Graves tackles the idea of nonjudgmental relativity. As the title suggests, the poem is a study of architectural styles in Oxford beginning with the delicate neoclassical curves of the houses on Beaumont Street to the red brick neogothic spires along Banbury Road. Eventually, we reach the individualistic postwar villas of Summertown, but all are seen in relation to Graves's tumbledown cottage in Islip: "A house self-certain, not divided, with a good feng shwee / Beaumont Street, Banbury Road and Summertown cannot come to see / Whom I can no more understand than they can me." The point of the poem is clear: each housing style reflects a different type of individual with a different life-style, but Graves's philosophy makes no attempt to comment on this diversity—the agreement is to differ.

In the verse-play "Antigonus: An Eclogue," a literary historian and a poet come together to discuss the characters affected by the death of Antigonus, the slain Sicilian lord in Shakespeare's *Winter's Tale.* The controversy of the poem originates from a discussion between historian and poet about the cowardly behavior displayed by Antigonus's companion, Fernando Campi, when he betrayed the island to the enemy Turkish fleet for revenge and for personal power. After recounting the tale, the poet asks the literary historian which characters are responsible for the tragedy. The historian replies that he strongly condemns Fernando for his nefarious behavior. The poet refuses to do likewise and "abstains from taking sides" because favoring one side over the other suggests "a strong self-interest" in the result. It is better to allow Providence to provide a "virtuous resolution: / Then from the ruin of opposing views / Securer friendship might again be borne." Thus, Graves returns here again to the idea of the relativity of truth.

The argument of these seldom discussed poems also appears in the analyses of the more frequently criticized poetry. Canary points out in his interpretation of "The Rainbow and the Sceptic" that "the argument is that all knowledge is partial, all truths temporary" (1980, 64). In his long and informative discussion of "Mock Beggar Hall," the title poem of the collection, Kirkham notes perceptively that the significance of the poem resides in the landlord's restraint "from imposing his will on another and . . . [preferring] to wait passively for the conflicts to die out. . . . 'Abstention and endurance' summarizes the trend of these poems" (Kirkham 1969, 80). Day examines "Knowledge of God" with the conclusion that

> to assert with assurance that He [God] takes an active part in the endless round of existence, directing the seasons, sporting with the Danae, fighting

with "rebel demons," and generally giving proof of his omnipotence, is wrong-headed: if God is God, then he must be invisible, unknowable, outside of Time and Space. (Day 1963, 65)

Furthermore, the conclusion of another of Graves's long poetic verse-plays, "Interchange of Selves," appears to be that conflict in any form is evil and that stoical endurance is the only sensible solution to the vicissitudes of life.

These, then, are the basic concerns of the collection, except for the odd inclusion of "Full Moon." It is a drily intellectual volume, and one does miss the sense of assimilation of these Mallik-influenced tenets into some form of poetic image. As in the later poems in *Whipperginny,* the movement is away from poetic self-involvement and toward an objective appreciation of theoretical structures and broad generalities. Graves embraced the theory of relativity so firmly that in his *Poetic Unreason,* published in 1925, he goes so far as to affirm that judgments of "good" poetry and "bad" poetry are relative to the experiences of the critic. This inability to take sides, to feel emotional involvement, to take seriously the agnostic stance, is what is wrong with *Mock Beggar Hall.* The content of this pseudophilosophical poetry is not particularly original, and the realization that all the poems will have the same unresolved relativistic conclusion quickly dissipates a reader's enthusiasm for, or enjoyment of, the poems. In 1926, in his critical study of modern literature, *Transitions,* Edwin Muir, a contemporary of Graves, compared "The Rock Below" from *Whipperginny* with the "stifling compromise" of *Mock Beggar Hall.* Muir states,

> On the one hand we have the consistent relativism of his later poetry, on the other, a determination to dig down until his mind produces "fruits of immortality." There is the mass of his busy, temporizing, hypothetical verse, verse which seems to say, "This may be true, or it may not"; there are a few poems which leave no room for the relative or for questions of this kind.
> . . .
>
> It is the difference between a state imagined and a state hypothecated and only dipped in the imagination to be given an intellectual convincingness. . . . It lacks the truth which we feel in poetry when there is an organic correspondence between external image and the inner conflict or desire—that correspondence which clamps poetry to reality and gives it an absolute force. (175, 173)

Fortunately, the poetic mood of *Mock Beggar Hall* did not last much beyond the return of Mallik to India, but the philosophical implications continued to affect Graves for the rest of the decade. The concept of relativism with which he always felt uncomfortable became a way of interpreting the world, and when one considers the difficulty that the opinionated and passionate Graves must have had in disciplining himself to the dispassionate, nonjudgmental stance advocated by Mallik, it becomes evident that the poet was grasping for some form of metaphysical standard by which he could live. Of course, in some areas of thought, Mallik's teachings were clearly in accordance with Graves's own conclusions and acted only as affirmations of what he already believed. They both agreed in the rejection of conventional societal values, the dismissal of an ascending order of moral values, and the disbelief in organized religion and its teachings. But if the intellectual maturing process of Graves's philosophical period assisted him in saying good-bye to the more conventional beliefs, it also made him aware of the hopelessness of clinging to a blighted love. This awareness is evidenced in his only love poem in *Mock Beggar Hall*—"Full Moon."

"Full Moon," written in 1923, first appeared in *Winter Owl,* a Graves-edited magazine financially supported by William Nicholson. The reason why Graves decided to include this love poem amid the many heady metaphysical speculations in *Mock Beggar Hall* has never been adequately explained. Kirkham's conclusion that the poem is "the symbolic counterpart, and the finest expression, of the morality presented exclusively in intellectual terms and laboriously argued in the majority of *Mock Beggar Hall* poems" (1969, 84) seems strangely out of keeping with the purport of the poem. Possibly, the emotional sentiments expressed in the poem were pressing enough for Graves to use despite their thematic inappropriateness.

The poem mirrors Graves's continuing unbalanced, emotional situation through 1923 with Nancy and may signal his realization that their love was on the wane. In the poem, the warmth and passion of the two lovers have been chilled by the passing of the silver moon, "the tyrannous queen above." The final stanza brings down the curtain on the love affair:

> And now cold earth was Arctic sea,
>   Each breath came dagger keen;
> Two bergs of glinting ice were we,

> The broad moon sailed between;
> There swam the mermaids, tailed and finned,
> And Love went by upon the wind
> As though it had not been.

The coldly objective stance in the conclusion of the poem does not mean, as Kirkham seems to suggest, that the poet has stoically resigned himself to the loss of love. Rather, the irony of the sterile moon turning its chill gaze upon the ardent and hopeful lovers and transforming their frenzied passion into marmoreal bitterness reveals the purpose of the poem to be the "freezing" of the reader into contemplation of the fragile nature of love. The poet asks for emotional, not intellectual, sympathy here.

After *Mock Beggar Hall* was published, Graves immersed himself in a number of projects, including the revisions of his ballad opera "John Kemp's Wager" and the composition of several poems for J. C. Squire's *London Mercury.* Many, such as "Alice" and "Ovid in Defeat," appeared in the 1925 volume *Welchman's Hose.* As the summer of 1924 wore on, Graves was revising *Poetic Unreason* and writing the first draft of his thirty-thousand-word biblical romance *My Head! My Head!* During this summer, too, Graves edited a number of poems by John Crowe Ransom for Hogarth Press and first came across Laura Riding's "Quids" in a copy of *Fugitive.* Graves's fury of artistic activity seems all the more impressive when we learn that he was also doing much of the housework for a family of four children because of Nancy's ill heath:

> Nancy had now been subjected to the physical strain of bearing four children in under five years; she had also had to cope with the nervous strain of living on an uncertain income; while references to physical symptoms such as goitre, loss of hair, and periods of exhaustion suggest that her health was frequently undermined by a thyroid problem which was aggravated by any unusual strain. (Graves 1986, 291)

Sassoon, for one, saw Graves as a victim of domestic drudgery and of a domineering wife, but Graves had much pride in his choice of life-style and wife. He bristled terribly when anyone dared mention his difficulties to him, and in a reply to a letter from Sassoon written on 19 February 1924, Graves defended his domestic conditions as follows:

> As for my drudging domestic difficulties I have none; My domestic duties . . . keep me happy and vigorous. As for money. We are absolutely broke at the moment and I am awfully grateful for your offer . . . to take money

from you as a friend and to feel no obligation, *but* [Graves's italics] friendship at World's End implies friendship towards the whole damn lot of us, and until you realize that I am completely satisfied with this life, debts and all, and am not so far as I know Nancy's drudge . . . or the Impoverished Genius with the Awful Wife and the Squalling Brats . . . you and I are at too cross purposes to be really friends again.

Much of this had to be a bluff on Graves's part. His poetry of this period showed a progressive disillusionment with the idea of love and marriage, and his "stiff upper lip" mentality was simply an extension of Mallik's teaching of the necessity of strict self-discipline in order to meet every demand placed on the individual. Graves was simply testing his own endurance during a very difficult time.

The realization that his two studies of poetic analysis (*Poetic Unreason* and *Contemporary Techniques of Poetry*) and recent volumes of poetry were not only overlooked critically but were also failures financially undermined Graves's confidence in himself. His insecurity was only heightened by the sudden deaths of many of his friends: Walter Raleigh, Graves's tutor; Sam Harries, his close friend; George Mallory, his tutor from Charterhouse; and even Rivers, his psychological mentor. Graves lamented at this time "that it seemed as though the death of my friends was following me in peace-time as relentlessly as in war" (*Goodbye*, 404–5). Furthermore, Mallik had returned to India, T. E. Lawrence was abroad in the Royal Tank Corps, and Blunden had traveled to Tokyo as a professor of English. In a real sense, Graves was intellectually alone and probably found refuge from his dissatisfaction and from his worries in his work, both domestic and artistic. R. P. Graves concludes much the same when he writes that "the harder he [Graves] worked the happier he appeared to be, as there was less time for worrying overmuch about Nancy's health or about his own continuing lack of success" (Graves 1986, 302).

The poems in *Welchman's Hose* echo most of Graves's concerns during the mid-twenties. The collection is in many ways a more sophisticated production than *Mock Beggar Hall.* Graves's belief in the relativity of all things is still in evidence, but he introduces the concept with a subtlety and smoothness that is lacking in the earlier volume. In addition, the collection is much lighter in tone than the previous volume and shows signs of ironic and even mocking awareness of the implications of the philosophic direction in which the poet was moving. This mocking tone was to be reintroduced later and with greater skill in *The Marmosite's*

Miscellany in 1925, but here it makes a refreshing change from the gravity of *Whipperginny* and *Mock Beggar Hall.* The volume even contains Graves's Olympic silver medal entry for the 1924 games, "At the Games," which is a paean for pure sportsmanship. Also included is the touchingly humorous four-line "Love Without Hope" in which the bird catcher doffs his tall hat to the squire's daughter as she rides by, while the escaped larks, unobserved (his poems?), sing about her head.

The most important poem in the volume is "Essay on Knowledge," later renamed "Vanity" and substantially rewritten for the *Collected Poems.* The poem is a symbolic presentation of Graves's struggle within himself to control the dark passionate emotions that seethe in him when he attempts to adopt a detached and philosophically neutral attitude toward the happenings in life. The dragon in the opening stanza symbolizes the awakening of passion and the death of innocence:

> Be assured, the dragon is not dead,
> Who once more from the pools of peace
> Shall rear his fabulous green head.
>
> The flowers of innocence shall cease
> And like a harp the wind shall roar
> And the clouds shake an angry fleece.

The awakening of the dragon throws the well-regulated aspects of daily living off course; the certitudes of rationality and reason are suddenly challenged by the whirlwinds of unbridged emotions. The intensity of this loosed passion frightens an innocent lover who cries out that love must be eternal and "unshaken." But the cries awaken only an ancient toad, symbol of the philosophic awareness of the Apollonian and Dionysian duality in man's nature:

> He knows that limits long endured
> Must open out in vanity.
> That gates by bolts of gold secured
> Must open out in vanity.
>
> That thunder bursts from the blue sky,
> That gardens of the mind fall waste,
> That age-established brooks run dry,
> That age-established brooks run dry.

The repeated last line emphasizes that man cannot legislate his rational qualities forever; they can "run dry." Out of the calmness of a serene and ordered blue sky can burst the thunder of untamed violence or lust, and even the most cultivated minds can fall victim to passion's dictates. Love is seen here as the opponent of rational detachment and objective observation, but the implication of the poem touches a more profound level: if the rationalist places his trust in the certainty of a reasonable response to all matters of life, what happens when the foundation crumbles? What happens when lust or desire insinuates itself into the well-ordered mind? Graves's answer in this poem seems to suggest that all previously held values would dry up like the brooklets in a hot summer's heat.

Graves clearly realized that the most effective weapon in keeping an objective hold over "the dragon" in himself was the promotion of a relativistic philosophy in both his work and life. *Welchman's Hose,* as an example, might be said to deserve the subtitle "In Praise of Relativity," for most of the major poems in the volume are examinations of the various ways one can view productively the mundane dictates of existence. Relativity, for Graves, had become a liberating experience that stood in opposition to the banal social conventions of Victorian expectations, the established church, and Georgian poetry. In *The Long Weekend,* Graves defines what relativity meant to him:

> The word "relativity" now came to be commonly used . . . to mean that a thing was only so if you cared to assume the hypothesis that made it so. Truth likewise was not absolute: "beautiful results" could be obtained by mathematicians from consistent systems based on the hypothesis, for example, that one could slide a left hand into a rigid right-hand glove—or simultaneously into a pair of rigid right-hand gloves. (97)

In "Alice," Graves examines this same vision of relativity in poetic form. The poems opens the *Welchman's Hose* volume and seems to continue directly the philosophical speculations in *Mock Beggar Hall.* Alice, "prime heroine of our nation," is well prepared for the oddness of the looking-glass world because she is "of true philosophical bent." That is, she refuses to look upon the world from only the restrictive perspective of logic and reason, because they are inapplicable to her current situation:

> "From hearthrug level, why must I assume
> That what I'd see would need to correspond
> With what I see now? And the rooms beyond,
> Why should they pair with our rooms?"

Without the preconceived expectations based on logical conclusions and rational explanations, Alice thrives in the world beyond the mirror—the unconscious—and very easily discovers how "to learn the rules and move and perfect them." Alice's special talent, however, resides in her recognition that the rules and "realities" are different on both sides of the mirror.

> For Alice though a child could understand
> That neither did this chance-discovered land
> Make nohow or contrariwise the clean
> Dull round of mid-Victorian routine,
> Nor did Victoria's golden rule extend
> Beyond the glass: it came to the dead end
> Where formal logic also comes;

There are two distinct worlds: the one beyond the glass and the dull world of mid-Victorian routine and expectation. The true heroine is at home in both places and recognizes the relativity of truth in both places. For Graves, Alice's easy balancing of the unconscious and conscious worlds demonstrates a new awareness that his inspiration for his poetry need not always require a dredging of his unbalanced subconscious—his nightmare state—for material. Rather, the poem optimistically suggests that the poet can move freely from conscious to unconscious without mental trauma. Day makes a similar observation when he says: "While the domain of unreason may be the proper dwelling place of the poet, we can infer from 'Alice' that the poet need not fear it as a limitless realm which must encroach on the boundaries of everyday reality" (1963, 87).

"Ovid in Defeat," originally titled "Ovid's Breeches," is another study of relativity; but this time the subject is love. Graves examines here the role of the woman in a love relationship from the chauvinistic, pro-male perspective of Ovid and then looks at men through the jaundiced eyes of sectarian feminists, a reversal which is shown to be as empty as Ovid's vision. The result of such a jaded view of the man-woman relationship is eternal conflict between the sexes with nothing gained by either party. Graves's view is to recognize both sexes as uniquely individualistic in themselves. Neither sex is superior to or more talented than the other; their interpretations of thoughts, deeds, and art simply differ. His plea is for empathy between the two similar but slightly different views so that conflict and struggle for dominance can cease.

> Thought, but not man's thought,
>   Deeds, but her own,
> Art, by no comparisons
>   Shaken or thrown
>
> Plough then salutes plough
>   And rose greets rose:
> While Ovid in toothache goes
>   Stamping through old snows.

"The College Debate," which purports to be from a letter addressed to Edith Sitwell, one of the new friends Graves made during the twenties (*Good-bye,* 404), takes the reader into the heady atmosphere of the debating hall where the trend of modern poetry is being heatedly debated by learned dons. As might be expected, this work reflects the relative poetical tastes of the various speakers. First, the centenarian dean of Saul Hall declares that there have been no true poets since Wordsworth and Tennyson; the sycophantic librarian agrees, but feels that Watson's and Bridges's lyrics deserve mention. The more liberal junior don then pontificates on the merits of Hardy and Housman, but the young undergraduates who make up the audience bounce "from their seats" to defend the modern poetry of Edith Sitwell. In the central stanza, Graves stands back and addresses Sitwell with the relativistic attitude that he proposed in his *Poetic Unreason.* There he stated that "the possible appreciation of any poem depends . . . on whether the allusive images are common to the poet and to his reader" (35), and that "no poetry can hope to appear to which an absolute permanent value may legitimately be accorded" (43). Graves humorously admits that in the heat of the moment he can sometimes sit "sceptred and orbed on the absolutist throne" and pass judgment on his friend's poetry, "but afterwards paid for each proud excess / With change of heart, fatigue, mere foolishness."

The proper spirit toward poetry, then, as toward life, is to realize that "poems alter by the clock and season / As men do, with the same caprice as they / Towards hate or concord." A poem may have its relevance for each generation, but it may mean very little to posterity. There is no absolute message that poets can give to future generations; the poet can be judged successful only if he touches the commonality of our personal experience.

"The Clipper Stater," the last of the "relativity poems" in the collection, is possibly the best known because of its purported allegorical

references to T. E. Lawrence. This poem, which not unexpectedly contains several of Graves's concerns, relates how Alexander the Great, the
Lawrence figure, suffers acutely from ennui when he discovers that there
are no lands left to conquer; for this reason, he gives up his status,
denying his godhead, to be carried off by a djinn to a frontier post in
China far from any civilization. Here he becomes an enlisted man and
quickly learns the rough lot of a frontier soldier's work. He stoically
endures humiliation and physical hardships until one day he is paid with
a coin that contains his own image, mutilated but recognizable. Alexander
then contemplates his own divinity and concludes that a god is a god
only for a certain group of people at a certain time. He impassively
accepts the discovery of his lost divinity and "then all he knows / Is, he
must keep the course he has resolved on." Spending his coin on a feast
of almonds and fish, Alexander rushes back to the ramparts to stand his
watch.

Clearly, Graves enjoys the use of irony at his friend Lawrence's
expense, but the poem also applies Graves's vision of relativity and
philosophy of strict self-discipline that he learned from Mallik. The poem
indicates that Alexander's conquest of the known world did not encom-
pass the wild frontier where he became a soldier and where his godliness
was unknown. The conclusion to be inferred is that God lives only in the
minds of his adherents. When Alexander is whisked off to a place where
he has no adherents, he becomes a mere common soldier:

> He, Alexander, had been deified
> By loud applause of the Macedonian phalanx,
> By sullen groans of the wide worlds he had vanquished.
> Who but a God could have so hacked down their pride?

But the argument in favor of the relative nature of God is not put to rest
here. Alexander's acceptance without complaint of his new role as stoic
man on the fringe of civilization is an affirmation of the soldierly virtues
that Graves valued during the war and that he saw as necessary in order
for him to survive his own hardships.

Two final poems, "From Our Ghostly Enemy" and "The Presence,"
deal with ghostly hauntings and remind the reader of the atmosphere of
The Pier Glass; both poems clearly demonstrate, however, that Graves's
poetic approach to his neurasthenic hauntings had changed considerably.
He points out in Good-bye that his continuing attempts to write a novel

of war memoirs brought back neurasthenic symptoms (408), but that the attacks became fewer and less intense after he met Mallik. "From Our Ghostly Enemy," first published in the *London Mercury* in December of 1924, demonstrates one method by which Graves learned to control his neurosis. The poem concerns a man constantly dogged by an unruly ghost—

> Who, without voice or body,
> Distresses me much,
> Twists the ill to holy, holy to ill,
> Confuses me, out of reach
> Of speech or touch;
>
> Who works by moon or by noon,
> Threatening my life.

"Filled with despair," the man relates to his wife the nature of his haunting experiences; she, in return, dispenses some "simple advice" that brings him peace:

> "Speak to the ghost and tell him,
> 'Whoever you be,
> Ghost, my anguish equals yours,
> Let our cruelties therefore end.
> Your friend let me be.'"

R. P. Graves sees this poem as evidence that Robert had grown completely dependent on Nancy during this period (1986, 292), but the critic has fallen into the trap here of taking Graves's poetry too literally. His interpretation forces one to ask why the man waited until he was in desperate straits before going to his wife. And what kind of wife would not recognize her husband's neurotic symptoms and come to his aid before being asked? More likely, the advice to confront one's fears and face the conflict calmly and without aggression sounds very much like Mallik's teachings.

The most damning evidence against Nancy's ability to dispense psychological balm to the troubled poet is in Graves's emphatic rejection of her in "The Presence." This poem, because of its similarity in tone to Graves's other neurasthenic poems, has been misread by most critics as simply another product of a diseased mind. Day, for example, describes the poem as "an inward haunting, the function of a tormented imagination, the real source of man's greatest fears." He adds, "Such poems as these prompt us to believe that there was more than a little justice in Graves's correlation between his neuroses and his best poetry" (Day 1963, 88). On the surface, the speaker is haunted by his dead wife's spirit, which continually accuses him of forgetting her. The speaker's reasons for despair are vague and ambiguous; ultimately, this ambiguity is detrimental to the success of the poem. Day's suggestion that this is the "most moving poem of this point in his career" (1963, 88) seems far too much of an overstatement to be accepted without further critical evidence.

In "The Presence," Graves laments metaphorically the diminishing of physical desire in a love relationship; when desire disappears on one side, he implies, the love is moribund. However, the death of love in this way is neither clean nor abrupt, for its memory lingers on in physical presence throughout the house:

> She fills the house and garden terribly
> With her bewilderment, accusingly
> Enforcing her too sharp identity,
> Till every stone and flower, bottle and book,
> Cries out her name, pierces us with her look.

That desire is no longer a part of the union and that the speaker is forced to be reminded of lost passion make the "horror" of her presence more painful than if she had left him alone. The failure of desire is torturing because one is reminded of past hopes and dreams that have been neither sustained nor, as in Graves's marriage with Nancy, fulfilled. "The Presence" is an admission of defeat, and by 1925, Graves must have known that his marriage was a failure; thus, not surprisingly, he was psychologically ripe for Laura Riding's entry into his life.

By 1925, Graves's financial situation was so bad that something had to be done to ensure a steady income. The care of his four children and Nancy's continued decline throughout the year compelled him to submit his B.Litt. thesis to the English department at Oxford in order to obtain teaching credentials. His thesis had been published earlier in February by Cecil Palmer under the title *Poetic Unreason,* but, as R. P. Graves points out, it had prompted destructive criticism in the *Manchester Guardian* and misinterpretation in the *Times Literary Supplement* (Graves 1986, 307). Graves summarized his attitudes towards poetry at that time in *Good-bye:*

> I then held the view that there was not such a thing as poetry of constant value; I regarded it as a project of its period only having relevance in a limited context. I regarded all poetry, in a philosophic sense, as of equal merit, though admitting that at any given time pragmatic distinctions could be drawn between such poems as embodied the conflicts and syntheses of the time and were literary hang-overs from a preceding period and were therefore inept. I was, in fact, finding only extrinsic values for poetry. I found psychological reasons why poems of a particular sort appealed to a particular class of reader, surviving even political, economic, and religious change. (406–7)

In fact, Graves's summary of a book with which, by 1929, he could have little sympathy, is quite succinct. In many ways, *Poetic Unreason* was a "downright denial" of the views held in *On English Poetry* (1). Its main tenets, obviously influenced a great deal by Mallik's philosophy, suggest that the poem becomes a two-way mirror in which both the poet and the reader see themselves, and that the poem in its initial draft "has no communication intention at all" (26). The only communication between poet and reader occurs between their subpersonalities and shared environment; the more varied the poet's experience or the more mixed his heritage, the greater the opportunity for him to become a "capable spokesman for his culture, because he can assimilate various discordant ideas and taken on various subpersonalities with ease. In the interim, the reader may create any interpretation that fits his own vision.

Graves also reflects that a poet is separated not only from the reader, but also from his own creation, the poem. Because the poem is a product of unconscious activity, the author's conscious purpose is not of great critical value in understanding the poem:

> From the poet's side, I wish to stress two important psychological phenomena: first, that no poet can ever rationally state beforehand what he is going to write about; second, that no poet can rationally state exactly what he has written and why; in effect, what the conflict is or what the factor is that solves the conflict, until after completely emerging from the mood that made him write the poem. (*Poetic Unreason,* 5)

The reader, too, is separated from the poem because of his limitations in experience or intelligence, which may deter him from grasping the implications of the poetry. Furthermore, Graves discusses how allusive images can be misinterpreted by various readers to produce divergent impressions of what the poet really means. Finally, Graves concludes that no poem ever remains static; it is a series of evolving events and meanings that change both temporally and subjectively. According to Graves, "no poem . . . has ever remained static but has always been steadily and waywardly developing both generally with the language and particularly with the mood of the individual reader" (188).

The meaning and effect of the poem, then, like everything in *Mock Beggar Hall,* is relative. Every person, every age, every mood, and every interpretation is relative to something. This leads Graves to the logical conclusion that value judgments as to what make a good or bad poem are invalid. Ultimately, the voice of Mallik can be heard when Graves, in defense of the term "bad," states, "As in ethics, I do not see the possibility of an absolute right or wrong, God against the Devil, so in an aesthetic sense I hold that the term Bad is in effect only relative" (*Poetic Unreason,* 22).

It might seem somewhat strange that, despite this relativistic view of poetry, Graves was inspired in the spring of 1925 after a trip to the zoo with his family and Sassoon to write a 421-line "long restless satire" (foreword, *Collected Poems 1938*) "ending with a description of many contemporary authors written by the marmoset as though he were the great satirist Samuel Butler come back to life" (Graves 1986, 312). The satire is leveled at writers from all schools of modern literature; Georgians, such as Blunden, Davies, Masefield, Marsh, and Squire, feel Graves's lashings as do the moderns such as Huxley, Eliot, Joyce, Strachey, and Yeats. Lawrence is seen "with dark robes of destiny hung," and Bennett deftly characterized as "eating ortolans from a paper bag." But the tragedy in Graves's mind is that his fellow poets have nothing to say to an audience of readers who are spiritually exhausted from the war and its aftermath. Graves recognizes that contemporary society and its cultural manifestations are as hollow as Eliot had depicted three years earlier in *The Waste Land.*

The Marmosite's Miscellany is more than just a poetic version of his *Contemporary Techniques of Poetry* (1925), in which Graves had placed the three contending schools of poetry into pseudoparliamentary factions and had critically scrutinized more than seventy poets' works. In the poem, Graves makes strong pleas for a pantheistic worship of God, for equality among men, for openness between individuals with different conceptions of life, and for what R. P. Graves calls the "exercise of 'associative' or 'analeptic' as against purely intellectual thought" (1986, 313). All of these concerns demonstrate that Graves was not as stoic as his tutor, Mallik, and his praise of associative thought would suggest that

Graves was retreating from the strictly rational sort of poetry that he had been writing. In the dedication to *The Marmosite's Miscellany,* "To M. in India," Graves describes himself sitting beside the Thames, awaiting a sign which will explain the purpose of life to him, just as Mallik sits beside the Ganges beneath his peepul tree. But Graves does not have the patience of his mentor. He feels "exiled" in England:

> Aghast at the long cruelty of tradition
> At so much pain yet to be harvested
> With the old instruments. In England I was
> Bruised, battered, crushed, often in mind and spirit
> But soon revived again like torn grass
> When, after battle, broken guns and caissons
> Are hauled off and the black swoln corpses burnt. . . .

Graves feels sure that his convictions about life are correct, but he is embittered and crushed by the loneliness of his vigil. His sole supporter is halfway across the world in India, and the only tie they have is their friendship, which "makes light / Of broad dividing seas, broad continents" between them. However with a family of four and a disintegrating marriage, Graves could not afford "to sit cross-legged . . . by the Ganges" awaiting "the clear morning waters for a sign" forever; nor—by the middle of 1925—did he wish to.

Graves, now armed with his B.Litt., decided to apply for a university post and spent most of July 1925 collecting letters of recommendation for a teaching post he would not be offered at Cornell (Graves 1986, 315). This rejection and news of the unexpected death of Sam Harries in India must have made his job of reviewing "dud poetry" for the *Nation and Athenaeum* even less inviting than before (*Good-bye,* 408). Finally, when Nancy fell ill and her doctor advised that she needed to spend winter in a dry climate, Graves must have felt the noose tightening even further around his neck, but as he describes in the 1957 edition of *Good-bye,* good fortune was about to descend:

> A week or two later . . . I was invited to offer myself as a candidate for the post of Professor of English Literature at the newly-founded Royal Egyptian University, Cairo. . . . The salary, including the passenger money, amounted to fourteen hundred pounds a year. . . .
>
> I got the appointment. The indirect proceeds from poem-writing can be enormously higher than the direct ones. (264)

The prospect of going to Egypt threw the Graves household into chaos. An offer was even made to Sassoon that he might join Nancy and the four children in the Graves retinue—an invitation that he wisely refused (O'Prey 1982, 159–60). Instead, Robert and Nancy extended the offer to join them on their Egyptian adventure to Laura Riding, and the disgruntled Riding surprisingly agreed to go. Graves's decision to invite along Riding—a poet whom he knew only by letter—and Riding's decision to follow this family of six have never been adequately explained. However, R. P. Graves's speculations do have a ring of truth, as does the possibility that Nancy saw in Riding the usefulness of a potential child-minder:

> Nothing could have pleased Robert more [than Riding's decision to come to Egypt]. He still had considerable misgivings about the way of life they would encounter in Egypt; and Laura's strength, for she was evidently a strong-minded woman, would enable both him and Nancy to face whatever lay ahead with greater confidence and greater equanimity. (Graves 1986, 321)

5

The Influence of Laura Riding: Collaboration and *Good-bye To All That*

The advent of Laura Riding in Graves's life on 5 January 1926 is well documented by biographers and critics alike. Some assess the ensuing partnership as having had very minimal influence on Graves's development, while some see in the figure of Riding the muse that influenced his critical and imaginative vision and that eventually spawned his conception of the White Goddess. In his biography, Seymour-Smith considers Riding's poetic influence on Graves as ephemeral, and points out that it was Graves who "helped teach her to write more lucidly. He also served as a source of information" (1982, 138). Seymour-Smith goes on to say that "her debt to him is considerable. But he had to be tactful, since no debt could be acknowledged" (1982, 249). Conversely, R. P. Graves claims that "the quality of Robert's literary work was dramatically improved by Laura's detailed criticisms in which her chief principle was that Robert should be precise and say exactly what he meant" (1990, 330). Randall Jarrell, George Steiner, and Daniel Hoffman see Riding as the muse who led Graves toward his eclectic theory of the White Goddess. Douglas Day in *Swifter Than Reason* presumes that the White Goddess is directly inspired by Graves's relationship with Riding, but Sydney Musgrove's "The Ancestry of *The White Goddess*" claims that this mythic character had been evident in Graves's writing since the early twenties. Perhaps Kirkham synthesizes the prevailing opinions of the Graves-Riding partnership best in his comment that the influence of Riding on Graves "was partly technical: the example of her personal criticisms were [*sic*] evidently largely responsible for a new terseness, sharpness of attack, and a surer intellectual control of his material" (Kirkham 1969, 110). Moreover, Kirkham points out that "during the four years from 1926 to 1929 he [Graves] absorbed Laura Riding's ideas concerning the nature and function of poetry, the nature of the poetic self, life in society and human existence; he acquired in the process a new set of poetic and moral values . . . a much clearer sense of purpose, and something like a Weltanschauung" (1969, 110–11).

The question of whether Riding permanently influenced Graves is outside the scope of this book, but by the beginning of 1926 Graves was looking for someone, anyone, with whom to share an intellectual relationship. What Graves may have glimpsed when he read Riding's "Quids" was a kindred spirit. He must have smiled at the "series of wry philosophical comments upon human behavior" (Graves 1986, 299) and felt that the satiric attack on conventional behavior and Divinity as well as on the patriarchal system was enough to begin a correspondence with the American writer. Eventually, he invited her to England to collaborate on an analysis of modern poetry, but when she finally arrived, she was bundled off to Egypt. There she spent the next six months in close relationship with the Graves family.

What happened in Cairo between the two can surmised from the "Recent Poems: 1925–1926" section of *Poems 1914–1926: Collected Poems of Robert Graves,* published by Heinemann on 2 June 1927. The majority of these poems were written while Graves was in Egypt and record the overwhelming effect that Riding had on him both intellectually and emotionally. In a letter written in reply to my speculation about the Graves-Riding relationship during Graves's brief tenure at the Royal Egyptian University, the biographer R. P. Graves sums up the development of their affair as follows:

> Robert clearly fell in love with Laura while they were at Cairo, just as you speculate. He and Laura were closeted together for long hours, discussing ideas rather more than writing anything down; and as he discovered for himself the formidable quality of her intellect he came first to admire and then to love her. (R. P. Graves to Quinn, 15 January 1987)

The most effective poems to appear in the "Recent Poems: 1925–1926" section all manifest some aspect of the developing love for Riding and intellectual excitement that Graves was experiencing through the first half of 1926. One of the most fervent expressions of his new awareness appears in "Pygmalion to Galatea," which was initially published in the *London Mercury* in May of 1926. In the poem, Pygmalion sings to the recently incarnated Galatea about the womanly qualities he would have her possess; Pygmalion wants his creation to be lovely, merciful, proud, constant in love and protean in thought, witty, kind, endearing, and unsubjugated. In short, she is to be the idealistic vision of a helpmate as well as an individual and independent woman. Having heard Pygmalion's song, Galatea reveals to him her human transformation:

> Down stepped proud Galatea with a sigh.
> "Pygmalion, as you woke me from the stone,
> So shall I you from the bonds of sullen flesh.
> Lovely I am, merciful I shall prove:
> Woman I am, constant as various,
> Not marble-hearted but your own true love.
> Give me an equal kiss, as I kiss you."

The love of Galatea will liberate the artist's mind from the "sullen flesh" and allow his spirit to soar to new heights. But the emphasis in this poem is on the concept of equality between the love partners. Galatea is said to be proud and unsubjected, and in the final line "an equal kiss" is shared. Earlier in the poem, Pygmalion urges, "Prize your self-honour, leaving me with mine." The sculptor has created Galatea from his own conception of beauty, but her spirit, like his, must be free to discover its own values and vision in order that she experience complete humanness. Equality, then, as D. N. G. Carter points out, "is based upon a free dependence, an accepting of what the other has to bestow without forfeiting 'self-honour'. In this case the result is envisaged as a union in which the idealistic and the physical reciprocally interact, softening the rigidity of the one, civilizing the brutishness of the other" (Carter 1989, 221).

The emphasis on the unsubjected and proud nature of Galatea has, not surprisingly, led several commentators, especially Kirkham and Canary, to see here an ur-White Goddess in the making. Kirkham stresses Galatea's "dominant role" and her commanding sense of independence (1969, 106), while Canary remarks on the positive correspondence between Galatea and Laura Riding as Graves's muse in Majorca (1980, 75). In fact, Graves is not so much creating a muse figure in this poem as communicating what he feels is missing from his marriage with Nancy. His later muses, the White Goddess especially, are neither kind, merciful, nor constant in love—and they are hardly endearing. In "Pygmalion to Galatea" he is not projecting his idealistic poetic muse, but simply clarifying to his new friend those attributes he values in a woman.

As Graves and Riding were closeted more and more in Cairo, they discovered that they had more than an intellectual sympathy for one another; the poem "The Nape of the Neck" exemplifies their growing intimacy. In what can only be called a bizarre sexual metaphor, based perhaps on Riding's opinion that thought flows along an inner path different from that of the senses (Wexler 1979, 29), Graves places a secret entrance to the intimacy of thought at the nape of the neck. The spine, which leads to this sensitive zone, is described as a "secret stairway by which thought will come / More personally, with a closer welcome, / Than through the latticed eyes or portalled ears." Reminiscent of D. H. Lawrence's theory of the solar plexus as the nerve center of consciousness, this direct route of thought-sympathy is judged as further evidence of special contact between friends:

> The tighter bound the chaplet, the more easy
> The door moves on its hinges; the more free
> The stair, then the more sure the tenancy—

In the concluding stanza of the poem, Graves admits that one can be fooled by a "hypocrite assassin" who can betray the preciousness of this organic communication (he does not say how, but he may be thinking of Nancy here); but the strength of this bond between true lovers is too strong to be destroyed, and one can appreciate the special bond even more after having been betrayed by previous, inferior lovers.

After seven years of disappointment in marriage with Nancy, Graves found it difficult to believe that he had discovered in Riding a lover who fulfilled his desires as completely as Galatea fulfilled Pygmalion's. Until Riding, Graves had been a monogamous lover—his background was puritanical, and in neither autobiography nor biography is there a hint of adultery before his departure for Egypt in 1926. It is safe to surmise, however, that after the birth of Sam in 1924, Nancy and Robert had not regularly been on intimate terms. The sudden awakening of physical passion must have been both frightening and wonderful at the same time, and the heat of the Egyptian spring and exotic feeling of exile might have made physical intimacy more likely than back in Islip.

In "This is Noon," Graves expresses his uncertainty about the constancy of his and Riding's newfound physical love. In contrast to his earlier "Song of Contrariety" and "Full Moon," where love could be consummated only in stealth and under cover of darkness, this poem's opening stanza states "that love rose up in wrath to make us blind," and that both lovers were carried away by a raging passion for each other. The next day the couple exchange smiles, perhaps a trifle guiltily, across the table, but the poet is not sure if his lover's smile is genuine. Day, who feels this poem implies that the love will not be able to withstand the scrutiny of daylight (1963, 96), fails to see that the poem is full of hope; each night that the poet spends with his lover helps dissolve any doubt he might have about their love.

> Now I too smile, for doubt, and own the doubt,
> And wait in fear for night to root it out
> And doubt the more; but take heart to be true,
> Each time of change, to a fresh hope of you . . .

Eventually, when the poet has gained full confidence in his lover, they will both be able to face the harsh light of the moon without fear of love's dissolution.

From an examination of Graves's poem of 1926, and from the hints that Graves gives in *Good-bye*, the scenario that unfolded in Egypt is not difficult to piece together. When Graves left for Egypt with his wife, four children, and Laura, his marriage was already failing; indeed, he wrote in *Good-bye* that "by the summer of 1926 the disintegration was already advanced" (437). While Graves did not see Riding as a potential lover when they left England, the discovery of similar intellectual and artistic views quickened their mutual attraction. Graves synthesized this attraction into his poetry as he moved from the idealism of "Pygmalion to Galatea" through the discovery of mental sympathy displayed in "The Nape of the Neck" into the question of the constancy of love displayed in "This is Noon." The culmination of this maturing love appears in the much criticized "Pure Death," which has been altered so much in subsequent editions that its original form needs quoting here:

> This I admit, Death is terrible to me,
> To no man more so, naturally,
> And I have disenthralled my natural terror
> Of every comfortable philosopher
> Or tall dark doctor of divinity:
> Death stands again in his true rank and order.
> Therefore it was, when between you and me
> Giving presents became a malady,
> The exchange increasing surplus on each side
> Till there was nothing but ungiveable pride
> That was not over-given, and this degree
> Called a conclusion not to be denied.

That we at last bethought ourselves, made shift
And simultaneously this final gift
Gave. Each with shaking hands unlocks
The sinister, long, brass-bound coffin-box,
Unwraps pure Death, with such bewilderment
As greeted our love's first accomplishment.

"Pure Death" provides an astute study of the powerful effect love can have on two people. Its opening stanza pronounces that the realization of love in all its dimensions can eradicate the consolation of conventional religious and philosophical teachings. No relief can be found in any dogma, because death can strip from them their otherwise inseparable union. The lovers continue to give all of themselves to each other until only their "ungiveable pride" remains, and even this they decide to offer to each other. This conclusion, as Hoffman succinctly points out, "moves in two directions at once: toward a hoped for, desperately sought fulfillment and at the same time toward a feared yet endurable ecstasy of terror, the frozen passion of death" (1967, 187–88). Their willingness to offer the "complete self," to have enough faith in the other, makes this death of the ego a "pure" death.

The poem is one of the most positive visions of love to issue from Graves's pen since the naïve and innocent songs in *Country Sentiment*. Graves had finally found in Laura Riding someone commensurate with his talent and emotions. In a letter to Sassoon on 31 March 1926, Graves wrote, "Laura and I are writing a book together about poetry and so on. It is extremely unlikely that Nancy, Laura, and I will ever disband, now we've survived this odd meeting and continue to take everything for granted as before" (O'Prey 1982, 165). And so began what Riding later termed the "three life," which was to have far greater consequences than Graves could possibly have envisioned at the time.

Graves stayed in Egypt as a professor of English at the Royal Egyptian University for fewer than six months. The reasons for his resigning the position were various: the poor health of his four children (*Good-bye*, 432), the hopes of obtaining a post at an American university, the feeling of futility in teaching at an institution where education was a farce, and a general dislike of the expatriate life in British society abroad. (This dislike of British pretentiousness and self-assuredness was later to be a contributing factor to Graves's leaving England for Majorca.) Despite the large salary for his position, Graves arrived back in England not only penniless, but with another financial responsibility in Laura Riding.

About the only manuscripts that Graves was able to complete in Egypt, outside the poems mentioned earlier, were *Lars Porsena, or the Future of English Swearing* and *Impenetrability, or the Proper Habit of English,* two books which have as their common theme the English language. The latter book, a history of the development of the English language with a great deal of attention paid to the loss of grammatical gender, case, and tense inflections, aims to demonstrate how flexible and exact the English language is for poetic expression. According to Graves the freedom of language is its greatest virtue. (Graves was later to expand the ideas in this book. With Alan Hodge he put together a handbook for writers—*The Reader Over Your Shoulder.*) *Lars Porsena* is a potboiler that attempts to examine the art of swearing in an objective manner.

Once back in Islip, the tensions of cramped quarters and noisy children made "The World's End" an impossible workplace, so with Nancy's blessing, the Graves family and Riding took up residence in London, and Robert and Laura began to collaborate on two books of criticism. This move, according to Seymour-Smith, was made simple because Nancy "had fallen under Laura's spell no less than her husband" (1982, 136). Seymour-Smith continues:

> Nancy seemed in no wise shocked by the moral considerations which concerned A. P. and Amy [Graves's parents], who were kept in the dark till the last moment. At this stage she felt glad that some other woman was willing to take her place. Her husband, for all his servitude and helpfulness and unimpeachable guilts, somehow possessed a demanding air, ghostly though this was. He had often made her feel that she was doing or being something wrong. Laura could handle him better. It would all work out very well. They were "dis-married" at last. She was, after all, a modern woman—and no one could have been more solicitous of her rights, or understanding about her feminist feelings, than Laura. She had never met anyone like her. At least Robert was right in that. And hadn't she agreed with him from the start? (Seymour-Smith 1982, 137)

Eventually, after less than two months in London and with the pressing need to leave England to avoid paying income tax on his Egyptian salary, Graves and Riding decided to go to Vienna for the winter. His escape from marital responsibility obviously disturbed Graves, but the anticipation of being alone with Laura must have been the impulse that spurred on such a daring move. In a letter written to Sassoon on 18 September 1926, just before the couple left for Vienna, Graves nonchalantly blurted out the news that he and Laura were leaving for Vienna to work. The stilted form of the letter and rather chopped logic suggest an embarrassed man trying to sound worldly and confident.

> What we came to tell you was quite casually that we are going to Austria for a bit: unconventional but necessary and Nancy's idea. She finds that now she's well she can't bring herself to resume the responsibility of the house unless we aren't there to force it on her: and that she can't begin to draw again unless she's alone, and she is longing to draw. We find in our turn that we can't get on with our work unless we have her equally busy. So we are going to Vienna . . . and be damned to scandal. (O'Prey 1982, 169)

A few months earlier, Graves had written to Sassoon to thank him for his suggestion to shorten the introduction to his *Collected Poems: 1914–1926*. Included in that letter was an evaluation of Sassoon's latest poems by Laura Riding strained through the diplomatic pen of his friend: "I am glad that she [Laura] liked you as a person and she now likes your poems more and more. They may be clumsy at times she says but they are real: which is the only thing that counts in the end" (Graves to Sassoon, 13 July 1926). Clearly, Graves was falling more and more under Riding's personal and critical influence; according to R. P. Graves, Riding's character was so strong that the controlling intelligence behind *A Survey of Modernist Poetry* was hers alone. He says "that Robert Graves's chief function was to help Laura to clarify her thoughts so far as was necessary in order for them to be expressed in the good, honest, prose which he regularly produced" (Graves 1990, 43). Graves the nephew makes his uncle sound more like an effective copyeditor than a collaborator.

The two stayed in Vienna for nearly five months, ostensibly to work on *A Survey of Modernist Poetry* and *Anthologies Against Poetry,* but also to be alone and to consolidate their newfound friendship. As R. P. Graves states quite emphatically in his letter to me of 15 January 1987: "Yes, Austria certainly was a liberating experience for Robert: a foretaste of what was to come." On their return to England in early 1927, Graves and Riding took an apartment in London and rented a barge nearby for Nancy and the children. The rationale for going to Vienna was conveniently forgotten, and the "three life" began afresh. Through early 1927, while Nancy was away at a farm in Cumberland (Seymour-Smith 1982, 140), both Graves and Riding completed their word-for-word collaboration—*A Survey of Modernist Poetry.*

In this book there emerged a new voice for Graves, a voice that had been glimpsed earlier but that had been submerged by his metaphysical interests and the relativistic teachings of Mallik. In the oft-quoted foreword to his *Collected Poems, 1938* Graves states unequivocally, "In 1925 I first became acquainted with the poems and critical work of Laura Riding, and in 1926 with herself; and slowly began to revise my whole attitude toward poetry" (xxiii). Riding's value-laden conceptions about poetry and other poets soon infected and destroyed Graves's relativistic standards which the metaphysical objectivism of Mallik disallowed. Riding convinced him that the poet was no longer the responsible spokesman for society because society was too corrupt and insensitive to judge the value of a true poet. The true modernist poet—of the likes of Ransom, Frost, or cummings—was independent of tradition and fashion and followed the dictates of his own unique poetic identity. This mentality, reflected through most of *A Survey*, gave Graves confidence to assert his own vision of poetic truth against the dictates of science and logic.

Canary points out that "the first freedom that Laura Riding brought Graves was freedom from the reader" (1980, 75–76). Indeed, a large segment of *A Survey* is devoted to a fervent attack on the lazy modern reader and critic who fails to spend time or effort delving into the significance of the poem. Graves and Riding see the central issue here as "clearness":

> The quarrel now is between the reading public and the modernist poet over the definition of clearness. Both agree that perfect clearness is the end of poetry, but the reading public insists that no poetry is clear except what it can understand at a glance; the modernist poet insists that the clearness of which the poetic mind is capable demands thought and language of a far greater sensitiveness and complexity than the enlarged reading public will permit it to use. (84)

The poor plain reader is caught between reliance on his own shaky critical opinions and reliance on the clichés and stereotyped expectations of traditional poetry; inevitably, the lazy reader will choose the safe route of familiarity in his selection of poetry. Some of Graves's evident contempt for the reader is reflected in "To the Reader Over My Shoulder" in *Poems: 1926–1930*. Here Graves admits he feels the pressure of the plain reader "peering beneath / My writing arm," so he scratches a few words of warning to the intruder:

> All the saying of things against myself
> And for myself I have well done myself.
> What now, old enemy, shall you do
> But quote and underline, thrusting yourself

> Against me, as ambassador of myself,
> In damned confusion of myself and you?
>
> For you in strutting, you in sycophancy
> Have played too long this other self of me,
> Doubling the part of judge and patron
> With that of creaking grind-stone to my wit.
> Know me, have done: I am a clean spirit
> And you for ever flesh. Have done.

In the first stanza quoted above, Graves admits that part of his poetic subpersonality was previously aimed at pleasing that voice within himself that spoke of society's expectations. But in the second stanza, the poet announces that worldly concerns will no longer dictate to him—that his new poetry will be judged for itself. It will not be written to satisfy outside needs or pressures; it will be complete in itself. Graves, then, sees poetry here as something free of the baser instincts. The writing of poetry has become "an act of purification; by isolating self from the impurity of contact with what is not-self the poet releases himself from the determinations of the flesh and existence in time" (Kirkham 1969, 114).

The poet, as described in *A Survey,* is primarily a transmitter of human experience, which is reified by the consciousness of the individual poet into poetic expression. This personalized view of experience is then presented to the poetry reader in order to put his perception of the universe in sympathy with the poet's sensitive vision. Thus, the poet's craft is to create with words an accurate depiction of what the world is *really* like:

> But the truth is that "the rest of mankind" is for the most part totally unaware of the universe and constantly depends on the poet to give it a second-hand sense of the universe through language. Because this language has been accepted ready-made by "the rest of mankind" without understanding the reasons for it, it becomes, "by progress," stereotyped and loses its meaning; and the poet is called upon again to remind people what the universe really looks and feels like, that is, what language means. If he does this conscientiously he must use language in a fresh way or even, if the poetical language has grown too stale and there are few pioneers before him, invent new language. (*A Survey,* 94–95)

This careful scrutiny of the poem's meaning and use of language leads naturally to advice about reading poetry, and about reading modern poetry in particular. Graves and Riding advise the plain reader to read slowly and to absorb the meaning of the words while noticing the relationships between the connotations and denotations. To prove their point, the authors spend a large part of the book analyzing e. e. cummings's "Sunset," a poem that is "just the kind of subject that the plain reader looks for in poetry" (*A Survey,* 11) and Shakespeare's sonnet 129. Their method of explication in these analyses is often credited with influencing Empson's *Seven Types of Ambiguity.* It can definitely be said to be the forerunner of the New Criticism.

The second piece of collaboration written at this time, although not published until 1928, was *A Pamphlet Against Anthologies,* a vituperative attack on just about everyone connected with the compilation of poetic anthologies: "the living dead" who write for them (164), the "dead heads" who read them, the "sapheads" who edit them (155), and the commercial exploiters who publish them. Anthologies, Graves and Riding claim, are generally negative productions unless they are used to publish poems not appearing elsewhere, because they pander to popular taste and sentiment and often bowdlerize many of the poems that appear. Graves and Riding analyze several popular anthology pieces here and find them to be lacking in logic, rhyme, and sensibility; but the pamphlet is not as well organized as *A Survey,* and some of the attacks seem petty and distorted. Anita Weinzinger, very heavily dependent on George Stade's research on Graves for her ideas, sums up succinctly the argument of *A Pamphlet:*

> The authors are chiefly concerned with the complaining that anthologies corrupt living poets and ruin the good poems of dead poets by putting them in bad company, enrich editors and publishers, and conform to popular taste. In the rest of the book they maliciously attack and ridicule a number of anthology favorites, subjecting them to the kind of close analysis they developed in *A Survey of Modernist Poetry.* Their point is to demonstrate that "it can be laid down as a fairly fast rule that any modern piece that has achieved . . . popularity . . . must be functionally half-witted or contain at least one crucial perversion of thought." (Weinziger 1982, 24)

In "Pavement," from *Poems: 1926–1930,* Graves offers a poetic version of this attack on anthologies. The sugary verse, which presents a highly romanticized portrait of a chimney sweep as seen through the innocent eyes of children, is contrasted with the sordidness of the reality. The description of the sordid reality is neatly bracketed in the poem so as to be easily edited out by the "discriminating" editor of the trade

anthology or ignored by the "sapheads" who enjoy reading such tripe
while ignoring the reality of the situation. The closing lines of the poem
should suffice to display the virulence of Graves's attack:

> . . . And when we children cried
> "Hello, Wm. Brazier, how are you, Wm. Brazier?"
> He would crack his whip at us and smile and bellow,
>
> "Hello, my dears!" [If he was drunk, but otherwise
> "Scum off, you dam young milliners' bastards you!"
> Let them copy it out on a pink page of their albums,
> Carefully leaving out the bracketed lines.
>   It's an old story—f's for s's—
>   But good enough for them, the suckers.]

Mrs. Fisher; or, The Future of Humour demonstrates just how hostile
Graves had become to his reading public. He claims, "[My purpose is] to
show you how little I care for you all and your jealously cultivated sense
of humour" (29). The book examines human alienation caused by the
"goddawful" elements of modern life: the classification, categorization,
and standardization of human behavior—even of humor. The only hope
for the human race, he maintains, is for man to participate so fully in
these antilife customs, institutions, and values that the system will
eventually self-destruct from within. Given this attitude, it is not at all
surprising that Graves was to lose all of his old friends (save Edward
Marsh) in the late twenties.

From 1926 to 1928, Graves's love for Riding became the central
factor of his life. He became devoted to her with the same kind of
fanaticism that had led him to be carried away with Mallik's teachings in
1924 and belief in pastoral idealism after the war ended. But Laura
Riding offered three special reasons for worship: she was full of ideas
that Graves could easily empathize with; she was already a fellow
craftsman in the art of poetry; and she was physically attractive to Graves
and could satisfy his uneasy sexual longings. While it seems surprising
that Nancy and Laura could manage to coexist peacefully for some time
in this rather complex triangular situation, R. P. Graves confirms that they
did so:

> Robert remained for some time in love with Nancy, and devoted to his
> children, and hoped that they could all remain together in perpetuity. Laura
> was also fond of Nancy, and this is the start of what Laura later called the

"three life." It worked surprisingly well, though inevitably there were many tensions. (R. P. Graves to Quinn, 15 January 1987)

R. P. Graves's comments here tend to oversimplify the situation. The rather casual attitudes of Nancy and Robert toward the impending trip to Vienna, where Robert's lungs could heal and Laura could explore her heritage while they worked together on *A Survey of Modernist Poetry* (Graves 1990, 36); the family's separation into different households in England, so that Laura and Robert could work together while Nancy left for Cumberland to follow her artistic desires (Graves 1990, 56); their eventual separate dwellings in London—all would suggest something other than a willingness on the part of the three to forge a closer bond of friendship. The truth of the matter may be simply that both Nancy and Robert had lost all love for each other and stayed in this rather unusual situation for the sake of the children and for fear of family scandal. The rapidity with which Geoffrey Phibbs was able to destroy the communion of the "wonderful Trinity" implies that all was not well in their relationships with one another. And Graves's poem "Quayside," written about this time, uses the symbol of a ship pulling away from shore to mirror his feelings of relief at moving away from an outdated love affair.

> And glad to find, on again looking at it,
> It was not nearly so good as I had thought—
> You know the ship is moving when you see
> The boxes on the quayside sliding away
> And growing smaller—and having real delight
> When the port's clear and the coast is out of sight,
> And ships are few, each on its proper course,
> With no occasion for approach or discourse.

The concept of leaving the baggage of old memories behind as the ship slips quietly out of the restrictions of the port and into the wide seas, where there is no "occasion for approach or discourse," anticipates the move to Majorca by Graves and Riding in late fall of 1929 when, "finished with nearly all . . . other leading and subsidiary characters" (*Good-bye*, 439), they would say good-bye to the old memories. This is a far cry from the earlier poem "The Dead Ship" in *Poems, 1914–1927* (renamed "Ship Master" for the 1926–30 volume), in which the journey of life is likened to a voyage aboard a vessel that is neither seaworthy nor charted for a particular destination. The feeling in the latter poem is that human life is an aimless journey with no direction or hope for contact with other human beings ("But hope no distant view of sail"). "The Dead Ship," written just before Riding entered his life, provides a stark contrast to "Quayside," where the voyage out into the unknown sea is welcomed with relish.

"Thief" is the third of the sea-motif poems to appear in *Poems: 1926–1930,* and like "Pavement" it suggests a freedom from the old self. The crimes of the poem's central character range from stealing "rings, flowers and watches" to shouting "oaths, jests and proverbs," for which he has been chained aboard a galley "steered toward battles not [his] own." Graves is, in fact, the thief who has too long attempted to escape from the realities of life by mouthing romantic platitudes or metaphysical philosophies that were not part of his poetic self. As a result of these deceptions, he has overlooked the starkness of life and has consequently been sentenced to face life beside the oarlock for ten years. The sentence is felt to be more of a chastening of the spirit than a strict punishment; one feels that after ten years of "comradeship with the damned," the thief will emerge more disciplined and strengthened than had he remained in his old corrupt environment.

Examples of Graves's newfound "realistic" approach to love poetry, obviously influenced by his awakened passion for Laura Riding, read significantly differently from anything he had written to Nancy. In "Between Dark and Dark" from *Poems, 1929,* written in a mood that echoes Robert Herrick and perhaps anticipates W. H. Auden, Graves advises young lovers on the realities of love relationships. The song is reminiscent of the mead hall scene in *Beowulf,* a moment of brightness amidst the darkness of the unknown outside. Graves, whose free expression of love had been thwarted for several years, now forewarns lovers to "be fed with apples while you may" and enjoy the delights of love as fully and passionately as possible, because such joy cannot last forever "with the grave's narrowness" always near. And this is the man of experience talking. His use of the old *carpe diem* theme is given its complete expression in the final stanza:

> Take your delight in momentariness,
> Walk between dark and dark, a shining space
> With the grave's narrowness, though not its peace.

The poem is an admission that the nature of love is transitory, and that a lover must be willing to grasp the physical pleasures when they are offered. Furthermore, the poem emphasizes the dual nature of love: its exquisite glory and its lust fever. The partaker of love must realize at the very moment of sexual fulfillment that love is fading and some part of him is dying. But the poet is perhaps less concerned with the ephemeral quality of love than with the passage of time between our waking adult hours and our death at some unknown point in the future. The lover must act quickly and decisively if he has an opportunity to experience a new love, lest his chance escape. The uncertainty as to how long the time span is between the two moments is what makes lovemaking frenzied and momentary. But what if the lover could find a woman who had the power to "stop time," who had the power to make all the tensions of an ordinary time-laden lover dissolve? Would this not make love eternal and secure?

In "The Terraced Valley" (*Ten Poems More*), probably written in 1929, Graves describes the abstract world into which his musing has led him. It is a world of opposites, a world turned inside out:

> The unnecessary sun was not there,
> The necessary earth was without care,
> Broad sunshine ripened the whole skin
> Of ancient earth that was turned outside-in.

Everything in this abstractly lifeless world is neat and tidy: everything conforms to an imposed standard:

> Neat this-way-that-way and without mistake:
> On the right hand could slide the left glove.
> Neat over under:

But the poet cannot find his loyal companion anywhere in this region and begins to search frantically for her:

> But found you nowhere in the whole land,
> And cried disconsolately, until you spoke
> Close in the sunshine by me, and your voice broke
> That antique spell with a doom-echoing shout
> To once more inside-in and outside-out.

The power of the lover to transform the "antique spell" (more aptly changed to "trick of time" in *Collected Poems, 1938*) is significant. Here the force of the lover's voice changes the gloomy world of formality, abstraction, and conformity into a vibrant, living world. Riding's restoration of vitality to Graves's life purged the burden of war guilt, the hapless marriage, the false philosophies and sentimental visions, and various other neuroses that Graves suffered; it gave him rebirth, freed him from his own history to start afresh. In his "Dedicatory Epilogue to Laura Riding" in the 1929 edition of *Good-bye,* he confirms this transformation when he states why there was no mention of Laura Riding in the book.

> By mentioning you as a character in my autobiography I would seem to be denying you in your true quality of one living invisibly, against kind, as dead, beyond event. And yet the silence is false if it makes the book seem to have been written forward from where I was instead of backward from where you are. If the direction of the book were forward I should still be inside the body of it, arguing morals, literature, politics, suffering violent physical experiences, falling in and out of love, making and losing friends, enduring blindly in time; instead of here outside, writing this letter to you, as one also living against kind—indeed, rather against myself. (443)

"Against Kind," which appeared in *Poems, 1929,* explains much of the ambiguous terminology in the passage above. Graves wrote the poem in praise of Laura Riding's integrity in being true to her own nature and not allowing herself to become sullied by conventions, categories, or societal tenets. As a result of her stance, she becomes "invisible by elimination / Of kind in her"; that is, she rejects that which other people value, turning inward instead to examine the "inner, timeless reality of the mind rather than the external, material reality of events, or even the physical existence indicated by laundry, light, fuel, drink, and food" (Kirkham 1969, 135). Lost in her internal search for poetic truth, Riding no longer requires any outside attention, but critics and other writers grow frustrated by her invisibility—her self-containment. In the final two stanzas, Graves indulges in a little wish fulfillment when he writes:

> She gave no sign; at last they tumbled prostrate
> Fawning on her, confessing her their sins;
>   They burned her the occasion's frankincense,
> Crying "Save, save!", but she was yet discrete.
>
> And she must stay discrete, and they stay blind
> Forever, or for one time less than ever—
>   If they, despaired and turning against kind,
> Become invisible too, and read her mind.

Graves's hope for himself is here. If he can transcend his own background and learn to become invisible (to overcome his past) like Laura, then together their love and their art will be independent of outside conditions, outside the ken of others "of kind." But by 1929, the tenor of this type of elitism and the kind of mentality it engendered had alienated most of Graves's remaining friends.

Graves's poetry through 1929 continued to attack humanity with vehemence. Often, in poems like "Hell," with its harsh staccato rhythms and half-rhymes—what Kirkham aptly calls "ejaculatory, impatient rhythms . . . [which add] up to a total effect of perfunctoriness" (1969, 119)—Graves even makes a grudging attempt to dissociate himself from the subject matter, as in the final stanza:

> But to their table-converse boldly comes
> The same great-devil with his brush and tray,
> To conjure plump loaves from the scattered crumbs,
> And feed his false five thousands day by day.

During this purging period, Graves's poetry manifests a sense of freedom and an independence of form that was not noticeable in the earlier poetry. In "A Former Attachment," for example, the severing of the love relationship is defined not only by the central image of the ship moving from the quayside (the objective correlative), but also through the vigor of the rhythm and tautness of the phrasing, while the half-rhymes give the verse its strength and balance. Commenting on this experimental use of half-rhyme, Gaskell notes that "the experience dealt with, like all experiences, is incomplete" and that the poem starts in the middle of a sentence and concludes on an "off beat rhyme" (1961, 217). This poem, along with "Nature's Lineaments," "Hell," "Lift-Boy," and much of the less successful, early Riding-influenced verse in the *Poems: 1926–1930* collection, all show a cleaner technique. The word selection is fresh and vigorous, while the rhythms seem simple but produce enough variation to keep the pace interesting and unexpected. Graves's colloquial style, with its experimental use of accentual line in reaction against smooth iambic, is often supported by a formal structure and almost always utilizes an orthodox and lucid syntax. If many of the poems mentioned above are harshly scoured of imagery and musicality, this is in keeping with Graves's newly acquired philosophy, voiced through his and Riding's *A Survey of Modernist Poetry,* that "truth" is revealed through poetic logic and that it should not be obscured by appeals to sense imagery and to the "cool web of language [that] winds us in" to becloud our intellectual detachment.

Most of the poems in *Poems: 1926–1930* reflect this new belligerence in Graves's attitude toward poetry and life. A revolutionary spirit, which was to find full outlet in *Good-bye,* runs through the collection; it wants to upset applecarts and begin afresh in a society free of corruption—one that could appreciate his and Riding's poetry. As Kirkham points out, the poems attack the whole socialization process, "the sacrifice of the personal identity in the interests of the group—and the substitution, in the life that social man makes for himself and the language he uses, of an artificial, abstract reality for personal truth" (1969, 120). The stance of the volume is that of looking at human existence from the perspective of an outsider, as one already willingly exiled from the morass and ready to certify clearly why he deserted the "sinking ship." *Poems: 1926–1930* is as much a justification for leaving England as was *Good-bye To All That.*

The unsavory story that unfolded between late October 1928, with the arrival of Geoffrey Phibbs, and the publication of *Good-bye* a year later, when Graves and Riding were settled in Majorca, has been carefully examined by at least four commentators: R. P. Graves in *Robert Graves: The Years with Laura* (71–137); Seymour-Smith in his biography (154–90); Joyce Wexler in her critical study of Laura Riding (49–67); and Frank O'Connor in his autobiography, *My Father's Son* (68–71). The entrance of Geoffrey Phibbs into the "three life" began with a note written to Riding in October of 1928. By January of 1929, Graves and Riding had recruited him to join their work at the Seizen Press, a private printing press that they had founded in 1927 in order to prove, they said, that "we were our own masters and no longer dependent on publishers who would tell us that our poems did not fit the image of poetry which they wished to present to the public" (Moran 1963, 35). The shifting of relationships and the absurdities of the following three months have all the makings of a theatrical farce. R. P. Graves, however, would have us glimpse the situation in a more serious manner.

When the four-life began in February 1929, with the introduction to the group of Geoffrey Phibbs, there was a brief period of some weeks when all four participants were perfectly happy. Nancy was rather on the outside. To understand the relationship between them at this stage, watch the classic film *Jules et Jim;* Nancy is the Frenchman's girl, whom he eventually marries.

But more important, see the German as Robert, the Frenchman as Phibbs, and Catherine as Laura. This will tell you an enormous amount about the true nature of their relationship. (R. P. Graves to Quinn, 15 January 1987)

Considering the brief period of the "four life" and Phibbs's neurotic behavior during that period, imagining the four in a state of happiness is very difficult. Eventually, a number of conflicting love triangles developed. At one point, Riding sent Graves to Huntingdon to find Phibbs, whom she then preferred to Graves, and bring him back to her. This task, which must have been exceedingly distasteful to Graves on both an emotional and a psychological level, the poet dutifully describes in *Good-bye:*

And then, later in the same month, my sudden journey to Hilton in Huntingdon, to a farm with memories of her [Nancy] as I first knew her, to burst in upon—as it happened—David Garnett . . . gulping his vintage port and scandalizing him with my soldier's oaths as I denied him a speaking part in your parable. (445)

Graves was successful in persuading his rival to go back to London, but the ensuing all-night discussion ended in catastrophe. Graves described these events in a letter to his confidante Gertrude Stein shortly after the incident:

Laura tried to kill herself with tablets of Lysol and then a jump of 50 feet into a stone area. This was because Geoffrey Phibbs was sort of a dual personality, part incredibly good, part very very ordinarily vulgarly bad. . . . He quitted. So she broke her pubis bone in two places and lumbar vertebrae were badly smashed but her spinal cord remained, curiously intact. (Graves to Stein, n.d.)

Graves fails to mention in this letter his own leap after Laura (probably from several floors below), or his own escape from serious injury. The attempted suicide, the strange and sudden decision for Phibbs to set up house with Nancy and with Graves's children, Graves's nursing of the injured Riding back to health, and the petty accusations that flew between the separated couples—all were carefully documented and gleefully disseminated by the local scandal mongers. Edith Sitwell's ungracious letter to Sassoon in Italy presents a fair sampling of the judgment of fellow writers at the time:

Then there is the Mormon Father of Islip [Robert Graves], or who used to be of Islip. The most terrific gossip is going on. . . . Everybody is saying that the Concubine [Laura Riding] is dead, having thrown herself out of a window, and I hear that some months ago, she imported a very bad Irish poet and married man to live with her and the Mormon Father, because she said he (the I.P.) was the most beautiful person she'd ever seen. But after a few months he escaped, first to his Aunt, and then to France and his wife, because *A* he was not allowed enough to eat, *B* he was made to scrub out the bath, and it took three hours every day, and *C* the Concubine wouldn't allow him to wear any underclothes, even in the depths of this awful winter, because she said they would spoil his figure. So he returned to his wife. (Sitwell to Sassoon, 18 May 1929)

While Riding was recovering in the hospital, Graves was busy on two projects: the first, with the help of Edward Marsh, was the pulling of strings to quash police proceedings against Riding's threatened deportation for suicide, and the second was the writing of his autobiography, at which time he felt free to "jettison as much of his family as he pleased" (Graves 1990, 103). Both projects turned out successfully.

Graves wrote *Good-bye* at a frenzied pace, finishing the first draft in just over two months. His mood while writing is captured in a letter to Gertrude Stein, with whom he continued to correspond during Laura's hospitalization.

I am busy . . . in writing my autobiography. It is a sort of goodbye to everyone but the very very few people to whom one never says goodbye or has ever said a formal how do you do. Quite ruthless; yet without indignation. (O'Prey 1982, 191).

Despite his ruthlessness, Graves admits in "Postscript to *Good-bye To All That*" that he followed a careful formula while writing the book. He first "put into the book all the frank answers to all the inquisitive questions that people like to ask about other people's lives" (*But It Still Goes On*, 12) as well as mixing in the ingredients of pulp fiction: food and drink, murder, ghosts, heroes, princes, kings, exotic characters, poets, and grand social events. He even added a special mention of Shaw and Galsworthy to ensure German and Scandinavian attention (16). Where the war was concerned, Graves claimed that he was neither writing an antiwar document nor attacking his regiment; rather, he "had tried not to show any bias for or against war as a human institution, but merely to describe what happened . . . during a particular and not at all typical one in which

[he] took part" (16). The same explanation is used to dispel attacks on Charterhouse in the book. Graves does admit, however, that ingredients are not everything in a story; for a book to be popular it has "to be written in a state of suppressed excitement, and preferably against time and with a shortage of money. And the sentences have to be short and the words simple. And the most painful chapters have to be the jokiest" (21).

This paragraph is what has led the American critic Paul Fussell to comment that of all the memoirs of the war, "the stagiest is Robert Graves's *Good-bye To All That*" (1975, 203). He sees Graves's remarks here as an indication that the formula for *Good-bye* is farce. For Fussell, Graves is a "joker, a manic illusionist" (1975, 206) who utilizes his personal vision of truth as a protection against "the positivistic pretensions of non-Celts and . . . the preposterous scientism of the twentieth century. His enemies are always the same: solemnity, certainty, complacency, pomposity, and cruelty" (1975, 206). All this seems reasonable, but when Fussell also claims that *Good-bye* "is rather a satire, built out of anecdotes heavily influenced by techniques of stage comedy. . . . Its brilliance and compelling energy reside in its structural invention and in its perpetual resourcefulness in imposing the patterns of farce and comedy onto the blank horrors or meaningless vacancies of experience," this goes too far.

Graves use of an anecdotal style incorporating a dramatic presentation of a series of actions, followed by a sparse, curt commentary, and then further action, would seem to match Diane De Bell's analysis of *Good-bye* closer than Fussell's vision of stage farce. De Bell sees this style as necessary because the narrator is still unable to face the full horror of the slaughter on the western front (1976, 163). Graves's narration, for example, of the first time he confronted a dead body as a young lieutenant is told with a laconic, dismissive air, which rings more of fear and disbelief than of satire. This grisly vision of the boy-officer trying to waken the dead man until he notices the bullet hole in the back of his head is beyond satire. The other officer looks on, dismissing the suicide as "business as usual": "While I remember, Callaghan, don't forget to write to his next of kin . . . I'm not going to report it as suicide" (*Good-bye*, 88). The author's deliberate attempt to distract the reader from the gruesome actualities of war by the mundane matters of officialdom is not material for Fussell's stage comedy, but a recognition of Graves's inability to capture the horror of the moment and its attendant trauma. Graves's neutral stance in the bathetic line at the end of the episode, "At stand to, rum and tea were served out" (89) might have had as its subtext,

"Somehow I [Graves] made it through another day amid the growing horror." This is not a comic punch line.

Good-bye is not a satiric comedy, although admittedly elements of satire do appear; it is an autobiographic *Bildungsroman* that carries its hero through the intense physical, intellectual, and social wasteland of the early twentieth century. Graves is a modern-day pilgrim carrying the chalice of his emerging individualism through sloughs different from those of Bunyan's allegory, but the effort required to avoid falling victim to temptation along the road is no less for Graves than for Christian. Although Graves at the end of *Good-bye* has not reached the Celestial City, he has found a safe harbor under the benign influence of Laura Riding's tutelage; and the autobiography, or what Frank has called the "anti-Romantic retrospective" (1976, 74), is partially the tale of the trials and tribulations along that road, the themes of which he had been exploring in his poetry since his days at Charterhouse.

The prewar sections of the autobiography are primarily an introduction to the hero in the formalized structure of Victorian middle-class society with all its genteel pretensions and virtues. The emerging pattern is that of a developing consciousness being thwarted by the combined forces of family expectations, scholastic regimentation, social conformity, and class distinction. The image of the hero in this section of the autobiography is that of a child who enjoys solitude as a kind of escape. He enjoys summers in Germany because he is free to behave as a child and not as a miniature adult. But more importantly, the early sections demonstrate how little Graves's upbringing prepared him for the realities of the war and its aftermath.

Both biographical accounts of Robert Graves's childhood record the rarefied environment of maternal protectiveness which generated within the youth a naïve vision of the outside world and with which he would always be in conflict. In fact, Robert Richman goes so far as to suggest that because of his protected upbringing, "what Graves was left with was a truly disabling horror of reality, particularly sex reality. . . . Graves's craving for purity was undoubtedly one source of his poetry, in which he creates a timeless realm beyond history" (1988, 68). R. P. Graves's biography, in particular, confirms that *Good-bye* demonstrates accurately how oppressive and rigid the Christian morality was in the Graves family. Perhaps only an individual who had been so fully imbued with these ideals could be as strongly affected as Graves was, when the authenticity of the ideals began to unravel as it did at Charterhouse and on the western front.

At the same time, the war acts as an excuse not to continue in the pursuit of the same empty values as those of his parents' generation. *Good-bye* relates how, full of romantic illusions and thoughts of heroic grandeur, Graves goes to war completely unaware of what awaits him on the grim battlefields of France, much as Christian is unaware of the subtle temptations that will meet the pilgrims on their journey through life. The war sections of *Good-bye,* which make up over half the book and lend unity to it, follow the familiar pattern of discovery, disillusionment, and death; but, providentially, Graves survives serious injury and is reborn on 22 July 1916 to proceed through the rest of the war more cautiously and cynically than before.

Still, by the time the war is over, Graves has paid a terrible price for his participation: his health is precarious, his belief in the Establishment is nil, and he has jumped into an ill-advised marriage to escape the ambiguity of his own sexuality. But the war has given him a few benefits in return: a belief in the power of literature and an endurance and strength of will that affirm man's individual tenacity. And these two beliefs see Graves through the hollowness of the postwar period, despite many false starts and inconsistent patterns of behavior. Frederick Frank seems to agree when he states,

> Memories of the Western Front bring Graves to an ironic realization of the opportunities which the War created for the spiritual and imaginative enlargement of sensitive individuals like himself. In fact, it is no exaggeration to say that the First World War became the great, directive force in his career. Because self-salvation and restoration of vision are old patterns for autobiography, Graves is able to superimpose these designs on his own particular struggle and to reconcile his ideals with harsh realities. Even his being listed as killed in action may be seen as a comic miniature variation of the theme of rebirth. (Frank 1976, 80)

Throughout the twenties, the struggles with English smugness, both in literary and personal circles, as well as his neurasthenic disorders and marital breakdown—not to mention the disfavor his work fell into—had all pushed Graves to the brink of despair. Besides providing a means of escaping his past, *Good-bye* also gave Graves a forum for an attack on the conventional proprieties of English life, an attack all the more profound because it came from someone within the system (Fraser 1962, 27). Graves himself confirms this to be true in his prologue to the 1957 edition, where he writes:

I partly wrote, partly dictated, this book twenty-eight years ago during a complicated domestic crisis, and with very little time for revision. It was my bitter leave-taking of England where I had recently broken a good many conventions; quarreled with, or been disowned by, most of my friends; been grilled by the police on a suspicion of attempted murder; and ceased to care what anyone thought of me.

But more than anything else—more than a war memoir, farce, autobiography, or satiric attack—*Good-bye* is a song of deliverance offered up to his liberator, Laura Riding. Graves uses her poem "World's End" as the introductory motto and dedicates the epilogue to her—an affirmation of Riding's lasting influence on him. Through purposely ambiguous personal allusions, Graves relates various incidents from earlier in the year (primarily involving his pursuit of Phibbs for the distraught Riding) which take on symbolic importance for him: the trip to Ireland with its stopover in Sligo, a city celebrated in song by his father; the return to Fishguard and the ride on the locomotive named "Wales of the Royal Welch Fusiliers"; and then the journey across the Channel to Rouen, where the "threesome" visited the spot where Graves had "died" in 1916 and where Laura (having been rejected by Phibbs earlier in the day) "seemed to die" (445).

Finally, *Good-bye* relates how Graves pursued Phibbs to Hilton, where twelve years before he had visited Nancy and proposed marriage while she was doing farm service as part of the war effort. Now in Riding's service, Graves had returned in time, erased the past memories, and overlaid them with a new and more vivid patina. Riding had, in effect, changed time for Graves. She had blotted out his past and made him free of the earlier encumbrances. Moreover, Laura had risen, like himself, from the dead after having jumped to her supposed death: "It was a joke between Harold the stretcher-bearer and myself that you did not die, but survived your dying, lucid interval" (445). Now together, they would carry on "against kind" and the detritus of modern life:

> . . . no more politics, religion, conversations, literature, arguments, dances, drunks, time, crowds, games, fun, unhappiness. I no longer repeat to myself: "He who shall endure to the end, shall be saved." It is enough now to say I have endured. (446)

This manifesto, then, is Graves's parting shot at his intellectual, social, and artistic contemporaries. He had, with his soldier-like dedication, endured for over ten years the "goddawful" conditions of postwar

England and searched for some kind of enlightenment that could make sense of his diverse experience; he had, to this point, made a number of false starts with his poetry. But with Riding's assistance, Graves was able to recognize his previous experimentation with poetry as part of the old order—part of the flotsam and jetsam that had to be jettisoned to make a new beginning under her tutelage. *Good-bye* became the prose record of the failed poetic world; after its completion, Graves's poetic life began anew with the firm conviction that Laura Riding's artistic influence was unique and vital for the progress of humanity:

> She was the one poet of the time who spun, like Arachne, from her own vitals without any discoverable philosophical or literary derivations: and the only one who achieved an unshakable synthesis. Unshakable, that is, if the premiss of her unique personal authority were granted, and another more startling one—that historic time had effectively come to an end. . . .

> Laura Riding was remarkable as being in the period but not of the period, and the only woman who spoke with authority in the name of Woman . . . without either deference to male tradition or feministic equalitarianism: a perfect original. (*The Long Weekend,* 200–201)

By the late summer of 1929, Graves was ready to leave England and establish himself with the recovering Riding somewhere on the Continent. He had effectively sundered his ties with the past and, not unlike Paul Morel and Stephen Dedalus at the conclusion of *Sons and Lovers* and *A Portrait of the Artist as a Young Man,* respectively, had set out on a voyage into exile to reaffirm his commitment to his art. But unlike the journeys of Paul and Stephen, Graves's voyage was to be carefully charted by a navigator who was to steer him into a golden age, an age of certainty where there would be no more good-byes.

> Content in you,
> Andromeda alone,
> Yet queen of air and ocean
> And every fiery dragon,
> Chained to no cliff,
> Asking no rescue of me.
>
> Content in you,
> Mad Atalanta
> Stooping unpausing

Ever ahead
Acquitting me of rivalry.

Content in you,
Invariable she-Proteus
Sole unrecordable
Giving my tablets holiday.

Content in you,
Niobe of no children
Sorrow no calamity.

Content in you,
Helen, foiler of beauty.

("The Age of Uncertainty," in *Poems: 1926–1930*)

6

Sassoon's Early Lyrical Poetry: Music and Nature

The amazing anomaly in Sassoon's career is not that he wrote poetry, for like Graves he had chosen his calling early in life, but that he wrote the kind of poetry that he did. There is very little in Sassoon's early writing to suggest, as Bergonzi states, "a potential rebel and defier both of public opinion and military authority" (1980, 92); and indeed Bergonzi might have added there was very little in his intellectual or social makeup to suggest the militant socialist crusader of the immediate postwar period or the metaphysical companion of Herbert and Vaughan that he later became, a period reflected in his *Heart's Journey*. Most of all, there appears little evidence that the hearty young fox-hunter of *The Weald of Youth* and Sherston's *Memoirs* would close his career writing Catholic devotional verse. The transition from country gentleman to religious quietist was long and tempestuous.

The early life of Sassoon is well documented by his critics and in his own fictionalized and autobiographical writings. If Robert Graves's observations in *On English Poetry* have any validity—that "a man is not a poet unless there is some peculiar event in his family history to account for him" and that this peculiar event is often due to "marriages between people of conflicting philosophies of life, widely separated nationalities . . . [which] are likely either to result in children hopelessly struggling with inhibitions or to develop in them a central authority of great resource and most quick witted at compromise" (33)—then Sassoon was well-equipped to become a poet. On his mother's side was the artistic, landed gentry of the Thornycrofts, with their roots deep in the soil of Cheshire. Joseph Cohen characterizes the maternal influence as promoting "leisurely living, acquiring the social graces, breeding horses and dogs, and hunting foxes" (1957, 170). The failure to note the artistic side of the

Thornycroft legacy is perhaps due to Sassoon's underplaying its importance in the *Memoirs*.

While his mother was a strict Anglican, Sassoon's father, Alfred Ezra, was a member of one of the richest Jewish families in England. The marriage of Alfred Sassoon to Theresa Thornycroft caused such hard feelings in his clan that Alfred's mother "refused to admit his wife or children to her house at Ashley Park, and cut them out of her will" (Corrigan 1973, 17). Not surprisingly, the marriage could not endure the social and cultural disparity, and when Sassoon was five, his parents separated. The job of raising the three children fell to his mother.

Not long after this separation, Sassoon's father contracted tuberculosis. His sons visited him periodically as he slowly weakened, and at one such meeting in Eastbourne, Sassoon met his paternal grandmother and was shown his place within the Sassoon family tree. This sudden awareness of his part in the family history is important, for Sassoon made contact with and recognized for the first time his Jewish antecedents, his place in a family that Corrigan claims was to play an ever-increasing part in his inner life.

> I [Sassoon] sometimes surmise . . . that my eastern ancestry is stronger in me than the Thornycrofts. The daemon in me is Jewish. Do you believe in racial memories? Some of my hypnagogic visions have seemed like it, and many of them were oriental architecture. (Corrigan 1973, 17)

Sassoon's diverse cultural and religious background forms the center of Joseph Cohen's perceptive article "The Three Roles of Siegfried Sassoon." So firmly does Cohen adhere to Graves's conception of differing ancestral origins contributing to the making of the poetic impulse that he concludes that two of Sassoon's poetic roles have developed from this.

> On one hand, he [Sassoon] has delighted in being the stern voice calling the multitudes to account for their wickedness and folly, and predicting their destruction if they failed to heed the warnings around them. On the other hand, Sassoon has seen himself as the gentleman-recorder of his mother's aristocratic, pastoral traditions. In short, he has lived the roles of angry prophet and country gentleman throughout the major part of his poetic career. (Cohen 1957, 170)

While this criticism does have a general validity, Cohen's stress on the Old Testament image of the prophet is too emphatic to lend his argument full justification. While Sassoon does virulently attack the profiteers, brass hats, and noncombatants during the war, his sense of outrage does not come from self-righteousness; rather it comes from a New Testament love of his fellow man and the disillusionment with a set of ideals that were disregarded by the ruling establishment during the conduct of the war. His postwar satiric verse was not written with an accusatory fire-and-brimstone voice, but with the voice of gentle Horatian satire, condemning not so much the actions as the folly and shortcomings of men.

Perhaps rather than the discovery of his Jewish roots, the death of his father may have been the most significant event in Sassoon's childhood. Many of the reviewers of *The Old Century* have simply seen the book as an evocation of the Edwardian twilight written by a man who wanted to forget the encroaching inevitability of a second world war. Lulled by the idyllic background of the prelapsarian "doomed patterns of English country life in the last years before 1914" (Mallon 1983, 83), critics have often overlooked the various distressing episodes that are recorded in Sassoon's autobiography. Sassoon's use of childlike language reflects the perspective of an eight-year-old trying to grasp the significance of his father's death, but the poignancy of that event still filters through the words of the adult:

> I felt desolate, because of so much happiness which could never happen now that he was dead; for he had made everything seem so promising when we were with him before he was ill. . . . It horrified me to think of poor "Pappy" being buried in a place [the Jewish cemetery] where people behaved like that [stealing flowers from a newly made grave]. I saw it all in squalid clearness; the thought of Heaven was no help to me when those imagined sounds of outlandish lamentation were in my ears. I felt death in a new way now, and it seemed as though our father had been taken from us by strangers. (*The Old Century,* 39–40)

The deaths of both his father and his maternal grandmother touched Sassoon deeply. It is not surprising that the next year the lines of "Queen Mab"—"How wonderful is Death / Death and his brother Sleep!"—influenced Sassoon to become a poet (*The Old Century,* 73–74). A brief glimpse of this juvenilia is afforded by Corrigan's study, *Siegfried Sassoon: Poet's Pilgrimage,* whose sampling of poems shows a fascination with the subject of death that would seem somewhat morbid in today's psychological climate. "The Sea of Death," "The Passing," "In the Churchyard," and "The Court of Death" all examine some facet of death, the inevitable plunderer of life. At this stage of his life, Sassoon saw the descent into "the palace of King Death" as full of terror and darkness, a journey that must be undertaken alone. Eventually, he was to try to distance himself from the idea of death in the "Lyrical Poems," but this theme would always linger relentlessly like a leitmotif behind his romantic musings.

The scenes of pathos in *The Old Century* are more than adequately balanced by Sassoon's positive reflections. Most of the memories in the book are in some way orchestrated by nature or under her benevolent aegis. Whether it be the brisk description of the freezing cold winter of 1895, when the red sledge was brought out of the stable and the family set off "along the glossy rutted lanes with all three of [them] snuggling in beside her [their mother]" (39), or the Gedges Wood "in the sun-flecked shade under the leafy chestnut poles" (98), Sassoon glories in nature's diversity.

Sassoon's awareness of nature was made even more acute when, recovering from pneumonia, he was taken out of doors in the late spring of 1895 to recuperate in a tent in the garden. Thorpe points out that a child's developing awareness is often intensified after the experience of a prolonged illness, and that H. G. Wells and Osbert Sitwell had similar experiences (Thorpe 1966, 121). Thus, as the young, recuperating Sassoon sat in his garden tent almost mystically aware of life surging back into himself as well as nature, a bond was forged that was to lead to a lasting sympathy between the man and the natural elements.

> To be out of doors again at that time of year was indeed like coming back to life. But it was more than that, for illness had made my perceptions detached and sensitive. I know how memory idealizes things; but I think . . . that this was my first conscious experience of exquisite enjoyment. The tent gave me a feeling of independence and security as I lay there and listened to a pattering shower or gazed at wisps and shoals of silvery cloud on mornings when the air was heavenly fresh and even the sky looked innocent —the mornings when I was alone and the dew not yet off the grass in the undiminished shadows of that garden world. (*The Old Century*, 52–53)

The experiences of that sickness are in many ways instructive about the kind of poet Sassoon would eventually become in *The Heart's Journey* and thereafter. The elements of his future poetic material are already noticeable in his sympathy with nature as well as in his love of solitude and quiet introspection. Furthermore, Sassoon informs the reader that his pneumonia had set him outside the ordinary realm of experience—that he had flirted with death, but unlike his father, had returned safely to health: the warmth of the "April sunshine flooding into his room" (44) assured him that he had returned safely from the "enormous flame-lit arches" of death (44).

The development of the poetic impulse in Sassoon as chronicled in *The Old Century* up to this point was almost entirely based on introspection. The inspiration of the juvenile poetry came from elaboration of dreams and of silent musings over his experiences, as limited as they had been in the protective environment of Weirleigh. But as Sassoon observes, in 1897 there occurred a dramatic change in his temperament—one which culminated in his leaving this Blakean garden of childhood innocence behind. Prompted probably by the onset of puberty, this change is documented in two different manuscripts that Sassoon wrote about his poetry at this time:

> The handwriting of the earlier volume has a sort of innocent refinement, and the decorations are really rather charming. In the later volume the calligraphy is large and untidy and the drawings have become crude and insensitive. The poems themselves . . . are similarly different. There is a transition from the serene simplicity of childhood to something uncontrolled, self-conscious, and wilfully lugubrious. The poetic impulse in me had become more impetuous, while the artistic sense, which so many children possess up to the age of twelve, was about to leave me to my own devices until such time as I was old enough to call it back. (*The Old Century*, 145–46)

This change, brought about by Sassoon's leaving his self-absorbed innocence, has much to do with his assumption of a more public life in his teens. The chapters of *The Old Century* that reflect the widening of the introvert's horizon stress two particular activities that drew his attention away from his semi-autistic musings: riding and cricket. His participation and interest in the sporting world (chronicled in loving detail in the fictional memoirs of Sassoon's alter ego, George Sherston) take the reader on a tour of the Kentish weald, where Sassoon introduces the reader to his developing relationships with several of its inhabitants. The author's friendship with his young tutor, Clarence Hamilton, takes him outside himself to worry about his cricket average; and certainly Richardson, the groom, whose knowledge of horses and ability to play cricket Sassoon admires, gives him a second male role-model to follow. But life in *The Old Century* is nothing if not leisurely, and Sassoon's introductions to the various "characters" of the area are delicately etched. Major Horrocks, the local country gentleman whose various interests in fine music and gardening make him an ideal companion for the gentle and sensitive boy, is contrasted effectively with his mother's gay and spontaneous friend, Florence Branwell. These portraits, then, aim to sketch for the reader an outline of Sassoon's early life, of his home and family background ("the world in which his poetic mentality was nourished," as he states in a letter to Blunden on 1 November 1939), and of the influences that they were to have on his literary career.

In the second part of the autobiography, entitled "Seven More Years," Sassoon's poetic development diminishes abruptly. In a letter to Blunden (1 November 1938), Sassoon suggests that childhood has a certain magic both for children and for adults who remember it fondly, while adolescence—"much the common light of day"—has far less to offer. He explains that his own progression through adolescence was so lacking in significance that in this section of his autobiography he is forced to rely heavily on humor and anecdote. He might have added that this was not a very productive period in his life, and that it must have been difficult to extract from his literary imagination very much of interest.

The second section of *The Old Century* covers the period from Sassoon's fifteenth birthday to his twenty-fifth birthday. It is divided into six chapters, the first two of which rather perfunctorily describe his school days at the New Beacon School and at Marlborough. Both chapters give reassuring portraits of schoolmasters, Mr. Jackson and Mr. Gould for example, that dispel some of the misgivings about public school education at the turn of the century. Sassoon remarks that while he was at the New Beacon School he looked on poetry "as an occupation to be almost ashamed of," but he continues that he still "had a feeling that [he] lost something wonderful which [he] still wanted, though [he] couldn't remember what 'feeling inspired' had felt like" (187). Not until his last year at Marlborough, when he came across Hood's "Bridge of Sighs" and thrilled to its "sense of powerful expression and memorable word music" (218), did Sassoon once again find comfort and direction through the assumption of his poetic vocation.

Chapter 3 of the second section follows a pattern established earlier. Once again, Sassoon is at home invalided with a strained heart, writing the occasional poem on a familiar theme: "Youth makes a six-stanza journey to Old Age, the moral being that Time's golden sands run all too fast" (227). His parody of "The Sands of Dee" named "The Extra Inch" looks forward to his parody of Masefield's "The Everlasting Mercy," but only in mimicking of style and rhythm.

The last three chapters of this section add very little to the history of Sassoon's poetic development. Chapter 4 recounts his days at Henley House, where he crammed for admittance to Cambridge; then follows a short description of his bicycle rides through the Kentish countryside, where the natural beauty of the landscape reawakens him to its loveliness. At Cambridge, we see the indolent and directionless undergraduate spending three months trying to write a poem about Edward I and ignoring his academic pursuits so completely that he returns to the womb of Weirleigh to celebrate his escape from textbook learning into the world of "intellectual freedom" (274). The final chapter is a rather strained attempt to give a rounded form to the book. We are asked to observe the seed that has sprung up from the Kentish soil much in the same way that the child in the "Prelude" wonders about the sowing of the farmer's seed: "What will the seeds be like when they come up?" he asks (13).

Finally, in chapter 6, we are introduced to a twenty-one-year-old Sassoon who has himself "come up" or come of age. What confronts us is an immature young man whose only desire seems to be a rather romantic one: to be a poet. His qualifications for such a role seem somewhat lacking, but to young Sassoon in the sunlight of an Edwardian summer afternoon, everything was possible:

> I was young; and what had death to do with me? To be dead was unbeliev-
> able, or at any rate as difficult to realize as last winter's snowfall. There was
> only the dazzling daydream of visible existence, and the serenity of poems
> and pictures, and the past and future meeting in a siesta of weather which
> was neither summer nor autumn. (283)

Thus armed with a fervent belief in his own worth and a romantic attachment to the unchanging values of time, Sassoon set out to capture in his art the essence of his experience.

The Weald of Youth opens in May 1909 with the naïve and overtly romantic twenty-three-year-old Sassoon riding home from a cricket match, his poem "Villon," printed in *The Academy,* tucked beneath his straw hat for safety. Very few changes are noticeable in Sassoon's character since our last glimpse of him two-and-a-half years earlier, except that we learn he has been dabbling in poetry in between shopping for riding equipment, visiting the Royal Academy, and playing cricket and golf.

At this point in his life, Sassoon had privately had printed a one-act play called *Orpheus in Diloeryum,* which was handsomely praised by family friend Edmund Gosse as a "delicate and accomplished little masque" that showed "richness of fancy and command of melodious verse" (*The Weald of Youth,* 15–17). But if the fragment of the play that Corrigan prints in her study of Sassoon (1973, 60–61) is indicative of the entire play, then we might surmise that Gosse's comments were written to encourage rather than to judge the young writer. Most certainly, the opening of the book strongly suggests that Sassoon had not yet found his vocation as an author. Bergonzi states in his assessment of the protagonist at this time:

> Sassoon has left a full and evocative account of his pre-war life . . . which can, not unfairly, be described as one of cultivated idleness: his energies were largely taken up with hunting and cricket, with collecting old books (rather more for their bindings than their contents) and with the composition of exquisite countrified verses that denoted a poetic talent minor to the point of debility. (Bergonzi 1980, 92)

The kind of poetry that Bergonzi writes about here is typified in Sassoon's sonnet "October," which depicts the typical adolescent weariness redolent of much pre-Raphaelite and Swinburnian poetry.

> Across the land a faint blue veil of mist
> Seems hung; the woods wear yet arrayment sober
> Till frost shall make them flame; silent and whist
> The drooping cherry orchards of October
> Like mournful pennons hang their shrivelling leaves
> Russet and orange: all things now decay;
> Long since ye garnered in your autumn sheaves,
> And sad the robins pipe at set of day.
>
> Now do ye dream of Spring when greening shaws
> Confer with the shrewd breezes, and of slopes
> Flower-kirtled, and of April, virgin guest;
> Days that ye love, despite their windy flaws,
> Since they are woven with all joys and hopes
> Whereof ye nevermore shall be possessed.

Although he admits that he seldom kept to the strict Italian sonnet form, Sassoon felt comfortable writing sonnets, as many of his early lyrical poems attest. These early sonnets, like "October," also suffer from the artificiality of subordinating ease of expression to a preordained rigidity of form. But "October" is a poor poem for any other number of reasons.

The poem is dilettantish; it is written by an objective observer who is standing emotionally outside the experience that is the subject of the poem. Sassoon's concern is to find the most effective word music with which to convey the intellectually realized experience, and his attitude seems to be that if logic and coherence are lost in the process of making the evocative music, then somehow this should be overlooked. The opening stanza of "October," indicative of a number of Sassoon's early lyrics, is an excellent example of such confusion: according to the poet, the leaves still hang on the silvan trees in the October mist, waiting for the first frost to make them flame, to change their color. However, in one group of cherry trees, the process of changing colors has progressed so far that the leaves on the trees are already shriveled. We are informed that all things decay, yet the leaves on the majority of the trees still wear their "arrayment sober." In the sestet, the reader is told that the dream of the coming spring with all its joys and hopes "nevermore shall be possessed." But the central metaphor, that of the trees for life, does not hold up. Next year the trees will afford another arrayment, so why should not the readers feel that their hopes and joys will be rekindled as well? The poem is somewhat lacking in logic and makes Edward Marsh's early comment to Sassoon clearly understandable:

> I think it certain that you have a lovely instrument to play upon and no end of beautiful tunes in your head, but that sometimes you write them down without getting enough meaning into them to satisfy the mind. Sometimes the poems are like pearls, with enough grit in the middle to make the nucleus of a durable work, but too often they are merely beautiful soap-bubbles which burst as soon as one has had time to admire the colours. (*The Weald of Youth,* 138)

The "pseudo-archaic preciosities" (28) that invaded Sassoon's vocabulary at this time also distract the reader from a musical appreciation of "October." The outmoded and obsolete usage of Middle English words such as "kirtled," "pennons," "shaws," "whist," and "ye" seriously diminish the freshness and spontaneity of the description. Furthermore, the redundancy of "silent and whist" in line 3 argues strongly that for Sassoon, rhyme and meter were of greater importance than sense. The concluding line of the sonnet, faintly reminiscent of Poe, sounds more like the conclusion of a medieval morality play than of a twentieth-century poet looking to say his "final word about life" (36).

Throughout *The Weald of Youth,* Sassoon reiterates that the only two themes that he was about to write about with passion were music and early morning. Sassoon was never to tire of these two subjects during his poetic career, but the latter subject would take on special significance in the war poems, where the morning stand-to became a time of silent, hopeful meditation in a sunless world. A brief glance at the "Lyrical Poems 1908–1916" in his *Collected Poems* also verifies Sassoon's claim that he wrote many sunrise poems: "Morning-Land," "At Daybreak," "Daybreak in a Garden," "Morning Glory," and "Before Day" are the most obvious examples. Almost all the poems are cloying and full of delicate imagery: "White misted was the weald; / The lawns were silver grey" ("Daybreak in a Garden") or "fair glimps'd vale / In haze of drifting gold" ("Storm and Sunlight"). Indeed, almost all the lines of this section are simply dreamy wanderings that lack any tension to contribute a spark of life to them. The poet simply tells the reader what beauties we are to experience, and then proceeds to describe them for us. In one case the poet even abnegates that responsibility:

> And I've no magic to express
> The moment of that loveliness;
> So from these words you'll never guess
> The stars and lilies I could see.
>
> ("A Poplar and the Moon")

One sonnet that is often singled out from the rest as having poetic merit and as being a signal that Sassoon's development was progressing is "Before Day 1909." Redolent of Swinburne's style and tone, the poem voices the plaintive adolescent cry of the solitary singer, the romantic loner in a secret turmoil. Felicitas Corrigan mysteriously calls this poem "a sonnet of exquisite perfection which, down to its least part, bears the individualizing touch of pure Sassoon" (1973, 62).

> Come in this hour to set my spirit free
> When earth is no more mine though night goes out.

And stretching forth these arms I cannot be
Lord of winged sunrise and dim Arcady:
When fieldward boys far off with clack and shout
From orchards scare the birds in sudden rout,
Come, ere my heart grows cold and full of doubt,
In the still summer dawns that waken me.

When the first lark goes up to look for day
And morning glimmers out of dreams, come then
Out of the songless valleys, over gray
Wide misty lands to bring me on my way:
For I am lone, a dweller among men
Hungered for what my heart shall never say.

Corrigan claims that this poem contains "all the poet's youth in it. The
song sings of his loves: sunrise, early morning mist across the valley, the
cherry orchards and the Weald and himself standing with arms out-
stretched . . . listening for a voice heard only in silence" (1973, 62). A
careful reading of the poem admittedly reveals beautiful imagery and a
well-evoked mood, but the significance of what the sunrise will bring to
the twenty-three-year-old is uncertain.

In *The Weald of Youth,* Sassoon gives a prose account of the
experience that probably shaped the content of the poem. This account,
despite being written some thirty-two years after the fact, contains more
vitality and vividness in its description than the stilted language of the
poem itself:

> And now I was beholding the sun himself as his scarlet disc rose inch by
> inch above the auroral orchards and the level horizon far down the Weald.
> A very Kentish sun he looked. . . . There he was . . . like some big farmer
> staring at his hay-fields and hop-gardens. And here was I, unconsciously
> lifting my arms to welcome the glittering shafts of sunrise that went wide-
> winged up through the innocent blueness above the east. But with the first
> rays slanting across the lawn everything somehow became ordinary again.
> . . . In the Arcadian cherry orchard across the road a bird-scaring boy had
> begun his shouting cries and clattering of pans. . . . I yawned; felt a bit lone-
> ly; and then went indoors to see if I could find myself something to eat. (40)

A sense of bathos is evident here that is missing in the poem, and the
loneliness is more acute because of the contrast it evokes. Moreover, the

pragmatic choice of following the dictates of a growling stomach over romantic musings causes us to smile at the vicissitudes of human nature: a humor that is absent in Sassoon's verse at this time. It seems incredible that a critic as acute as Edmund Blunden could write that this sonnet "would alone entitle him to resemblance among those many Englishmen who have answered 'the nods and becks' of thrilling tranquillity with an added pleasantness" (1950, 314).

Nearly all of Sassoon's poems of this period were concerned with solitude and tranquility, and many of them still incorporated the imminent death motif that Sassoon favored in his early writing. Poems such as "Wisdom," "Today," and the very Keatsian poem "The Heritage" all view death with the romantic detachment of a Burne-Jones painting. Many of the poems were similarly experimentations in mimicry and technique. In "Ancestors," Sassoon catches the echoes and voice of Fitzgerald's "Omar"; "Villon" has the flow of Swinburne, while "Goblen Revel," a poem which Marsh favored, is a healthy cross of Christina Rossetti and Keats's "Eve of St. Agnes." It contains imitative lines like "With flutes to brisk their feet across the floor,— / And jangled dulcimers, and fiddles thin / That taunt the twirling antic through once more." Corrigan is correct when she dismisses most of the "Lyrical Poems" as a "derivative mass of experiments [which] can be dismissed for the most part as being musical, grandiloquent, and mindless" (1973, 61). Still, occasionally a poem appears that looks forward to the more careful and original craftsman that Sassoon was to become.

"Haunted" is not a great poem, but it exhibits two developments that were to serve Sassoon when he later came to write war poetry. The first development is his use of concrete description to evoke a sustained sense of place, as opposed to the brief visual images that are so ephemeral and unsubstantial in the earlier works. Here an unnamed brooding man is making his way home through the woods on an exceedingly hot summer's evening. A sense of dryness is evoked by the poet's careful selection of vivid detail:

> Evening was in the wood, louring with storm.
> A time of drought had sucked the weedy pool
> And baked the channels; birds had done with song.
> Thirst was a dream of fountains in the moon,
> Or willow-music blown across the water
> Leisurely sliding on by weir and mill.

The dying sunset is "burning thro' the boughs / . . . in a smear of red" when an unnamed anxiety causes the protagonist to dread being in the forest at nightfall. He hurries down the woodland path, but in his agitation, he becomes confused and turns deeper into the forest. Lost in the thicket, he panics; and Sassoon captures this claustrophobic moment with deft, solid imagery that functions both on a literal and figurative level.

> . . . his throat was choking.
> Barbed brambles gripped and clawed him round his legs,
> And he floundered over snags and hidden stumps . . .
> Butting and thrusting up the baffled gloom,
> Pausing to listen in a space 'twixt thorns,
> He peers around with peering, frantic eyes.

Despite the unfortunate repetition in the last line, Sassoon manages to keep his concrete images consistent throughout the poem, and they illuminate, through the use of the pathetic fallacy, the character of the protagonist.

The second improvement of this poem is its almost complete lack of archaisms and redundancy. Sassoon finally seems to have found the voice of a twentieth-century poet. The jarring medieval English words of his previous poetry are replaced by modern terminology. The "shaws" have become English woods and there are no "ye"s or "nary"s to be found. The so-called plot line of the poem flows smoothly from beginning to end, and while it is fair to criticize the stereotyped ending for lack of imagination, the concluding lines leave little doubt as to what has happened to the protagonist: "Then the slow fingers groping on his neck, / And at his heart the strangling clasp of death."

Ultimately, the poem fails because Sassoon cannot convince us of what horror the protagonist is trying to escape. The personification of this evil, "squat and bestial," looping down upon its victim, is little more than rehashed Bram Stoker. Still, despite its melodramatic conclusion and "blots of green, and purple in [the victim's] eyes," "Haunted" is a marked improvement on the majority of Sassoon's earlier work and was to lead him to a flirtation with realism through his parody of Masefield's "Everlasting Mercy" in 1911.

In September of 1912, Sassoon turned to his second theme—that of music—and wrote under the combined influence of "ecstatic afflatus" and

Francis Thompson's "The Hound of Heaven" his "Ode to Music," which, he felt, liberated him "from anaemic madrigals about moonlit gardens, thrummed by the lutes of ill-starred lovers" (*The Weald of Youth,* 122). As Sassoon accurately stated in later life, this poem was little more than "rhapsodic bombilating in the void" (Corrigan 1973, 63), but it does substantiate his desire to throw off the constraints of subject matter and write about concerns which he truly felt. Unfortunately, as Sassoon himself notes in a critical summing up of his poem, he "had tried to produce a glorious effect by exclaiming 'Gloria in excelsis' and asking everyone to believe how wonderful I felt" (*The Weald of Youth,* 123). Nevertheless, he was so excited at the time by his creation that he sent it to T. W. H. Crosland, the editor of *The Antidote.*

Sassoon was in the process of completing "The Daffodil Murderer" when word came from Crosland that his "Ode to Music" had been accepted for publication, and in the flush of this latest success he decided to send Crosland his burlesque of Masefield's "Everlasting Mercy." After some careful editing, Sassoon and Crosland produced a sixpenny pamphlet called "The Daffodil Murderer" under the pseudonym of Saul Kain (a play on the name of Masefield's protagonist Saul Kane). Michael Thorpe dubs this Sassoon's most promising prewar poem, reprints its entire 556 lines in his appendix to *Siegfried Sassoon,* and judges it in some ways superior to the Masefield original (Thorpe 1966, 10). This is high praise indeed for a poem whose intention had been simply to pastiche what Robert Ross, author of *The Georgian Revolt,* has called "the seminal work of the new realistic school" (1967, 37).

Thorpe's energetic discussion of "The Daffodil Murderer" leaves little room for embellishment (see Thorpe 1966, 9–13). The critic touches lightly upon Sassoon's "unhappy mixture of the common man and the upper class schoolboy" in his choice of language in the quarreling passages, as well as on his seeming lack of social conscience throughout the work. On the positive side, Thorpe feels that several lines of the poem show that Sassoon had the capacity to feel empathy for the suffering victim—a capacity that would be tapped in great measure during the war. Thorpe might also have mentioned that the poem does succeed in depicting with great accuracy the rural life of Sussex (which Sassoon had carefully observed during the various Southdown hunting seasons) as well as the natural beauties of the changing seasons. Furthermore, Albert Meddle's gradual recognition of the eternal quality of nature and the transience of man in the pattern of existence as Meddle sits in prison "like a rat in a cage" waiting for his hanging suggests a significant divergence from Saul Kane's melodramatic conversion by the Quaker lady. In fact there is a nobility in Meddle's acceptance of his punishment and in his dismal future:

> O all pure things I've known,
> Let now my feet be shown
> The way that leads aright
> My spirit through the night;
> And when my breath shall cease,
> Grant me to sleep in peace.

This noble acceptance of what fate has in store reminds one of the conventional idealism that was embraced by the soldiers during the early phases of the First World War. But the greatest significance of "The Daffodil Murderer," Sassoon says, was "that it was the first sign of my being capable of writing as I did during the war, and the first time I used real experience. It also revealed my gift for parody, which is considerable" (Corrigan 1973, 68).

The poem was actually to have significance, despite its questionable literary merits. Sassoon sent a copy to his friend Edmund Gosse, who, in turn, passed it on to Eddie Marsh, whose curiosity was stimulated enough to ask for more of Sassoon's work to survey. Previously, Marsh's response to Sassoon's sheaf of work had been mixed; but now he recognized the overworked "vague iridescent ethereal" quality of Sassoon's poetry and advised the poet that one should "write either with one's eye on an object or with one's mind at grips with a more or less definite idea" (*The Weald of Youth*, 138).

The exchange with Marsh led to a luncheon in which Austin Dobson (whose poetry Sassoon admired) dropped by; after this meeting, as Christopher Hassall points out in his biography of Edward Marsh, "Sassoon began to take his literary life more seriously" (1949, 211). In fact, Sassoon even asked Marsh to find him lodgings in London so he could get away from the fox-hunting mentality that had permeated his life up until then. With his new protégé in tow, Marsh took great care to launch Sassoon actively into the literary and cultural milieu of London. By March 1914, Sassoon was ready to attempt writing poetry as a serious vocation.

The last quarter of *The Weald of Youth* demonstrates how unsuccessful Sassoon was in capitalizing on his new poetic environment. A typical day was spent gazing out of his window and wandering around his rooms, until he could dress in his impeccable style and go to lunch at his club and read the latest sporting newspapers and literary periodicals. In the afternoons, he would stroll through the city's galleries or museums, growing quickly bored. His evenings were spent at the occasional dinner party at the Gosses or with Eddie Marsh. But perhaps Sassoon's rather frivolous existence in London did have some effect on his poetic imagination, as he points out near the end of *The Weald of Youth:*

> I had grown up looking at it [London] as a place whose grime and noisiness made one doubly thankful for living in the country. But there came a moment during that summer when I realized that I was acquiring a liking for its back-street smells and busy disregard of my existence. . . . I was learning to love the city breezes; the country thoughts they carried with them gave the town intensity, and taught one the value of its trees. The skies had never meant so much to me as they now did in dingy London. Sunsets beyond those roofs and chimneys, those miles of brick and mortar, affected me with a newly-discovered emotion, inexpressible and alluring with the vague regrets of my ignorant twenties. There was a sort of poetry behind it all which fed my mind and created stirrings of expectation. (217–18)

Sassoon could not have known that the stirrings of his expectations would soon be enlivened with the onset of a world war, and surely, it is difficult to imagine anyone whose background or sensibility was less prepared for the reality of war than the man who was busily discovering the Russian Ballet while the rest of Europe prepared for armed conflict.

In a letter, written to H. M. Tomlinson, Sassoon says that he felt that writing *The Weald of Youth* enabled him to recall life at age 25, with all the "rich emptiness and immaturity [and with] all [its] gaps and impetuosities [and] intolerance [and] omniscient misapprehensions" (Sassoon to Tomlinson, 14 November 1941). The overt sympathy in the book toward this rich emptiness of immaturity is what makes its content somewhat unsatisfying. Sassoon harkens back to a time when his nebulous dreams of poetic success were yet to be realized, but his lack of perseverance and intellectual effort to realize these desires is irritating. The Sassoon figure projected in the book is described by Paul Fussell as "his hobbledehoy country self in embarrassed contact with literary and stylish London" (1983, 92), but this depiction is somewhat deceiving. If Sassoon's characterization was simply another gloss on the innocent being introduced to the reality of big-city life, i.e. the conflict between rustic simplicity and urban sophistication, then we might feel some empathy for

Sassoon. But the gentleman of leisure presented in the book seems quite content to take on the dilettantish trappings of the literary world without earning his keep. Throughout the autobiography, the protagonist fails to develop; he just lumbers awkwardly from one scenario to another with only the vague aspiration of poetic success to offer him some sort of direction to an otherwise purposeless meandering. The mature Sassoon, with much authorial intrusion, would have the reader believe that his young self was a well-intentioned youth truly in search of something significant, but the figure that appears is that of the twenty-five-year-old whose major concerns are inducing his family solicitor to let him "have an extra hundred pounds this quarter" or paying for another of his poems to be privately printed in vellum for circulation among his influential friends. This leisured world, depicted with such loving detail and care, was a world where stultifying inertia and sterility dominated.

It might have been Sassoon's object in *The Weald of Youth* to reconstruct a portrait of a serene Edwardian world from a standpoint of "mature sensibility and self-knowledge" (Sassoon to Tomlinson, 24 August 1942), but the book gives us precious little by which to assess the development of poetic awareness in the aspiring writer. Sassoon's omission, for example, of any mention of romantic awareness in these years might cause the reader to raise an eyebrow. There is very little significant material in the book; there is too much essay and not enough intimate substance by which one can understand the man. In fact, Sassoon sensed this inadequacy when he wrote to Blunden in September of 1941 that he feared the work might be judged as an "amiable irrelevance," with its strongest factor being its "quiet craftsmanship." Even if Sassoon was writing the autobiographical work in order to avoid facing the realities of yet another war, this does not excuse the omissions and gaps he leaves in recording his personal and poetical development. The result is a feeling on the part of the reader which Thorpe sums up as follows:

> Acceptance [of idealization] becomes more difficult where *The Weald of Youth* is concerned, largely because the paradisal unity is broken and the world as a whole comes more into view. It is no longer just a "local, limited world," but one that includes London and glimpses of "Country" life on a grand scale. The author still takes arms on the side of this enlarged world—so far as he saw it—but in such a way as to elicit a more serious response from the reader, who is now more strongly aware of what has been omitted. (Thorpe 1966, 153)

The Weald of Youth offers little room for doubt that if the war had not brought the insulated, leisurely world down around Sassoon's head, he would have remained in the same state of dreamy lethargy that had characterized his first twenty-eight years. In fact, at the conclusion of the autobiography, the twenty-eight-year-old Sassoon is as prepared for a life of poetry as he was for confronting the Germans: "I had rushed to the conclusion that war was a certainty, so what else could I do but try to have a gun in my hands when the Germans arrived, even if I didn't know how to fire it properly?" (271). Thus, after a short bicycle ride to Rye, two days before the declaration of war, Sassoon enlisted as a cavalry trooper in the yeomanry, and his distinguished military and poetic career began in earnest.

7

Sassoon's Early War Poetry:
From Idealism to Disillusionment

In his introduction to *Sassoon's Long Journey,* Paul Fussell characterizes Sassoon at the outbreak of the war as a "healthy, naïve, unthinkingly patriotic, horsy" young man (1983, x). Sassoon describes his early days as a cavalry trooper in the Sussex yeomanry with nostalgic affection in *Memoirs of a Fox-Hunting Man,* a fairly accurate portrait of the "outside self" of a young soldier unthinkingly engaged on a noble task. In the following extract, George Sherston, Sassoon's fictional self, has just joined the yeomanry and reflects on his first month of training:

> For me, so far, the War had been a mounted infantry picnic in perfect weather. The inaugural excitement had died down, and I was agreeably relieved of personal responsibility. . . .
>
> The basis of my life with the "jolly Yeo-boys" was bodily fatigue, complicated by the minor details of my daily difficulties. . . . But my fellow troopers were kind and helpful, and there was something almost idyllic about those early weeks of the War. The flavour and significance of life were around me in the homely smells of the thriving farm where we were quartered; my own abounding health responded zestfully to the outdoor world. . . . Never before had I known how much I had to lose. Never before had I looked at the world with any degree of intensity. It seemed almost as if I had been waiting for this thing to happen, although my own part in it was so obscure and submissive. (219–20)

The healthy and economical life depicted here continues for two months until Sherston is thrown off his horse in an effort to jump a barbed wire obstacle. During the tumble, Sherston breaks his arm and is eventually transferred to his home in Kent to recover. Sassoon, in fact, suffered similar injuries, but unlike his fictional self, he used the period of

recuperation creatively. In *Siegfried's Journey,* he carefully describes
what went on from the break in October of 1914 until he reported to
Litherland Camp in late April of 1915:

> During this period of inactivity I had experienced a continuous poetic
> afflatus, of which I took the fullest advantage, regarding it—not unnaturally
> —as my final chance of being visited by the Muse. This productiveness had
> indeed been almost like a recovery of the vernal raptures of my juvenilia,
> but I had been conscious of a newly-acquired technical control, while
> pervaded by an exultant sense of verbal freshness. My main performance
> had been a poem of nearly two hundred blank verse lines, vigorously
> impersonating an old huntsman remembering better days; but I had been
> happiest in a dozen war-oblivious lyrical pieces which had arrived spontane-
> ous and unexpected. It had been something of an ordeal when April recalled
> me to the Army as an officer in the Royal Welch Fusiliers. (17)

The two-hundred-line poem referred to here is "The Old Huntsman,"
which also later became the title poem of Sassoon's first volume of war
poetry. The poem is a recollective dramatic monologue spoken by an
infirm old innkeeper, once a successful huntsman for the local squire,
who now spends a great deal of time thinking about those "good old
days" and the dismal future to come. All measure of life and even
afterlife revolves around the hunt and its accompanying activities: hell is
envisioned as "the coldest scenting land [he's] known" while heaven is
akin to the joy he feels when he hears "the cry / Of hounds like church-
bells chiming on a Sunday." The old huntsman feels that somehow he has
not tasted all of life's fruits; his regret for never having been aware of the
munificence of nature is genuine.

>   Now I know
>   It's God that speaks to use when we're bewitched,
>   Smelling the hay in June and smiling quiet;
>   Or when there's been a spell of summer drought,
>   Lying awake and listening to the rain.

The portrayal of the old huntsman gives a sense of Sassoon's realization
of his own dilemma. The huntsman's self-reproach for his lack of
sensitivity to all opportunities for experience and for his blinkered vision
of the overimportance of hunting life is seen as a tragic oversight. He has
taken for granted the richness of the natural landscape; he has let the
dairymaid who loved him escape:

> I never broke
> Out of my blundering self into the world,
> But let it all go past me, like a man
> Half asleep in a land that's full of wars.

As he prepared for the possibility of violent death on the battlefield, Sassoon must have recognized how incomplete his previous life had been. Faced with the grim prospect of extinction, his desire to live and participate in the whirl of artistic and cultural opportunities seemed imperative. Furthermore, Sassoon wished to understand his own philosophical and theological speculations about existence before, like the old huntsman, he went "to sleep." The poem, then, is an affirmation of Sassoon's desire to transform his hitherto insensitive fox-hunting self into someone more intensely aware of the beauties and complexities of life. This was a transformation that had begun earlier with his new acquaintance with Eddie Marsh, but its impetus had been quickened significantly by the preparations for war.

Sassoon found very little time to nurse his newfound sensitivity during officer training at Litherland, although he did manage to compose "Absolution" which "was manifestly influenced by Rupert Brooke's famous sonnet sequence" (*Siegfried's Journey*, 17). The first of a number of poems written by Sassoon in what Bergonzi calls the "Brookian mode" (Bergonzi 1980, 92), and full of the self-glorifying ideals of a young inexperienced soldier, the poem "apostrophizes war as the agent of nobility" (Silkin 1972, 133). Of course, the training in camp bred this heroic feeling in the early years of the war, and the following excerpt from *Memoirs of a Fox-Hunting Man* shows that Sassoon looked back upon his experiences there quite favorably:

> It must not be assumed that I found life in the Camp at all grim and unpleasant. Everything was as aggressively cheerful and alert as the ginger-haired sergeant-major. . . . In May, 1915, the recruits were men who had voluntarily joined up, the average age of the second lieutenants was twenty-one, and "war-weariness" had not yet been heard of. I was twenty-eight myself, but I was five years younger in looks, and in a few days I was one of this outwardly light-hearted assortment, whose only purpose was to "get sent out" as soon as possible. (236)

Sassoon was able to maintain this rather heroic spirit even when news of his brother's death at Gallipoli reached him while he was in training camp. And once he had joined the Royal Welch Fusiliers in France, he

began work on his poem "Brothers," which he completed before seeing
any military action.

> Give me your hand, my brother; search my face;
> Look in these eyes lest I think of shame;
> For we have made an end of all things base;
> We are returning by the road we came.
>
> Your lot is with the ghosts of soldiers dead,
> And I am with the fighters in the field;
> But in the gloom I see your laurelled head,
> And through your victory mine shall be revealed.

The poem is an unabashed idealization of death in war. The two brothers
have made a noble covenant to fight and cleanse themselves of the baser
aspects of life; somehow the Homeric ideals of honor and duty in war
will vanquish the corruption of baser things. There is even a suggestion
of a welcoming of death by the brother who still lives. But the problem
with the poem is that in reality, the dead do not appear amid the gloom
with "laurelled head," that Sassoon simply overlooks the physical truth
about death, and that he had not yet come to realize what war was all
about. In fact, a reading of Sassoon's diary for the early months of his
duty in France suggest that he not only found a great deal of satisfaction
in war at this time, but that he felt it to be a surprisingly positive
experience.

> But I am happy, happy; I've escaped and found peace unbelievable in this
> extraordinary existence which I thought I should loathe. . . . We're safe for
> another year of war, too, so next summer ought to do something for me.
> Anything but a "cushy" wound! That would be an awful disaster. I must
> endure, or else die. (*Diaries 1915–1918*, 26)

Many of Sassoon's early war poems reflect this positive attitude
toward death. "The Dragon and the Undying" celebrates the beauty in the
bodies of the dead soldiers and their eternal spirit; and "France" expresses
how fortunate soldiers are to sacrifice their lives in a country as beautiful
as France. However, his poem "To Victory" (according to Graves the first
poem Sassoon showed to him, and which Graves dismissed as being
naïve) is perhaps the closest Sassoon came, before the death of David
Thomas, to expressing artistically his patriotic fervor. In fact, Lady
Ottoline Morrell found the poem so moving that she was inspired to write

to the editor of the *Times*, where the poem first appeared on 15 January 1916, to ask the identity of the mysterious S. S. She then wrote him a letter praising the "real beauty . . . [which] kept vibrating in my memory" (Morrell to the *Times*, 90).

"To Victory" continues Sassoon's transformation from fox-hunter to sensitive artist. A prose description of the Somme Valley, written in his diary the day before he completed the poem, gives us a glimpse of the artistic process involved in the creation of this poem; here is the raw lode from which the ore of "To Victory" was mined:

> . . . it was my happy heart this morning, my heart singing its praise of life and landscape. The men trudging behind chattered their war jargon, but I was back in an English day, walking alone on the hills with the mystery of my joy strong in me. O the beauty, the glory of what I saw, and see every day—so easily lost, so precious to the blind and the weary; so heavenly to men doomed to die. (*Diaries 1915–1918*, 31–32)

The next entry continues in a similar vein:

> O this joy of to-day! My voice shall ring through the great wood, because I am glad for a while with the beautiful earth, and we who live here are doomed to fall as best befits a man, a sacrifice to the spring; and this is true and we all know it—that many of us must die before Easter. (*Diaries 1915–1918*, 33)

The early days of Sassoon's war experiences could be seen as a release from his apathetic vision and his prewar lethargy. He now belonged to a collective crusade on which he and thousands of other young men had entered as "swimmers into cleanness leaping." The new and intense awareness activated by the war became a stimulant for his mind and feelings. The nobility of the cause, the healthiness of the outdoor activity, the freedom from financial responsibility, the companionship of fellow soldiers like David Thomas—all contributed to the outpouring of unrealistic, sugary verse; but at the same time, there was an ever-developing sense of identification with the forces of nature and a refining of sense impressions. In fact, the early diary entries are crammed with careful descriptions that testify to a conscious attempt on Sassoon's part to sharpen his already intense sensitivity to nature. Writing of his excitement at being in the neutral zone and lobbing bombs at German working parties, Sassoon wrote that "the great thing is to get as many sensations as possible" (*Diaries 1915–1918*, 51).

These sensations, accumulated throughout the winter of 1916, led, however, to a gradual revelation that not everything at the front was as ideal as Sassoon would have desired. In his "first admonitory war poem" (Corrigan 1973, 77), "In the Pink," Sassoon returned to the colloquial voice of the old huntsman in order to contrast the prewar life of a young farmer with his current life in the trenches. Sassoon concentrates here on a number of details which show the two worlds in deliberate contrast. The soldier's rotten boots worn for a five-mile march in "stodgy clay and freezing sludge" are contrasted with the best suit he wore when he was off to walk with "brown-eyed Gwen." The infantry man is given a warm potion of rum and tea to put him back in the pink, but the gloomy prophecy of the last two lines dispels any optimism: "Tonight he's in the pink; but soon he'll die. / And still the war goes on—he don't know why."

The importance of "In the Pink" lies not so much in its literary quality or profundity of thought, but in its sentiments about the terrible conditions in camp during the hard winter of 1915–16. In *Siegfried's Journey* Sassoon admits,

> . . . the more I saw of the war the less noble-minded I felt about it. This gradual process began, in the first months of 1916, with a few genuine trench poems, dictated by my resolve to record my surroundings, and usually based on the notes I was making whenever I could do so with detachment. These poems aimed at impersonal description of front-line conditions, and could at least claim to be the first of their kind. (17)

But on 19 March 1916, the sudden death of David Thomas (the Dick Tiltwood of *Fox-Hunting Man*) brought a shocking realization of the personal nature of war home to Sassoon. From then on, nearly all of his poetry was to contain bitter vituperation aimed at any political, religious, or national organ that sanctified or supported the machine of war. The description in *Fox-Hunting Man* makes clear that Thomas had been a close friend of Sassoon since their officer training days in Cambridge; moreover, the lamenting tone of his diary entry for his "young Galahad's" death suggests that Sassoon felt a strong homoerotic longing for the "angel with the light in his yellow hair" (*Diaries 1915–1918*, 45). In one of the rare portions of emotional outbursts of homoerotic passion left intact by his editor, Hart-Davis, Sassoon admits he was "longing for the bodily presence that was so fair." Similarly, his touching gesture of chalking Thomas's name on the beech tree stem and placing a garland of ivy and yellow primrose around it all strongly suggest the actions of a distraught lover (*Diaries 1915–1918*, 45). Within two weeks of Thomas's death, Sassoon had sublimated his realization of sudden and unexpected death into another poem: "A Working Party."

"A Working Party" is an account of the gruesome conditions of nightlife in what Fussell calls the "troglodyte world" of the trenches as soldiers blindly crawl up to the front line under cover of darkness. The blurred images and the disembodied voices are evoked with startling precision in the second and third stanzas, which engage the reader and force him or her to share the stark reality of the trek:

> Voices would grunt "Keep to your right—make way!"
> When squeezing past some men from the front line:
> White faces peered, puffing a point of red;
> Candles and braziers glinted through the chinks
> And curtain-flaps of dug-outs; then the gloom
> Swallowed his sense of sight; he stooped and swore
> Because a sagging wire had caught his neck.
>
> A flare went up; the shining whiteness spread
> And flickered upward, showing nimble rats
> And mounds of glimmering sand-bags, bleached with rain;
> Then the slow silver moment died in the dark.
> The wind came posting by with chilly gusts
> And buffeting at corners, piping thin.
> And dreary through the crannies; rifle shots
> Would split and crack and sing along the night,
> And shells came calmly through the drizzling air
> To burst with hollow bang below the hill.

The description of those horrors leads to the final picture of a fine Midland soldier—father of two children—who, in the process of busily building a sandbag shelter in the freezing cold, is shot by a sniper and instantly reduced to "a jolting lump / Beyond all need of tenderness and care." In this poem, Sassoon's satiric vitriol has not yet surfaced, for he had not yet been able to assimilate the shock of David Thomas's death. Instead, the poem grimly recounts the reality of death at the front: that it is indiscriminate and sudden. Sassoon, later cogitating on this phenomenon in his diary, writes that "bullets are deft and flick your life out with a quick smack" (*Diaries 1915–1918*, 48).

To sit inert and wait for his turn to die without taking some kind of revenge on the enemy for his personal losses does not sit well with Sassoon; his diary is suddenly full of descriptions of trudging out to No Man's Land to throw bombs at Germans. At one point he even admits, "something drives me on to look for trouble" (*Diaries 1915–18,* 15). In *Good-bye To All That,* Graves has no difficulty in attributing the cause of this recklessness: he claims that after Thomas's death, Sassoon was so angry that he volunteered to go out on night reconnaissance patrols looking for Germans (251). Sassoon confirms Graves's analysis in his perspicacious journal entry for 1 April 1916:

> I used to say I couldn't kill anyone in this war; but since they shot Tommy I would gladly stick a bayonet into a German by daylight. Someone told me a year ago that love, sorrow, and hate were things I had never known (things which every poet SHOULD know!). Now I've known love for Bobbie [Hamner] and Tommy [Thomas], and grief for Hamo [his brother] and Tommy, and hate has come also, and the lust to kill. Rupert Brooke was miraculously right when he said "Safe shall be my going, Secretly armed against all death's endeavour; Safe though all safety's lost." He described the true soldier-spirit. (*Diaries 1915-1918,* 52)

The reference to Brooke's sonnet "Safety" is a peculiar one considering that Sassoon had just written a poem reflecting the nonheroic nature of modern war, but perhaps he felt the need for some self-motivating philosophy which would justify his need for revenge on those who took Tommy and Hamo away from him.

The part of "the happy warrior" was not an easy one for the essentially pacific Sassoon to play, and by mid-April some of his enthusiasm for this role had begun to wane. An unpublished poem entitled "The Giant Killer," written about this time in his diary, strongly suggests that his desire for revenge was gradually being superseded by another instinct: the wish to survive.

> When first I came to fight the swarming Huns,
> I thought how England used me for her need;
> And I was eager then to face the guns,
> Share the long watch, and suffer, and succeed.
> I was the Giant-Killer in a story,
> Armed to the teeth and out for blood and glory.
>
> What Paladin is this who bleakly peers
> Across the parapets while dawn comes grey,

> Hungry for music, and the living years,
> And songs that sleep until their destined day?
> This is the Giant-Killer who is learning
> That heroes walk the road of no returning.

Sassoon's use of the medieval word for champion, "paladin," in the seventh line is neatly juxtaposed with the cautiousness of "bleakly peering" across the parapets. The hero in this poem wishes only to survive for another day and realizes that those that have gone before him will not return in a blaze of righteous glory. Clearly, the sentiments that this rather lifeless poem evokes are the inspiration of the nonheroic vision of "Stand-to: Good Friday Morning," the first poem that "anticipated [Sassoon's] later successes in condensed satire" (*Siegfried's Journey*, 17).

"Stand-to: Good Friday Morning" uses the realistic details of the trench conditions much in the same way as in "A Working Party," but the last three lines introduce a cynicism that becomes almost a signature for the remainder of Sassoon's war poems. Here Sassoon mixes the colloquial language of "The Old Huntsman" and the formulaic language of the supplication prayer in an ironic demonstration that the traditional belief in Christ's resurrection has very little significance in the hell of the trenches. The soldier, however, might be jogged into believing Christ if he receives a cushy wound on this Good Friday. Silkin's criticism of the poem for its crude metrics and awkward antithesis between the lark and the narrator and his comment that the poem's irony is "never serious enough to engage the real problems in the situation it clumsily raises" (1986, 141–42) seem to underestimate the importance of the poem's method. The first ten lines simply describe the weariness and condition of the watch in the trenches; the denouncement of the last three lines, however, not only captures the mood and reflection of the soldier, but also brings out his awareness of the futility of his sacrifice on this Good Friday. The irony cuts both ways:

> O Jesus, send me a wound to-day,
> And I'll believe in Your bread and wine,
> And get my bloody old sins washed white!

Christ's sacrifice has been useless if no one accepts him as God, and the soldier's sacrifice is useless to him if he dies. So the soldier proposes a bargain; he will believe in Christ's resurrection if he can be saved from oblivion by a wound which will send him home. Silkin's concern that

Sassoon's language here is weak seems strangely concocted; the use of "frowst," "damn," and "bloody" would seem in accordance with the language of the trenches and consistent with the interior monologue of the persona. Furthermore, the simplistic rhyme scheme suggests the language and muddled thoughts of one who has been on duty through the night and is dead tired on yet another damp and cheerless morning.

Not long after writing this poem, Sassoon was sent off to Flixecourt for a month's training course. The month behind the lines helped him gain some perspective on the previous few months and appreciate the glories of a French spring. Convinced that a major push was being planned for the early summer, Sassoon tried to concentrate on his poetic development by observing nature and forgetting the chaos that surrounded him. During his stay, he made friends with a young officer named Marcus Goodall (the Allgood of *Infantry Officer*), who according to Sherston "was quiet, thoughtful, and fond of watching birds" (292). Sassoon's diary for the period of this leave strangely lacks much mention of poetic productions, and indeed, once he was back in the trenches at Morlancourt in late May of 1916, his existence was "so completely identified with the battalion and those nearest [him] in it that [he] had lived very little with [his] private self" (*Siegfried's Journey*, 18), a fact that is confirmed by later entries for the time leading up to the Somme offensive. About all that the journal registers of Sassoon's poetic progress are his attempts to capture in words for later use in his poetry the various shades of the Somme skies and the nuances of landscape hues. Even during the bombardments on the Somme, Sassoon kept his poetic eye:

> Still we remain in this curious camp, which leaves a jumbled impression of horse-lines and waggons and men carrying empty deal shell-boxes, and tents, and bivouacs, and red poppies and blue cornflowers, and straggling Meaulte village a little way off among the dark-green July trees, with pointed spire in the middle, and a general atmosphere of bustle while we remain idle at this caravanserai for supplies and men and munitions. There is a breeze blowing and grey weather. (*Diaries 1915–1918*, 92)

On 21 July, Sassoon was given the false news of Robert Graves's death, followed the next day by news of the death of Marcus Goodall. The emotional shock of these blows might have contributed to the general and thorough exhaustion that led to a case of trench fever which took him out of the lines and back to England. In an unpublished poem written during this period, "Elegy: For Marcus Goodall," Sassoon vented his inner feelings and reflections about a war which was becoming for him less and less bearable. The opening stanza reveals a concern that was to haunt both Graves and Sassoon throughout the war and after: what had they done to be spared the violent death that had befallen their comrades? In "Elegy," Sassoon laments that while Goodall was being killed, he himself was daydreaming about some "hummock'd" field in England. And while he dreamed, the victim's body was "thrown / Into a shallow pit along that wood / Thronged by the dead." Melodramatically, he describes the dead ("discontented slain") prowling around the mass grave site "with moans and tears," and in the final stanza, draws an image vaguely reminiscent of the day of judgment in the Book of Revelation. A monstrous shell throws up enough earth to release the dead from their corporeal bondage, and they dance "through fields of heaven to meet the day, / . . . [and] the red-faced God who lit your mind." The ambiguity of the final line looks forward to the scarlet majors of "Base Details."

The poem itself is technically awkward, with the bizarre images detracting from the grief of the elegy and coming close to farce; nevertheless, the poem does depict those gruesome realities of death on the western front that are more perspicuously described in prose in *Infantry Officer*. Commenting on the first dead German soldiers he has seen close up, Sassoon writes:

> It gave me a bit of a shock when I saw, in the glimmer of daybreak, a dumpy, baggy-trousered man lying half sideways with one elbow up as if defending his lolling head; the face was grey and waxen, with a stiff little moustache; he looked like a ghastly doll, grotesque and undignified. Beside him was a scorched and mutilated figure whose contorted attitude revealed bristly cheeks, a grinning blood-smeared mouth and clenched teeth. (*Infantry Officer*, 337)

Sassoon's diary for the time he spent recovering from trench fever at Somerville College, Oxford, and at home in Weirleigh is empty from August until early December 1916. The only available evidence of his mental and physical condition at this time is in his account in *Siegfried's Journey*, but there the reader is given only a simplified version of the experiences detailed in *Infantry Officer*. As Thorpe points out, the early chapters of *Journey* make for "sketchy and somewhat disjointed reading" (1966, 159). *Siegfried's Journey* discusses the effect of Sassoon's stay at Garsington while he was recuperating from his illness. The comfort and care that Lady Ottoline Morrell lavished on him were important for his physical condition; discussions about the war with a largely pacifist group of visitors to Garsington soon opened his mind to the complexities of the political situation. In fact, Garsington became the catalyst for the "beginning of a process of disillusionment which afterwards developed into a fomentation of confused and inflamed ideas" (*Siegfried's Journey,* 22). During the summer of 1916, Sassoon heard stories that the British government had rejected a German peace proposal, that the war was being continued for less than noble motives, and that the young men of all warring nations were being sacrificed for the benefit of nationalistic pride. These ideas did little to reassure the already disillusioned soldier-poet.

The other concern that Sassoon pursued while he was at home was to have his friend Robbie Ross assist him to find a publisher for his first volume of war poetry. Ross eventually convinced Heinemann to publish what was to become *The Old Huntsman;* it included twelve of Sassoon's poems written in the satiric vein, including "Died of Wounds" and "The Hero." In *Siegfried's Journey,* Sassoon attempts to explain the development of this new technique of satirical epigram:

> Nothing I had written before 1916 showed any symptom of this development. It was as if I had suddenly found myself to be an expert boxer without having undergone any training. I have never been able to ascertain that my method was modelled on any other writer, though the influence of Hardy's "Satire of Circumstance" is faintly perceptible in a few of the longer poems. I merely chanced on the device of composing two or three harsh, peremptory, and colloquial stanzas with a knock-out blow in the last line. (29)

Sassoon would later continue to use this formula in his second volume of war poetry, *Counter-Attack.*

The letters written to Ottoline Morrell during Sassoon's period of convalescence offer an insight into his intellectual development at this time. He was reading *The Cambridge History of Literature,* concluding with reckless abandon that the minor poets of 1800–1840 were "absurd with their bloated featureless epics and footling album lyrics" (18 August 1916). He studied books on Slavonic folk music (24 August 1916), visited Hardy at Max Gate, and attended the ballet regularly. And with a growing trust in Lady Ottoline, his confidante, he disclosed his flamboyant fantasy: that after the war he intended to buy only snow-white horses, to dye them blue-green and to wear a flowing cloak to match (20 October 1916). While he was recovering, Sassoon also spent a good deal of time hunting, golfing, and playing cricket, thus keeping the Sherston side of his personality alive.

The combination of exercise and good care found Sassoon back at the regimental depot near Liverpool in the last month of 1916. His buoyant mood had given way to one of depression and despair:

> The year is dying of atrophy as far as I'm concerned, bed-fast in its December fogs. And the War is settling down on everyone—a hopeless, never-shifting burden. While newspapers and politicians yell and brandish their arms, and the dead rot in French graves, and the maimed hobble about the streets. . . . Those garden-dawns seem a very long way off now. And nothing before me but red dawns flaring over Ypres and Bapaume. (*Diaries 1915–1918*, 105)

For the rest of the war, Sassoon consumed a steady diet of Hardyesque fatalism and Wellsian pessimism, while the role call of his dead friends grew longer: Richardson, Edmund Dadd, Davies, Jackson, Pritchard, Thomas, Bayness. There is little wonder that he opened his diary for 1917 with a quotation from Hardy's *The Dynasts* which needs no comment:

> I have beheld the agonies of war
> Through many a weary season; seen enough
> To make me hold that scarcely any goal
> Is worth the reaching by so red a road.

8

Counter-Attack:
The Solitary Revolt

The year 1917 was to be a very eventful one for Sassoon. He was to be wounded in the shoulder and as a result of this injury to return to England for the publication of *The Old Huntsman*. He was to stage a protest against the continuation of the war and would have been placed in a mental institution but for the timely intervention of his loyal friend, Robert Graves. He was to spend a few months at Craiglockhart War Hospital as a victim of shell shock and shortly afterward to effect a rapid recovery—rapid enough that he was allowed back into the trenches. And during this period, he was still able to gather material for his attack on the established powers through his poetry, which was published extensively during the year in *Cambridge Magazine* and the *Spectator*.

In early 1917, Sassoon was at Litherland camp with Robert Graves, the two of them excited about their futures as poets. This companionship was an important support for Sassoon, but their company together was short-lived, for Graves was sent out to the trenches in late January. (Sassoon discusses Graves's decision to return to the front in *Memoirs of an Infantry Officer*; Cromlech [Graves] is given the opportunity to stay on home service, but an "angry pride" causes him to select overseas service for a third time [392].) Not surprisingly, a week later Sassoon was found fit for general service, and less than a month after Graves had left for France, Sassoon was in Rouen waiting to be sent up the line. His diary entry for 27 February captures his mood at the time. Referring to himself in the third person, he writes:

> He had loathed the business of "coming out again," had talked wildly with his pacifist friends about the cruel imbecility of the war, and the uselessness of going on with it. He came out with his angry heart, resolved to hate the whole show, and write his hatred down in words of burning criticism and

180

satire. Now he is losing all that; he has been drawn back into the Machine; he has no more need to worry. "Nothing matters now." He must trust to his fate: the responsibility of life has been taken from him. He must just go on until something happens to him. And through his dull acquiescence in it all, he is conscious of the same spirit that brought him serenely through it last year: the feeling of sacrifice.

He doesn't know for what he is making the sacrifice; he has no passion for England, except as a place of pleasant landscapes and comfortable towns. He despises the English point of view and British complacency. (137)

The staff officers whom Sassoon observed behind the lines guzzling their port wine and gobbling their chicken casserole while "good men" at the front were turned into cannon fodder appear in a long sketch entitled "Lunch on Sunday in Rouen," written on 4 March in his diary. This portrait and the slightly amended version that appears in *Infantry Officer* describe a blimp-like staff officer glaring darkly at slightly rowdy infantry subalterns back from the front. The glares are ignored by the young officers, but Sherston notes with a sense of pride that "the contrast between the Front Line and the Base was an old story, and at any rate the Base Details were at a disadvantage as regards the honour and glory which made the War such an uplifting experience for those in close contact with it" (*Memoirs*, 406). Sassoon's mellowed memories in his fiction, however, are sardonically sharpened in the diary entry, where the brigadier general and his complacency come under vicious attack:

> Why can't you go and show the Germans how to fight instead of guzzling at the Base[?] You have never been within thirty miles of a front-line trench, and yet you call yourself a general. And *you* will be alive, over-eating yourself in a military club, when I am dead in a shell-hole up on the Somme. *You* will guzzle yourself to the grave and gas about the Great War, long after I am dead with all my promise unfulfilled. (*Diaries 1915–1918*, 139–40)

Out of these experiences comes the much anthologized "Base Details."

> If I were fierce, and bald, and short of breath,
>   I'd live with scarlet Majors at the Base,
> And speed glum heroes up the line to death.
>   You'd see me with my puffy petulant face,
> Guzzling and gulping in the best hotel,

Reading the Roll of Honour. "Poor young chap,"
I'd say—"I used to know his father well;
Yes, we've lost heavily in this last scrap."
And when the war is done and youth stone dead,
I'd toddle safely home and die—in bed.

"Base Details," evidently generated from Sassoon's experiences in Rouen hotels, is representative of one of the themes that Sassoon would explore in his second volume of poetry, *Counter-Attack:* the incompetence of the general staff to direct men into battle. Here Sassoon imagines himself as one of the "brass hats" whose only task is to send "glum heroes up the line to death." Verbal irony abounds in the poem from the first line. His use of the word "fierce" suggests the harsh, rigid outer demeanor of these base officers, yet the poet makes absolutely clear that all these men lack the courage and bravery to be at the front with the rest of the soldiers. These officers are not "scarlet majors" only because of their red tabs, but because they are red-faced, "short of breath," and choleric. There is also a connection between their tabs and the bloody death to which they complacently send their subalterns. Sassoon meticulously describes the gluttony with which they gobble up their food in much the same way in which they guzzle away the lifeblood of their men until they turn "stone dead." The understatement of the word "scrap" for the mass slaughter of the Somme or Loos shows the ignorance of the general staff, and the verb "toddle" in the final line suggests virtual senility. In his interpretation of "Base Details," Silkin adds as a final irony that "there is a suggestion that these men [base officers] considered themselves to be in control of events, as though, being officers, the threads of destiny ran through their hands" (1972, 159–60).

Sassoon's mistrust of military leaders is also the theme of "The General," where the poet returns to the jaunty singsong rhythm of colloquial speech. While the general speaks a few hearty greetings to his men as they march up the line toward Arras, two smiling soldiers see him innocently as a "cheery old card." The name "Arras" immediately brings to mind yet another botched offensive, and the following line, "Now the soldiers he smiled at are most of 'em dead," confirms our suspicion of what is to happen there. Sassoon leaves no doubt where the blame for their deaths should lie: "But he did for them both by his plan of attack." The terse statement of the cause of their death confirms that the smiling general is an incompetent bungler, not worthy to be trusted with the lives of many better men.

Despite the rancor and bitterness apparent in these snipes at the general staff's incompetence, Sassoon's overriding purpose in *Counter-Attack* was to open the eyes of British civilians to what really was happening on the western front and to shake them out of their complacency and apathetic disregard for the horrors of war. But ironically, once Sassoon had left Rouen and moved back to the front, he reverted to his "happy warrior" mentality. Caught up in the machinery of the war, he was even to claim that if he had to choose between being in England or being at the front, he would choose the front because of the "quiet elation and absolute confidence" he felt in preparing for battle (*Diaries 1915–1918,* 151). This seemingly contradictory statement is explained somewhat by a letter he wrote to Graves just before another Arras offensive opened. He states that he envies Graves recuperating from his illness back in Wales and adds, "I am up to the neck in the war now. It's queer how it gets hold of me" (Sassoon to Graves, 4 April 1917). For Sassoon, the welfare of the men under his command took precedence over all other considerations; and the diary entries which describe his return to the Second Battalion on the Somme reflect this dedication:

> My party . . . were in a very jaded condition owing to the perfectly bloody time they've been having lately, but they pulled themselves together fine and we soon had the Bosches and pushed them back nearly four hundred yards. (*Diaries 1915–1918,* 155)

Not surprisingly, the continuing din and destruction of trench warfare gradually changed the tone of Sassoon's diary entries from a tone of bravado and orderliness to one of sadness and chaos as the survivors were forced to pass over the mutilated victims of yet another failed breakthrough. "Dead and living were very nearly one, for death was in all our hearts" reads a solemn entry the day after Sassoon was wounded (*Diaries 1915–1918,* 157). The wound took Sassoon out of the battle zone and back to England for recovery. There, almost immediately, he wrote the first draft of what he felt to be the best poem in *Counter-Attack* (Sassoon to Roderick Meiklejohn, 25 February 1918). In "Rear Guard" Sassoon transforms the hideous experience of the relief journey down from the Hindenburg Line into a poem destined to shock the complacent Englishman into an awareness of the actual conditions of war.

The poem opens with a lost officer groping his way by the "patching glare" of a lantern back to headquarters via the subterranean depths of gas-filled trenches. He passes the remains of former inhabitants, now destroyed and discarded, while above the "rosy gloom of battle" continues on with its muffled tones. The descent into this hell is reminiscent of book 6 of the *Aeneid*, in which Virgil describes the shadowy world of Tartarus. Like Aeneas meeting the fallen heroes of Troy, the officer finds one of his fellow soldiers and asks for directions. When an immediate reply does not follow his question, the protagonist shouts that the reclining soldier should help him get out of these Stygian depths and kicks the huddled man from sheer frustration. Finally, in desperation, he shines the light of his beacon directly into the soldier's face. The vision reflected back from the beam is staggering; it confirms, unexpectedly and frighteningly, the immensity and totality of death.

> Terribly glaring up, whose eyes yet wore
> Agony dying hard ten days before;
> And fists of fingers clutched a blackening wound.

Horror-stricken by his encounter with death, the protagonist wanders on until he finds a muted shaft of light which leads him to some stairs, and he dazedly struggles upward from the underground "with sweat of horror in his hair" to the twilight of the raging battle above ground. The officer's escape from subterranean death into battle is what gives the poem its situational irony; the protagonist has returned from the dead only to face the crushing destructiveness of heavy artillery above.

In essence, then, the emergence from one kind of death experience on the western front is just an initiation into another. The officer's callous kicking of the corpse of a fellow combatant and his blind groping along the gaseous slime of sodden trenches certainly attempt to explode the myth of the stolid, intrepid captain leading his troops to victory. Certainly, "Rear Guard" succeeds in conveying the helplessness of those victims caught up in a war which offered, instead of honor or nobility, only dark underground gropings and annihilation by huge shells. The prose analogue of this experience is vividly captured in *Infantry Officer* when George Sherston is on the march from Camp 13 to the front line.

Now we were groping and stumbling along a deep ditch to the place appointed for us in the zone of inhuman havoc. There must have been some hazy moonlight, for I remember the figures of men huddled against the sides of communication trenches; seeing them in some sort of ghastly glimmer . . . I was doubtful whether they were asleep or dead, grotesque and dis-

torted for the attitudes of many were like death, grotesque and distorted. .
. . Nevertheless that night relief had its significance for me, though in human
experience it had been multiplied a millionfold. I, a single human being with
my little stock of earthly experience in my head, was entering once again
in[to] the veritable gloom and disaster of the thing called Armageddon. And
I saw it then as I see it now—a dreadful place, a place of horror and
desolation which no imagination could have invented.

Concrete strong-posts were smashed and tilted sideways; everywhere the
chalky soil was pocked and pitted with huge shell holes; and wherever we
looked the mangled effigies of the dead were our memento mori. Shell-
twisted and dismembered, the Germans maintained the violent attitudes in
which they had died. The British had mostly been killed by bullets or
bombs, so they looked more resigned. But I can remember a pair of hands
. . . which protruded from the soaked ashen soil like the roots of a tree
turned upside down. . . . Such sights must be taken for granted, I thought,
as I gasped and slithered and stumbled with my disconsolate crew. Floating
on the surface of the flood trench was the mask of a human face which had
detached itself from the skull. (*Memoirs*, 430–35)

It was the loss of individual identity in such dehumanizing conditions
that Sassoon wanted the British public to recognize; but ironically, during
his recuperation at Lord and Lady Brassey's Chapelwood Manor, he
realized how little his poetic effort had touched the consciousness of the
aristocratic Brassey family and, for that matter, the rest of England. Only
when Sassoon contrasted the horrors of the Somme with his life spent
lounging amidst the yew-hedges and formal gardens and listening to the
blackbirds scolding one another, did he finally realize that poetry alone
would not change the course of the war; this realization confirmed the
idea that had been intermittently on his mind since he had been wounded.
As early as 23 April, when he was still recovering at the 4th London
Hospital at Denmark Hill, he had written confidentially to Robert Graves:

I can't make up my mind which course to adopt. (There can only be *two*.)
If I decide that I must keep up my reputation as a hero, I must go back *as*
soon as possible—in June, if necessary. The alternative is to scheme & plot
& wriggle for a reasonable job at home—(*not* hanging around Litherland—
that is out of the question). In other words, I must either go back tout de
suite, or (tacitly) *refuse* to go back at all (& tell everyone what I'm doing).
(Sassoon to Graves, 23 April 1917)

Less than a month later, Sassoon noted in his journal after a discussion with Lady Brassey about religion that he had better go back to the front "unless [he could] make some protest against the war" (*Diaries 1915–1918*, 171). However, only when he had escaped from the uncomprehending Lady Brassey to the sympathetic environs of Garsington was Sassoon motivated to act. In June of 1917, the Garsington pacifist circle suggested that Sassoon write something akin to Barbusse's *Under Fire*, but they eventually agreed that a statement of protest about the war (to be read in the House of Commons) together with a refusal to serve would do just as well. In her memoirs, Lady Ottoline Morrell claims that her husband Philip advised Sassoon to see Bertrand Russell and J. M. Murry to help him draw up a protest which he could give his commanding officer (Morrell 1975, 181–82). The statement was a simple catalog of reasons protesting the prolongation of the war; Sassoon stated that the war "upon which [he] entered as a war of defence and liberation, ha[d] now become a war of aggression and conquest" (*Diaries 1915–1918*, 173). In *Siegfried's Journey*, written thirty years later, Sassoon analyzes the causes which led him to this act of defiance:

> Realities beyond my radius had been brought under my observation by a European war, which had led me to this point of time and that sheet of paper on the table. . . . And somehow the workings of my mind brought me a comprehensive memory of war experience in its intense and essential humanity. It seemed that my companions of the Somme and Arras battles were around me; helmeted faces returned and receded in vision; joking voices were overheard in fragments of dug-out and billet talk. These were the dead, to whom life had been desirable, and whose sacrifice must be justified, unless the War were to go down in history as yet another Moloch of murdered youth. Let indignant civilians and phrase-coining politicians think what they chose. It was for the fighting men that my appeal was made, for those whose loyalty and unthinkingness would have betrayed, whatever acquisition the Peace might bring to the British Empire. (53–54)

And finally, these reflections led Sassoon to write the poem which he felt demonstrated the sincerity of his protest: "To Any Dead Officer." Sassoon gives full vent here to his disgust at a nation that deceives its men in order to extract from them the final sacrifice. The opening stanza presents us with the contrast between the "everlasting day" and the "everlasting night" of death that awaits the dead officer. The suggestion implicit in the poem is that politicians would rather have the common man believe in everlasting day (some kind of light, heavenly paradise) rather than in everlasting night—the dark nothingness of death, which would a far more likely conclusion. This contrast extends into the second stanza, in which the speaker recollects the young officer's disgust at living conditions in the trenches and juxtaposes the sights that await him there with scenes of peaceful, prewar life, when he could "join the crowd / Of chaps who work in peace with Time for friend." The third stanza reflects the speaker's realization that those who "were so desperate keen to live" are always those that "get done in"; and the penultimate stanza confirms that this is what has happened to the officer in question:

> So when they told me you'd been left for dead
>   I wouldn't believe them, feeling it MUST be true.
> Next week the bloody Roll of Honour said
>   "Wounded and missing"—(That's the thing to do
> When lads are left in shell-holes dying slow,
>   With nothing but blank sky and wounds that ache,
> Moaning for water till they know
>   It's night, and then it's not worth while to wake!)

Here, the contrast between what the speaker believes and what he feels extends the poet's motif of opposites; so the euphemistic phrase "wounded and missing" misrepresents the reality of the officer's death throes. In the final stanza, a send-up of the "happy warrior" mentality, the speaker informs the spirit of the dead officer in a rush of patriotic fervor that England will continue the struggle against "Prussia's rule" because there are "stacks of men" yet to use in battle. But the satire and irony have been carried on long enough; now the antiphon is to be heard. An ellipsis follows this statement, and the poem concludes with the words of a more authentic voice—that of the poet, perhaps:

> I'm blinded with tears,
> Staring into the dark. Cheero!
> I wish they'd killed you in a decent show.

The breakdown of the snappy, telephonic language near the end emphasizes the final contrast: all the posturings and euphemistic jargon of the politicians and of the military machine cannot conceal that these theoretical "stacks of men" are individuals with hopes and aspirations like those men whose lives have already been cut short in a meaningless war. Silkin, in his analysis of the poem, points out that "the futility of the man's [the dead officer's] sacrifice in yet another hopeless dud attack [is] a sacrifice that is merely one in an endless series of sacrifices" (1972, 163). The final words of Sassoon's war protest are a demand for public recognition of this fact:

> I have seen and endured the suffering of the troops, and I can no longer be a party to prolonging those sufferings for ends which I believe to be evil and unjust. . . .

> On behalf of those who are suffering now, I make this protest against the deception which is being practised on them. Also I believe that it may help to destroy the callous complacence with which those at home regard the continuance of agonies which they do not share and which they do not have sufficient imagination to realise. (*Diaries 1915–1918,* 174)

The month between writing his protest and being sent to Craiglockhart War Hospital for shell-shocked officers proved to be a difficult period for Sassoon. His firm decision to be a martyr for the pacifist cause did not make the already nerve-strained soldier's life any easier. Indeed, the letters that Sassoon received during the hiatus suggest the various emotional and intellectual attitudes that were gnawing at his consciousness. His fellow soldier and friend, Bobbie Hanmer, could not understand the "madness" of his action; Robbie Ross was "appalled" at what he had done; and Eddie Marsh used an intellectual approach, nicely spiced with idealistic phraseology, to convince Sassoon of his wrongheadedness. Arnold Bennett claimed that Sassoon was not knowledgeable enough to "judge the situation." Of the sample letters printed by Hart-Davis, only those from Ottoline Morrell and Edward Carpenter offered support and praise (*Diaries 1915–1918,* 178–81). Ironically, except for the writers of these letters who sought to offer him friendly advice, Sassoon's statement had little effect on anyone, so he was forced to overstay his leave deliberately to attract the attention of the military authorities. When ordered to return to his unit at Litherland, he sent a copy of his protest statement to his commanding officer informing him that "it [was his] intention to refuse to perform any further military duties" (*Diaries 1915–1918,* 177). Somehow, a copy of this letter reached Robert Graves, whose response to Eddie Marsh at the Colonial Office was that he thought Sassoon "quite right in his views but absolutely wrong in his action" (O'Prey 1982, 77). In the meantime, Sassoon had been ordered to Litherland, where, although he was treated very kindly by his acting

C.O., he still refused to abandon his stand. R. P. Graves claims in *Assault Heroic* that Sassoon was actually hoping for a court-martial arrest to arouse maximum publicity for his protest, but that he was dissuaded by Graves, who felt that a plot had been devised by the War Office whereby Sassoon would be locked in a lunatic asylum for the duration of the war (Graves 1986, 179–80). Feeling adequately checkmated, Sassoon relented and a medical board was convened. Its jury judged Sassoon to be in a state of mental collapse and sent him to Craiglockhart, where he was placed under the care of W. H. R. Rivers, the famed psychologist and neurologist. Eventually, Sassoon's protest was read out in the House of Commons, and his letter published in newspapers throughout England. By this time, Sassoon was busy walking around Edinburgh, playing golf, and writing the many antiwar poems that would eventually be included in *Counter-Attack.*

Sassoon spent just over five months at Craiglockhart, and from *Sherston's Progress* and *Siegfried's Journey,* we can glean a fairly accurate assessment of his time there. Rivers appears to have been the perfect father-confessor figure to cure Sassoon of his "antiwar complex." The psychologist's humane treatment consisted of giving his patient freedom during the day and of conducting three interviews a week with him during the evening, the results of which led Rivers to diagnose Sassoon's protest as having been "evoked by personal feelings" (*Infantry Officer,* 521). Eventually, Sassoon was brought around to agreeing with Rivers's argument that his selfish protest was not bringing the war any closer to an end; only at this point did his fixed belief in the claims of his protest begin to waver.

What finally brought the protest to its close was the growing friendship that developed between Sassoon and Wilfred Owen, a relationship that "reveals an influence almost as strong as that of Rivers in enabling him to make up his mind to drop his 'stop the war' attitude" (Thorpe 1966, 161). When Owen was passed as fit for general service, little doubt remained that Sassoon would soon follow him back to the front. Sassoon's and Owen's sympathies with each other grew so strong during the final month they were together at Craiglockhart that Sassoon's highly evocative and somewhat ambiguous remark in *Siegfried's Journey*—"I received his [Owen's] fullest confidences and realized that he could give me as much as I gave to him"—suggests that both men had admitted to each other their homosexual tendencies, and that perhaps Owen had owned to his "poetic crush" on Sassoon (Fussell 1983, 289).

Whatever the case, the two poets obviously shared an intellectual and emotional intimacy that made Owen's return to the battlefield an example for Sassoon to follow, albeit with reluctance.

During his stay at Craiglockhart, Sassoon had a good deal of free time to devote to poetry, and the poems he wrote there give a fairly accurate indication of his thought processes. However, the death of his prewar fox-hunting friend, Gordon Harbord, during the first month in the hospital threatened to unravel all the positive therapy Rivers had accomplished. Sassoon's personal response to Harbord's death is captured in an unpublished poem, "A Wooden Cross," in which Sassoon claims that his last link with the prewar past had been severed and laments his "helplessness" at being unable to prevent the death which sped Harbord on his "hidden way." The lament in the poem is not only for the loss of a dear friend, but for the loss of the innocent vision of life as well. The last two stanzas, however, turn to bitter invective:

> The world's too full of heroes, mostly dead,
> Mocked by rich wreaths and tributes nobly said,
> And it's no gain to you, nor mends our loss,
> To know you've earned a glorious wooden cross;
> Nor, while the parson preaches from his perch,
> To read your name gold-lettered in the church.
>
> Come back, come back; you didn't want to die;
> And all this war's a sham, a stinking lie;
> And the glory that our fathers laud so well
> A crowd of corpses freed from pangs of hell.

The forced rhymes and pedestrian sentiments, along with the spewing out of raw emotion, clearly indicate why Sassoon did not publish the poem; however, he effectively transformed this vituperative spleen against everyone in general into a particularized attack on the press and politicians in "Fight to a Finish."

Rivers's impression of the latter poem when shown a copy was that it was "very dangerous" (Sassoon to Ottoline Morrell, 29 October 1917), for the poem—a wish fulfillment fantasy which presages a successful end to the war—damns both press and parliament. Sassoon's use of understatement here is insidiously clever. The yellow pressmen, who wrote so falsely about conditions at the front and prolonged its continuance with stories of heroism and glory, are among those cheering "the soldiers who'd refrained from dying." The "refraining" soldiers, on the other hand, who have been curbed by military discipline from doing what they would have liked to do all along, now no longer need abstain from the pleasure that is theirs: "Snapping their bayonets on," the fusiliers break ranks and pig-stick the yellow pressmen. (Silkin suggests the link with cowardice here.) In the meantime, Sassoon and his company of bombers "turned and went / To clear those Junkers out of Parliament." The juxtaposition of the Prussian word for ruling class with the English parliament demonstrates the solidarity of the fighting man, whether German or British, against the politicians whose machinations kept them all at war. And while it is difficult to credit Silkin's claim that "Fight to a Finish" is the poem that comes "nearest to envisioning a revolutionary change" (1972, 160), it is apparent that Sassoon's frustration with the growing death list of friends was gnawing at him. Unable to effect a change, Sassoon settles for sniping at the shallow and largely unsympathetic press and self-seeking politicians.

This "home front versus military front" mentality received the full brunt of Sassoon's indignant imagination while he recovered at Craiglockhart. One by one, Sassoon picked off members of the complacent population. In "Glory of Women" and "Their Frailty," he ambushes the blind nobility of the female population who refuse to see behind the facade of war and continue to send their "glum heroes" out to die. In "Suicide in the Trenches," he assaults the mindless home crowds who cheer the soldiers marching by but who lack the imagination to realize what kind of hell they are sending their young boys to die in. "Does It Matter" demolishes the idealized vision of the noble war wound and brings home the reality of the suffering and handicaps of a lost leg or blindness. Thorpe remarks pointedly on the quality of this type of poetry:

> In *showing* the dreadfulness of the War, in its surface aspects, he preceded Owen and surpassed him and all English poets who had previously written of war. His satires have, quantitatively, greater "bite" than those of his fellow war-poets and a sheer brutality of utterance that matches the reality. No English satirist since Byron had had such power of invective. . . . He relieved the pressure of his emotion by *speaking* the brutality, over and over again. (Thorpe 1966, 26)

Considering his own cozy situation, Sassoon soon grew slightly uncomfortable with his pronounced disdain of noncombatants. He points this out in *Sherston's Progress* through George (his fictionalized self), who is lovingly wiping down one of his golf clubs after yet another successful day at the links.

> While I continued to clean my clubs, some inward monitor became uncomfortably candid and remarked, "This heroic gesture of yours—'making a separate peace'—is extremely convenient for you, isn't it? Doesn't it begin to look rather like dodging the Kaiser's well-aimed projectiles?" Proper pride also weighed in with a few well-chosen words. "Twelve weeks ago you may have been a man with a message. Anyhow you genuinely believed yourself to be one. But unless you can prove that your protest is still effective, you are here under false pretenses, merely skrimshanking snugly along on what you did in the belief that you would be given a bad time for doing it." (*Memoirs,* 537)

On 17 October 1917, Sassoon admitted in a letter to Ottoline Morrell that he had decided to return to France, saying, "After all I made my protest on behalf of my fellow-fighters, and . . . the fittest thing for me to do is to go back and share their ills" (*Diaries 1915–1918,* 190). At the end of the letter, he enclosed a copy of "Death's Brotherhood" (renamed "Sick Leave" in *Collected Poems*) which, he claimed, would show her the issues involved in his stand. The poem is a self-evident attempt to explain Sassoon's dilemma: how to explain his noncombatant status to his fellow soldiers for whom he is supposedly making this protest.

> When I'm asleep, dreaming and drowsed and warm,
> They come, the homeless ones, the noiseless dead.
> While the dim charging breakers of the storm
> Rumble and drone and bellow overhead,
> Out of the gloom they gather about my bed.
> They whisper to my heart; their thoughts are mine.
>
> "Why are you here with all your watches ended?
> From Ypres to Frise we sought you in the Line."
> In bitter safety I awake, unfriended;
> And while the dawn begins with slashing rain
> I think of the Battalion in the mud.
> "When are you going back to them again?
> Are they not still your brothers through our blood?"

The poem is impressive for its cleanness of expression and restrained emotional impact. The opening stanza sets up a stark contrast between the warmth and serene security of the protagonist's bedroom, far from the "rumble and drone and bellow" of war-torn France. While he rests, the homeless and noiseless dead gather round his bed and softly accuse the sleeper of his own unspoken thoughts. When, in the second stanza, the sleeper wakes in "bitter" safety (the adjective here is startlingly effective in the verbal irony implicit in the vision of his warm, friendly bed juxtaposed with his memories of Ypres and Frise), his mind is back with his battalion in the muddy fields of the Somme. The only answer to the rhetorical question posed in the final line is an unequivocal "Yes." The poem augurs accurately the decision that the poet was soon to make.

The memoirs of Lady Ottoline Morrell contain a chapter that relates her visit to Craiglockhart on 9 November 1917 to visit Sassoon. She states that "the last few weeks he [Sassoon] had become restless and felt that he could not stay there in safety and comfort while his regiment were still at the Front fighting. His compassion and sympathy for the men made him exceedingly miserable and his protest had apparently failed" (1975, 229). Rivers was evidently putting subtle pressure on Sassoon to go back, and by the time Ottoline Morrell arrived, he had made up his mind to return to France. The state of Sassoon's nerves at this time, not unlike Graves's over the same period, seemed acutely strained by the pressure of the decision. Indeed, Morrell writes that "he told me how haunted he was by the thought of men at the Front. Their spirits seemed to come and rap on the window calling him to go out to them" (1975, 230). The next day, Sassoon apparently opened himself up fully to Lady Ottoline, confessed his homosexuality, and admitted that "women were antipathetic to him" (Morrell 1975, 230). He had felt a good deal of guilt and had suffered great emotional damage until he had confessed his sexual inclinations to his brother, who had simply laughed and told him that he felt the same way. Not long after this admission, Sassoon began to chide and scold Ottoline Morrell for her artificiality and complex nature—he even left her without uttering a farewell.

The report of this experience is invaluable for two reasons. The first is that it shows how mentally unstable Sassoon was about the implications of his failed protest; peer pressure was pulling him back into the trenches. Second, the discussion clarifies that at least a part of his motivation to return was due to homosexual guilt. Sassoon was transforming his suppressed homoerotic interest for Owen, Graves (who had just announced to him his decision to marry Nancy), Bobbie Hanmer, and others into a more generalized and acceptable form of love: a loyalty to those men who served with him.

"Banishment," which has correctly been called a public apologia for Sassoon's attitude against the war (Thorpe 1966, 29), is more than that; it is a sublimated love poem in praise of the soldiers who are still fighting and dying on the western front. The poem has great flaws in its artificial language and worn-out clichés ("They went arrayed in honour" and "sent them out into the night"), but the poet's sentiment appears genuine. The cry here is for understanding, understanding by the men whom Sassoon left behind in the trenches. He wants them to understand that he has made his protest in the hope of saving these fine men from the "grappling guns"; "Love drove me to rebel. / Love drives me back to grope with them through hell; / And in their tortured eyes I stand forgiven." Love, then, is what finally conquered, and on 26 November 1917, Sassoon was passed for general service and sent back to Litherland to await his next duty assignment. Ironically, he told Ottoline Morrell in a letter from Liverpool that he had just heard from Edward Marsh how impressed A. J. Balfour had been by "Death's Brotherhood." Sassoon, in a scathing rebuttal of the compliments of politicians, responded: "Isn't it kind of them to be impressed by youth saluting them all prior to execution? God damn them all!" (Sassoon to Morrell, 22 December 1917).

At the end of 1917, a physically healthy but mentally fatigued Sassoon decided that less thinking might do him good. He vowed to "try and be peaceful-minded for a few months—after the strain and unhappiness of the last seven months." He continued, "It is the only way by which I can hope to face the horrors of the front without breaking down completely. I must try and think as little as possible. And write happy poems (can I?)" (*Diaries 1915–1918*, 197–98).

The remainder of the poems which appeared in *Counter-Attack* on 27 June 1918 were written while Sassoon was in Limerick, where he was sent early in 1918 to train new recruits. In *Siegfried's Journey,* he explains that the experiences in Limerick and Palestine that befell George Sherston were largely his own (69); a glance at Sassoon's diary tends to verify many of the occurrences and movements. The journal that he kept during these postprotest days also clearly indicates a shift in poetic focus which results in a different tone from the aggressively angry voice heard in the earlier works.

Sassoon's outdoor self clearly found living in Limerick to his taste. His journal is filled with remarks about the healthiness of the physical training and the resultant mental relaxation. Furthermore, his reunion with four brother officers of the Royal Welch Fusiliers lifted his spirits considerably. The countryside surrounding Limerick proved a great improvement over the industrialized area around Litherland, and Sassoon was soon part of the hunting scene of Jerry Rohan's Hounds. In many ways, the month in Ireland was a month of prelapsarian splendor only occasionally interrupted by an awareness of exactly why he was preparing his young recruits. His 12 of January diary entry reflects the ambiguity of his mental position:

> Peace of mind; freedom from all care; the jollity of health and good companions. What more can one ask for? But it is a drugged peace, that WILL not think, dares not think. I am home again in the ranks of youth—the company of death. The barrack-clock strikes eleven on a frosty night, "Another night; another day." (*Diaries 1915–1918*, 203)

But being with these young, naïve soldiers and attempting to prepare them for the unexplainable horrors of the western front could not be something that the recent protestor of the continuation of the war found easy to countenance. The poem "In Barracks," which Sassoon wrote while in Limerick, clearly conveys the mixed feelings he had at the time.

> The barrack-square, washed clean with rain,
> Shines wet and wintry-grey and cold.
> Young Fusiliers, strong-legged and bold,
> March and wheel and march again.
> The sun looks over the barracks gate,
> Warm and white with glaring shine,
> To watch the soldiers of the Line
> That life has hired to fight with fate.
>
> Fall out; the long parades are done.
> Up comes the dark; down goes the sun.
> The square is walled with windowed light.
> Sleep well, you lusty Fusiliers;
> Shut your brave eyes on sense and sight,
> And banish from your dreamless ears
> The bugle's dying notes that say,
> "Another night; another day."

The opening stanza of the poem captures the positive aspects of the military experience in Limerick. Here, in juxtaposition to the "flapping veils of smothering gloom" found on the Somme in "Counter-Attack" is the order of the pristine barracks square where strong-legged fusiliers repetitively march through the drill. Even nature seems in sympathy with their youth and boldness, for the sun benevolently shines warm and white as they practice their marches. Only in the final line of the first stanza is there an intimation that this drilling is serious business. The line itself is rather banal and lacks the potency to carry the message or image Sassoon desires, but the implicit suggestion is that these soldiers have been purchased not to fight something knowable—like the German army—but to fight against an amoral, Hardyesque power that destroys randomly and greedily without deference to any cause or concern. Inherent in the poem is the suggestion that no matter how well-trained or prepared the bold fusilier is, his survival is simply a matter of whim, a caprice of fate.

The second stanza is like an adagio; it is much slower and more precise than the first. The men move unhurriedly back to their barracks at the completion of a long day on the parade ground. The soldiers return to their beds where they sleep an untroubled sleep (like the dead they will soon become) unable to imagine the grisly conditions ahead. Sassoon uses the "knockout line" with its usual effectiveness, but the result of "another night; another day" is hardly shocking. Instead the ambiguity of the line makes Sassoon's point: on one level, the concluding line simply states that all these men have survived yet another day of the war. This survival is worth something. But beyond that is the realization that every passing hour (the eleventh hour) brings these unsuspecting victims closer to the appalling sights and potential annihilation at the front. The speaker in this poem is aware of the horrors that await his men, but he hopes that "another night; another day" might bring the ever-elusive peace closer.

For Sassoon, this "drugged peace" in Limerick was only real if he did not think about the implications of what he was doing and if he dedicated himself mechanically to training his recruits in the manner he described in a letter to Graves on 14 January 1918: "You would have laughed had you seen me this afternoon—lecturing 12 roseate Lance-Corporals on 'Patrolling'—one of my usual rambling discourses—no beginning or end to it, and punctuated with grins." This, then, was the masque that Sassoon had decided to present. He would become the jolly, mindless training officer happily lecturing his young recruits and escaping to his outdoor Sherston-self when opportunity permitted. Still, in the back of his mind the poet and protestor had not been completely silenced: "For my soul had rebelled against the War, and not even Rivers could cure it of that" (*Sherston's Progress*, 557).

The section of *Sherston's Progress* concerning George Sherston's encounter with the hunting world of County Limerick and its multifold diversions suggests that this period was one of the most mindless, escapist periods during the war for his alter ego, Sassoon. But unlike Sherston, who was able to escape into the world of hard riding and accept the master's motto "we may all of us be dead next week, so let's make the best of this one" (574) as valid, Sassoon was writing poetry each night in which his identification with the men continually grew stronger. And as this empathy grew stronger, the rancor and vituperation which characterized his earlier poetry began to mellow. "The Dream," written while at Limerick, is an excellent example of this developing focus on the men under his command.

"The Dream" opens with the description of the weary fox-hunter returning from his hunt in a "drizzling dusk." When upon his return he wanders by a cow shed, the acrid odor of the cow dung involuntarily transports him back to his war experiences. The third stanza is a flashback to France. The narrator recounts the fatigue and weariness of his men after a long march as they stumble "into some crazy hovel, too beat to grumble." The hovel is cold and filthy, but the men drop their heavy packs and begin unlacing their "sodden boots." The narrator dutifully examines his men's blistered feet; he says, "Young Jones / Stares up at me, mud-splashed and white and jaded; / Out of his eyes the morning light has faded." The emphasis on Jones's gazing up trustfully at his officer is the telling feature of the poem. The narrator's distress at being powerless to change the sordid conditions that he loathes as much as his men constitutes the theme of the poem; all the helpless narrator/officer can do is *share* his men's burdens. Further, the narrator must shoulder a heavier onus:

> Can they guess
> The secret burden that is always mine?
> Pride in their courage; pity for their distress;
> And burning bitterness
> That I must take them to the accursed Line.

In a real sense, he is their executioner, for under his command they will mindlessly be led ten miles down the road to the battlefield where "the foul beast of war that bludgeons life" awaits them. For Sassoon, the remembrance of the past is merged with the present because his duty of preparing men for the slaughter of the battlefield remains the same, whether in Limerick or in France. Thorpe's criticism—that the poem fails because the poet's emotions and not the tragedy to which he bears witness are the central concern—fails to grasp that the dream and the response are purposely individualized (Thorpe 1966, 30). Sassoon is no longer firing all his broadsides at the civilians and ineffectual "brass hats," but is trying to comprehend his own individual struggle. Moreover, the narrator/officer is as much a part of the tragedy as his men, if not more so, because he is fully cognizant of the ramifications of his internal struggle. Sassoon's abortive protest was made for these men, and back in Limerick he was preparing them once more for the kill.

"Dead Musicians," also written in Limerick, uses the pastoral and romantic sounds of classical music in apposition to modern fox-trot and ragtime tunes to contrast the prewar idyllic world with the strident chaos of wartime. The speaker was raised on the noble, rapturous harmonies of Bach, Mozart, and Beethoven; but the war has obliterated his capacity to appreciate the order and concord inherent in these musicians' works. The most significant "living" memories are now of the war. Amid its cacophonous blasts the polished fugues and glorious symphonies have no place. When the speaker reflects on his past now, he does not hear the dulcet songs of the prewar world, but the slangy speech of the dugouts or barracks so closely akin to fox-trotting musicality:

> "Another little drink won't do us any harm."
> I think of rag-time; a bit of rag-time;
> And see their faces crowding round
> To the sound of the syncopated beat.
> They've got such jolly things to tell,
> Home from hell with a Blighty wound so neat . . .

These lines, reminiscent of Eliot's use of ragtime in *The Waste Land*, conjure up memories of the dead too vividly for the speaker, who demands that the gramophone be turned off in order to disperse the ghosts that haunt his dreams.

Clearly, these two poems indicate that in Limerick Sassoon had not forgotten the realities of the war, nor had he compromised his own beliefs there; nevertheless, he appeared determined to carry on with his duties and get back to the front with his old battalion as quickly as possible. However, on 21 January Sassoon discovered that he was being sent to Egypt; and after failing to achieve a transfer to the western front, he accepted the new assignment with resignation.

His experiences of the journey to and arrival in Palestine are accu-

rately depicted in *Sherston's Progress*. Once on active duty, Sassoon left
the actual writing of poetry behind, as was his habit. In his letters to
Graves, Ottoline Morrell, and Roderick Meiklejohn, he substantiates what
is obvious from the autobiography and his diary: that he was bored. He
was appalled by the mental deadness and lack of intellectual capacity of
his fellow officers ("I haven't caught any of them reading Keats in a tent
yet. Keatings and French letters are probably more in their line" [Sassoon
to Graves, 4 March 1918]). For diversion, he began to read Walter Pater
and was inspired by a new awareness of the beauty in the landscape. He
wrote in a letter that the grandeur of the landscape was gradually pouring
into him "like water into an empty well" (Sassoon to Ottoline Morrell, 2
March 1918). Sassoon also found some interest in bird-watching, and his
vivid natural descriptions of the flora and fauna of Palestine suggest the
beginnings of a mental healing process. However, this serene interlude
came abruptly to an end when rumors of the German offensive of 21
March 1918 reached Palestine. This breakthrough, which Liddell Hart
characterizes as "the breaking of a storm which, in grandeur of scale, of
awe, and of destruction surpassed any other in the World War" (Liddell
Hart 1972, 384), eventually led Sassoon back to the familiar world of the
western front.

By this time, all the poems that were to make up Sassoon's second
collection of poetry had been sent to Heinemann. The volume was judged
remarkable not only for its bloodred and yellow paper cover, but also for
its "quantitatively, greater 'bite' than those of his fellow war-poets and
a sheer brutality of utterance that matches the reality" (Thorpe 1966, 26).
Like the French master of the short story, Guy de Maupassant, Sassoon's
effect depended on a twist of expectation, a situational irony which forced
the reader to feel uncomfortable and responsible for the slaughter on the
western front. By using the raw material of his own experiences and
transforming this "documentary realism into an angry didactic outcry"
(Bergonzi 1980, 102), Sassoon hammered home his lesson with simplicity
and power.

Sassoon's techniques in *Counter-Attack* were varied, but his most
effective method was to open the poems with rich descriptions of natural
beauty akin to the pastoral lyricism of early Georgian poets in order to
lull the reader into a false sense of security:

> They march for safety, and the bird-sung joy
> Of the grass-green thickets

Suddenly the reader is reminded where these men are marching to:

> . . . to a land where all
> Is ruin, and nothing blossoms but the sky
> That hastens over them where they endure
> Sad, smoking, flat horizons, reeking woods,
> And foundered trench-lines volleying doom for doom.
>
> ("Prelude: The Troops")

A further example of this technique is evident in "Attack"; the poem opens with a vivid image of dawn breaking over the battlefield.

> At dawn the ridge emerges massed and dun
> In the wild purple of the glow'ring sun
> Smouldering through spouts of drifting smoke that shroud

What the breaking mist shrouds, though, is not the babbling brook or the warbling nightingale, but rather

> The menacing scarred slope; and, one by one,
> Tanks creep and topple forward to the wire.
> The barrage roars and lifts. Then, clumsily bowed
> With bombs and guns and shovels and battle-gear,
> Men jostle and climb to meet the bristling fire.
> Lines of grey, muttering faces, masked with fear,
> They leave their trenches, going over the top. . . .

This technique has one paramount intention: to awaken the apathetic public to the horrors of war. And whether Sassoon is able to shock by his use of colloquial language ("bloody," "frowst," "blighty") or simply by exploding the myth of nobility in death as in "The Effect" ("When Dick was killed last week he looked like that, / Flapping along the fire-step like a fish, / After the blazing crump had knocked him flat"), the intent is the same.

In the postprotest poems, though, there is a muting of rancor and a stronger feeling of sympathy and solidarity with the men for whom Sassoon's protest was conceived. The poems are a comingling of a number of impulses and include a generalized admiration for the innocence and youthful vigor of the men going to battle (it is often overlooked that Sassoon was thirty-two years old in 1918; most of those

who served under him were under twenty), as well as a very strong
sexual attraction to young men such as Jim Linthwaite (*Diaries 1915–
1918*, 236), who brought Sassoon's affections to a more personal and
intimate level. In this later poetry, there is also a weariness with the war
and an appreciation of the simple pleasures of the past, a desire to find
them still satisfying; but the war has made that return impossible. In
"Repression of War Experience," a poem which Silkin finds a relative
failure (1972, 163–66), primarily because he feels the final lines fail to
convey an adequate sense of hysteria due to the narrator/poet's objective
separation from the soldier in the poem, Sassoon demonstrates how the
"fruits" of the war (the neurasthenic hallucinations, the shortness of
breath, the fear of loud noises) have infected and forever altered the
minds of the participants.

The tragic vision in "Repression" and throughout most of *Counter-
Attack* is that of the annihilation of the soldier—both physically and mentally—as a sacrifice for a people who are too busy with "business as
usual" to empathize with or understand the scope of these soldiers' perils.
Counter-Attack is an attack on complacency and an assault on the flaccid
sensibilities encountered throughout the year, but it is also a paean to his
"brave brown companions . . . [whose] unvanquished hardihood is spent"
("Prelude: The Troops").

9

Picture Show: War, Socialism, and Love

One of the most poignant reflections in *Sherston's Progress* comes during the account of a concert party given at Kantara base camp in Egypt just before Sassoon and his men embarked for France in late April 1918. In the lightly fictionalized account, Sherston reflects on how little the brave soldiers expect out of life, huddled around their makeshift stage. He muses about the inferior quality of the entertainment and how the soldiers respond to the sentimental remembrances of home with an awe and reverence. Then, in very un-Sherstonlike language, George describes the scene as it appears to him from just outside the charmed circle of the rapt audience:

> In the front rows were half-lit ruddy faces and glittering eyes; those behind sloped into dusk and indistinctness, with here and there the glowing spark of a cigarette. And at the back, high above the rest, a few figures were silhouetted against the receding glimmer of the desert. And beyond that was the starry sky. It was as though these civilians were playing to an audience of the dead and the living—men and ghosts who had crowded in like moths to a lamp. One by one they had stolen back, till the crowd seemed limitlessly extended. (*Sherston's Progress,* 605)

Sassoon completes this experience more piquantly in his diary entry, where the stress falls almost entirely on his sympathy for the men who are excluded from the joys of home because they are engaged in making war. The memories of all the dead he has known over the last four years come to haunt him; they, too, have been denied a chance to live and partake in the festivities as characterized by the women in their short silk skirts and by the jangling ragtime piano (*Diaries 1915–1918,* 235). For Sassoon, the war had continued to be a personal affair, but his sympathies had grown beyond his "happy warrior" or protest poses. "Concert Party," one of the earliest poems included in his next volume of verse, *Picture Show,* was Sassoon's attempt to display a growing attachment to and identification with his men.

The poem echoes very closely the fictionalized description. It opens in the early twilight as the men from the base camp drift like moths to a flame toward the sound of a piano tinkling in the night air. (Sassoon also used this moth image with greater symbolic power in "Repression of War Experience.") The soldiers arrive at the show to find "warbling ladies in white" singing songs that take them hypnotically into their past—a past now beyond and barred to the listeners. Songs are sung and enjoyed until the music stops, when the illusion of home and all it evokes fades away like the show itself. Silently, the soldiers disperse back into their own private worlds of despair, fear, and loneliness.

The poem works well in capturing the melancholy of the crepuscular desert as "over the grey-blue sand, / Shoals of low jargoning men drift. . . . / Out of the glimmering lines of their tents, over the shuffling sand." The narrator of the poem fully understands the emotions of the men, and the delicate shift from observer to participant ("They are gathering round" to "We hear them, drink them") clearly delineates a movement toward identification with their feelings. Indeed, Sassoon's admiration for his men was to be a sustaining factor in the weeks ahead. His journal entry of 23 April at Kantara confirms his broadening of outlook and growing sympathetic awareness:

> When I compare my agony of last year with the present, I am glad to find a wider view of things. I am slowly getting outside it all. Getting nearer the secret places of the heart also, and recognizing its piteous limitations. I recognize the futility of war more than ever, and, dimly, I see the human weakness that makes it possible. . . . Sometimes I feel as if this slow and steady growth of comprehension will be too much to bear. But, if I am not mad, I shall one day be great. And if I am killed this year, I shall be free. Selfishness longs for escape, and dreads the burden that is so infinitely harder to carry than three years, two years, one year ago. The simplicity that I see in some of the men is the one candle in my darkness. The one flower in all this arid sunshine. (*Diaries 1915–1918,* 238)

In "Night on the Convoy," Sassoon's sympathy is stirred for the three thousand innocent soldiers sleeping on the hurricane deck while the troop ship relentless carries the "victims" from Alexandria nearer to the western front. For Sassoon, the "lads in sprawling strength" are victims because they unquestioningly respond to whatever is asked of them, bravely and nobly. Paul Fussell, in his discussion of homoerotic impulses in the Great War, draws attention to the use of the word "lad" in much of the poetry. He concludes that it suggested the warmest degree of erotic heat, that the "lads who populate the poems and memoirs of the Great War have about them both the doom of Housman's lad and the pederastic allure of John Gambril Nicholson's" (Fussell 1983, 283). Sassoon's attachment to his men definitely had a homoerotic basis, but unlike earlier attachments to David Thomas and Robert Graves, his love was now broader and more generalized in its application.

Sassoon's letters during this period are filled with references to Georges Duhamel's *Vie des martyrs,* which suggest that he was also trying to find a philosophical perspective by which to justify his participation in the war. Furthermore, he still felt it imperative to believe that the dead and soon-to-die would be sacrificed for some valid purpose. Even Sherston is allowed a taste of Duhamel's philosophy:

> "It is written that you should suffer without purpose and without hope. But I will not let all your suffering be lost in the abyss," wrote Duhamel. That is how I feel too; but all I can do for them is to try and obtain them [his troops] fresh vegetables with my own money, and teach them how to consolidate shell-holes, and tell them that "the soul of defence lies in offense"! (*Memoirs,* 617)

Sassoon's continued anxiety for the safekeeping of his soldiers achieves its finest statement in "The Dug-Out," conceived just before he was wounded in the head in July of 1918:

> Why do you lie with your legs ungainly huddled,
> And one arm bent across your sullen, cold,
> Exhausted face? It hurts my heart to watch you,
> Deep-shadow'd from the candle's guttering gold;
> And you wonder why I shake you by the shoulder;
> Drowsy, you mumble and sigh and turn your head . . .
> YOU ARE TOO YOUNG TO FALL ASLEEP FOR EVER;
> AND WHEN YOU SLEEP YOU REMIND ME OF THE DEAD.

The speaker here enters the dugout and sees one of his fellow officers in a simulacrum of death. The ungainliness and unnaturalness of his bent limbs are reminiscent of the mangled bodies the speaker has seen on battlefields all over the western front. The image becomes so painful in the light of the guttering candle (suggestive perhaps of the briefness of life) that the speaker shakes the soldier, who drowsily turns his sullen face away. The final two lines capture succinctly Sassoon's predicament: in order to justify for himself the slaughter that he has witnessed on the field of battle—and the deaths that are yet to occur—he needs to establish some reason for the war's happening at all; he can attempt to accept what has happened if only there is a clear purpose. Michael Thorpe's analysis offers a further interpretation of the poem with a slightly different focus:

> He [Sassoon] avoids the sentimental treatment the subject invites . . . he focuses attention instead upon the symbolic ugliness of the youth's posture, which is reinforced by the body's alienation from the candle. Sleep is a cruel mockery of death: not just the youth's, or of all those that have died, but of the poet's own that may be imminent. When he shakes the youth by the shoulder, it is the instinctive reaction of one who shares his vulnerable humanity. The poem is not obviously . . . self-regarding: there is a subtle tension between the sense of pity—"You are too young"—and the sense of identification with the youth—"you remind me of the dead." (Thorpe 1966, 34)

The didactic voice of Sassoon has evidently mellowed since his last stint at the front; he no longer rants and shouts for the reader to see the injustice of the likely death of his fellow officer, but instead, in "Night on a Convoy," gives the reader a glimpse of the vulnerability of the soldiers in their innocent attitude of sleep. Sassoon also reminds us here of the same person's susceptibility to a gruesome death. He then leaves the reader to ponder why these mere youths should have to sleep forever. Quite simply, if the war were stopped, the question would be superfluous.

In "I Stood With The Dead," Sassoon extends his sense of identification beyond the living to those who have fallen and are "so forsaken." And while in the second stanza there is a personal lament for a lost lover (perhaps Gordon Harbord), the third stanza lifts the personal loss to a universal lament for all the dead. The ironic last line strongly intimates that the dues of the soldiers now dead were annihilation and painful death, and that on this day, more victims would be paid for their services in the same fashion:

> I stood with the Dead . . . They were dead; they
>   were dead;
> My heart and my head beat a march of dismay:
> And gusts of the wind came dulled by the guns.
> "Fall in!" I shouted; "Fall in for your pay!"

Sassoon's payment on a warm evening in July 1918 was a free ride down to the base hospital at Boulogne and an eventual transfer to the American Red Cross Hospital in London, where he penned a humorous version of the incident for Graves:

> I'd timed my death in action to the minute—
> (The *Nation* with my deathly verses in it)—
> The day told off -13- (the month July)—
> The picture planned—O Threshold of the dark!
> And then, the quivering Songster failed to die
> Because the bloody Bullet missed its mark.

(Sassoon to Graves, 24 July 1918)

From London, the poet was sent to Lennell in Berwickshire to convalesce. There he assumed a "comparatively cheerful and unspeculative frame of mind" (*Siegfried's Journey,* 73), and spent his days riding his bicycle and writing the poetry that would appear the next year in *Picture Show.* During his stay in Scotland (Sassoon was delighted to be in Surtees country), he was able to admit that "army life had persistently interfered with my ruminative and quiet loving mentality. I may even have been aware that most of my satiric verses were to some extent prompted by internal exasperation" (*Siegfried's Journey,* 74). In fact, throughout his convalescent period and until the end of the war, Sassoon moved further and further from actual battlefield concerns.

The effect of distancing himself from the front was wholly positive. During the late summer and autumn of 1918, Sassoon filled his time with visits to famous men: Churchill, T. E. Lawrence, Thomas Hardy, John Masefield, Robert Bridges, and many others who were willing to lionize the now notorious war-poet. In *Siegfried's Journey,* he explains, however, that the first time he felt completely remote and absolved from the war was during a private performance of cello music by Madame Suggia at Lindisfarne (76). In fact, music, with its healing power, was to be one of the key remedies in Sassoon's recovery from the experiences of the war, and it became a theme of several of his important poems of the twenties.

In November 1918, the unexpected ending of the war caught him off guard. Wandering alone through the water-meadows at Garsington, he suddenly heard the peal of bells and noticed Union Jacks being hung decorously outside the windows. He rushed into London to join in the victory celebrations, but closed his diary for 1918 with the words: "It was a wretched wet night, and very mild. It is a loathsome ending to the loathsome tragedy of the last four years" (*Diaries 1915–1918*, 282). Part of the reason for that feeling of loathsomeness is expressed in "Memory," a two-stanza poem which may be conventional in its sentiments, but which describes with sincerity the conundrum that Sassoon faced at the end of the war years.

The opening stanza of "Memory" is a delightful evocation of youth with its freedom from responsibility and addiction to natural beauty. However, the final stanza, where the speaker's heart is "heavy-laden" and his dreams have been burned away by the realization of death, provides a stark contrast to the first. Death has made him "wise and bitter and strong," but these are not characteristics the speaker values; instead, he longs for the stability of his world before it was fractured by the cataclysm of war:

> O starshine on the fields of long-ago,
> Bring me the darkness and the nightingale;
> Dim wealds of vanished summer, peace of home,
> And silence; and the faces of my friends.

It is to Sassoon's credit that even though his emotional self longed to forget the war and escape into some type of artificial environment like the orchidaceous world of Ronald Firbank (*Siegfried's Journey*, 135–37), he opted instead to become involved in the political concerns of the period. The influence of the pacifist discussions at Garsington and his own growing awareness of working-class virtues during the war led him to support Philip Snowden actively in the general election of 1918. This new adherent to the philosophy of the Labour Party even took him to tour the districts of the lesser privileged and he noted in *Journey* his perceptions of Lancashire's industrial mill towns:

In so far as Blackburn, Burnley, and Accrington were concerned, there seemed no prospect of a better world until they had been demolished and rebuilt. I had been spouting about freedom of thought, emancipation from social and industrial injustice, and the need for a clean Peace. But what use was a clean Peace to people whose bodies were condemned to such dirty conditions? How could the plans and promises of the politicians have any meaning for their minds until Social Reconstruction had improved these places? (*Siegfried's Journey*, 114–15)

In the election, Snowden used Sassoon more or less as a showpiece to offset the attraction of his political adversary, a war veteran who had been awarded the Victoria Cross for his part in battle. And Sassoon, much influenced by Snowden's nonvindictive peace proposals and working-class sympathies, reflected his new socialist leanings in several of the poems which appear in *Picture Show*.

"Memorial Tablet" at first glance appears to be a simple antiwar poem describing yet again the waste of life in the Great War. However, a more insightful reading yields significant political implications. The posthumous speaker tells how he was "nagged" and "bullied" by the local squire to join the war "under Lord Darby's scheme." The soldier dutifully obeyed his betters and sank as a result into the "bottomless mud" at Passchendaele. Sassoon's stress on the class distinction in the first two lines cannot be coincidental, for the entire poem turns on the dichotomy between upper and lower social levels.

The second stanza presents the squire in his pew reading the names on the war memorial. The speaker's name is "low down upon the list," but he is there in gilded writing and that is his due. So for two years of insufferable anguish and death, the speaker is rewarded a less-than-prestigious spot on the plaque. The question that concludes the poem— "What greater glory could a man desire?—needs no answer. The purposely ambiguous use of the word "man" here is also telling, for the soldier, who has given his life ostensibly for nothing more than a reservation on the local war memorial, is far more a "man" than the squire, whose single great glory is to urge others into battle for the preservation of England and its social order. The irony of the poems is brutal.

"Everyone Sang" was written just after Sassoon, now full of optimism and idealism about the coming socialist revolution, became literary editor of the *Daily Herald*. The opening stanza reflects a general "expression of relief" and signifies a thankfulness for liberation from the war years which came to the surface with the advent of spring" (*Siegfried's Journey*, 141). It also presents us with a liberating sense of harmony and community that was to expel the gloom from the land:

> Everyone suddenly burst out singing;
> And I was filled with such delight
> As prisoned birds must find in freedom,
> Winging wildly across the white
> Orchards and dark-green fields; on—on—and out of
>   sight

Sassoon explains the conclusion of the poem in *Siegfried's Journey:*

The singing that would "never be done" was the Social Revolution which I believed to be at hand. In what form that Revolution would arrive I cannot now remember foreseeing . . . No doubt I anticipated that there would be some comparatively harmless rioting . . . and everyone being obliged to admit that the opinions of *The Daily Herald* were . . . worthy of their serious consideration. (141–42)

Yet even Sassoon's rather glib interpretation of the coming revolution cannot blunt the hopeful energy of the last stanza of "Everyone Sang." Here, the death knell to exploitation of the lower classes is majestically sounded, and justice is brought to those who have profited from the war—who directed innocent, working-class soldiers to their death with empty promises of a world made better by their efforts. The revolutions would set the record straight.

> Everyone's voice was suddenly lifted;
> And beauty came like the setting sun:
> My heart was shaken with tears; and horror
> Drifted away . . . O, but Everyone
> Was a bird, and the song was wordless; the singing will
>   never be done.

The superficiality of Sassoon's vision of the socialist revolution leads one to the conclusion that his fervor for the new order was not intellectually binding. In fact, Thorpe—along with Sassoon's fox-hunting friends—wonders why one brought up in such a privileged and paradisal world (the world described in *The Weald of Youth* and the early chapters of *Fox-Hunting Man*) should wish to involve himself in a "socialist experiment" with *The Daily Herald* (Thorpe 1966, 155). No evidence exists that the prewar Sassoon or Sherston was aware of the industrial unrest or potential civil war brewing in Ireland; he was, as de Sola Pinto describes him, like "the majority of the Edwardian middle class [who] lived their lives . . . among the cricket and garden societies of 'suburban villadom'" (1951, 116). His knowledge of the appalling social conditions was minimal at best. Even his support of parliamentarian Philip Snowden was based more on pacifist sentiments than on socialist sympathy; and his reactions to the squalor and poverty of towns such as Burnley suggest more a good heart than any real socialist tendencies.

In his own defense, Sassoon suggested to Michael Thorpe in *Letters to a Critic* that he had been aware of the disgraceful living conditions that

East End London hop pickers had to put up with, and that their uncultured behavior made him aware "of what extreme poverty could produce" (Thorpe 1976, 22). He continued rather defensively, "I knew something about the Fabian Movement, as Uncle Hamo's brother-in-law, Sydney Olivier, was active in it. . . . I wasn't so devoid of social conscience as you have assumed" (22). But in spite of such protestations, Sassoon's lack of dedication to the socialist movement can be charted by his inability even to finish Beer's *History of Socialism*. He states in *Siegfried's Journey* that "its unbeguiling pages had only sent my mind rambling in other directions" (118). Furthermore, he followed Rivers's advice to study political economy at Oxford as a "useful preparation for my participation in the Labour Movement" (121) with only a *pro forma* intention. In fact, Sassoon's preparatory studies at Oxford lasted less than two months, and his letters to Graves during this period suggest a less-than-strenuous academic routine. Although he affected the appearance of a Bolshevik by wearing a "dark-green shirt, bright red tie and corduroy trousers" (Sassoon to Graves, 2 March 1919), he spent much of his time in socializing and in playing numerous rounds of golf. Quite clearly, the fascination with socialism and social reform was not deeply ingrained in Sassoon; it was simply a vestige from the Great War—he wished to make life more palatable for his fellow countrymen in the same manner as he had wished to make life for his troops as comfortable as possible. The few poems written on socialist themes as well as the paucity of references to socialist concerns in his letters suggest that this flirtation was to be exceedingly short-lived.

Sassoon's almost frenetic activities after the war all point to an attempt on his part to escape the haunting memories that the war had engendered. *Siegfried's Journey* is crowded with the names of famous people, especially those of writers and musicians, who functioned as interesting diversions for Sassoon but then, except for Thomas Hardy, disappeared from his life. In "Picture Show," he attempts to capture the superficiality of his life just after the armistice.

> And still they come and go: and this is all I know—
> That from the gloom I watch an endless picture-show,
> Where wild or listless faces flicker on their way,
> With glad or grievous hearts I'll never understand
> Because Time spins so fast, and they've no time to stay
> Beyond the moment's gesture of a lifted hand.

> And still, between the shadow and the blinding flame,
> The brave despair of men flings onward, ever the same
> As in those doom-lit years that wait them, and have been . . .
> And life is just the picture dancing on a screen.

The second line suggests that the speaker is aware of the dispirited superficiality of his position. His participation in the war has set him outside the deceptive flicker of life that drifts by him and that fails to engage him in its realities. He can only observe it much in the same way a viewer relates to life portrayed on the cinema screen: he is sympathetic and even empathetic to what is being observed, but is always aware that he is not really part of the action; he cannot engage these flickering shadows as they pass by him, oblivious to his presence. Being prevented from participation in the community of existence allows him no understanding of life's direction. In this condition, all he can observe is an endless stream of images dancing across the retina.

Sassoon's sense of detachment suggests that the war had not been exorcised from his psyche. In fact, the poem "To Leonide Massine in *Cleopatra*" gives a further example of his unsteady condition at this time. As the famous dancer plays her role in *Cleopatra,* the speaker is enthralled but is reminded how similar her death poses are to those of the bodies he observed on the field of battle. The difference is, of course, that the actress will rise again in glory to play the part the following day, but those "who sleep in ruined graves, beyond recall" for what was "phantom glory" will not find resurrection. This stark contrast between mock death in art and the finality of actual death in war overcomes the speaker, and in what Thorpe calls the "hollow rhetoric of the ending" (Thorpe 1966, 40) the poet concludes: "O mortal heart / Be still; you have drained the cup; you have played your part." Sassoon's conclusion reflects his unsatisfactory attempts to throw off the sorrowful memories of the war and somehow move on to new visions and ideas; however, the painful memories obstruct this endeavor and infect even the artist's appreciation of art—and by extension his ability to create art. The artist cannot digest his experience of war as easily as he desires.

The ironic "To A Very Wise Man" examines the difficult question brought up in "To Leonide Massine": how can the artist prevail over the intrusive thoughts of death that constantly invade his creative process? The opening stanza examines a wise man's sources of knowledge; he is said to be have gathered his wisdom from "blind-faced, earth-bound gods

of bronze and stone," but the Old Testament-like prophet's hoarding of
these secrets smacks of elitism and smugness. The second stanza shifts
abruptly to the speaker's perception of what constitutes human anxiety
and fear:

> In a strange house I woke; heard overhead
> Hastily-thudding feet and a muffled scream . . .
> (Is death like that?) . . .

The speaker's intention is to transform these fears (memories of the war
and its neurasthenic aftermath) into something natural and beautiful.

> I quaked uncomforted,
> Striving to frame to-morrow in a dream
> Of woods and sliding pools and cloudless day.
> (You know how bees come into a twilight room
> From dazzling afternoon, then sail away
> Out of the curtained gloom.)

Finally, in the last stanza, we return to the subject of the wise man who
appears to smile indulgently at the speaker's unsuccessful attempt to
shake off his irrational fears. The old sage has the consolation of his
religious beliefs; he is "the flying man, the speck that steers / A careful
course far down the verge of day, / Half-way across the world," while the
poor speaker is limited to his romantic notions of the healing power of
poetry, symbolized by bees flying out of a gloomy room. (This unusual
imagery of swarming bees is also used to great effect in Graves's "The
Pier Glass.") The speaker is willing to accept the wise man's teachings
if he can answer the question "Is death so bad?" but no answer is
forthcoming. The result is a stalemate; the wise man's ancient wisdom is
inapplicable to the uniqueness of the speaker's situation, and the speaker
is left in no better situation than he was in before.

"Butterflies," a pleasant and delicate analogy of Sassoon's situation
as a poet, opens by characterizing butterflies as "Frail Travellers" who flit
amid the charms of natural beauty. The poet reflects on what possible
force could send them "dancing through / This fiery-blossom'd revel of
the hours," but the second stanza explains that the butterflies are the
"musing silences" that fill the summer woods in contrast to the "enrap-
tured crying of shrill birds." The final stanza presents the reader with the
predictable poet-butterfly analogy: the poet's growing sensitivity is

characterized as being as delicate as the butterflies' flight; his poetic vision will lead him to the light from dark obscurity and allow him to observe the world with an unblurred view. The verbal juxtaposition inherent in the "phantom glare of day" of the final line creates at the same time a sense of black and whiteness, which may suggest that only the poet was born to see the world as it really is—without prejudice.

Sassoon touches upon the role of the poet in the postwar world in "The Goldsmith." The brief ten-line lyric tells of a craftsman who sculpts his golden vessels with meticulous labor and painstaking care. At the same time, the goldsmith is fully aware that his masterpiece will go unmerited in a society that has become crass and unappreciative. The craftsman's thoughts are in "a forgotten language, lost and dead"; that is, his innermost values are lost on the current generation. Only the goldsmith himself is aware of the finesse of his work, but when he has finished this task, he automatically begins to create another thankless piece of art: this time a necklace, whose value will also be underestimated. The last two lines, seemingly superfluous, place the action in Knossos, Crete, to give the poem a sense of antiquity as well as to evoke images of the Daedalian labyrinth. There might be a suggestion here that, like the seven youths and seven maidens who each year were placed in a maze and forced to struggle unsuccessfully to find their way out, so modern civilization is lost in a maze of misplaced values. Like the goldsmith, the modern poet-craftsman is fated to see his work undervalued and forgotten.

Perhaps the most important result of Sassoon's poetic musing occurs in the "Prelude to an Unwritten Masterpiece," a self-parody of his own work up to 1919. The first stanza echoes his lyrical poems of before the war, where "bird sung gardens" and "calm landscapes" were his poetic forte. A critical voice, printed in italics to underscore the contrast, passes judgment on the poet's efforts. They are lacking any depth of thought to accompany their melodious, soporific rhythms. In the next stanza, Sassoon pokes fun at his own Georgian poems such as "Haunted," where dark, irrational forces pursue the victim through old gloomy orchards and wild woods until he manages to escape. In the third stanza, however, the speaker continues on his journey:

> That's where it used to stop. Last night I went
> Onward until the trees were dark and huge,
> And I was lost, cut off from all return
> By swamps and birdless jungles. I'd no chance

> Of getting home for tea. I woke with shivers,
> And thought of crocodiles in crawling rivers.

This verse makes light of the sinister war poetry with its heavy psychological overtones to which Graves clung for so long. The play on Sassoon's mentor/analyst's last name in the final line of the stanza certainly clinches the point. The gentle tone of parody carries over into the final stanza, in which the speaker promises in the future to build "a dark tremendous song" from his prophetic visions; but even then he fears he will meet with critical disfavor:

> My beard will be a snow-storm, drifting whiter
> On bowed, prophetic shoulders, yet by year,
> And some will say, "His work has grown so dreary."
> Others, "He used to be a charming writer."
> And you, my friend, will query—
> "Why can't you cut it short, you pompous blighter?"

But beneath the gently ironic characterization of himself as Tennysonian sage, an effect that Sassoon pulls off with humor and self-effacement, there was a question of self-direction. Although the poet chose to turn back to his former style and content with tongue in cheek, his regression betrays a lack of inspiration and of subject matter now that the war was over. In the previous few poems, he appeared to be searching for a subject which could engage him emotionally and intellectually as completely as the war had done; but thus far, his search for poetic purposes had led only to incomplete and insubstantial answers.

One hope for inspiration that surfaced in 1919 was his love affair with Gabriel Atkin. Although the rather stylized and stilted love poetry that celebrates the relationship in *Picture Show* reveals that their love was not to become the overriding event of Sassoon's life, it certainly signifies that this relationship was instrumental in shifting Sassoon's attention, albeit temporarily, away from the war. Sassoon met Gabriel Atkin in Margate in December of 1918; he first mentions Atkin one month later in a letter to Graves on 9 January 1919, which describes the organization of an Oxford debating society: "Gabriel will play the harp on Saint's Days."

Gabriel Atkin was an artist, but not a successful one. Sassoon's *Diaries 1920–1922* reveals him to have been the poet's kept lover in

London. As the progress of the relationship unfolds through the diary entries, it becomes apparent that Sassoon enjoyed dominating the rather delicate Atkin and wanted to transform his undisciplined character into his vision of what a lover should be. But in the early stages of the relationship, the mention of which Sassoon scrupulously avoided in *Siegfried's Journey,* Sassoon showed obvious feelings of tenderness and concern. It may have been one of the first sustained sexual relationships of his life.

Sassoon had been experimenting with love poetry as early as 1918 when, at Limerick, he had produced "Idyll," a poem that Thorpe calls a "wistful piece of imagination or conventional reticence that tells against the individual expression of feeling" (1966, 44). The poem is a throwback to his earlier lyric poems and sonnets of the prewar period; crammed with flowery images and a rather conventional Georgian tone, its greatest weakness is its very outmoded Pre-Raphaelite quality—as if the awakening of a new love can be imagined only in the traditional, stylized manner. The speaker's heart will make him aware of the onset of love "from dreams into the mystery of morn / Where gloom and brightness meet." Once the couple has been brought together by love, it will share "the league spread, quiring symphonies that are / Joy in the world, and peace, and dawn's one star." The verse has little substance; it is cerebral, derivative, and lacking any of Sassoon's ironic realism.

"The Dark House" is a much better poem. Here the scene is conveyed simply, and an engagement of sympathy is felt for the parting lover. The narrator describes the early morning departure of a lover from the house where he has spent most of the night, but as dawn begins to break he has to steal away "in the chilly, star-bright air" while his lover is still awake upstairs. All is quiet as the lover passes through the garden, but he disturbs a thrush who voices the unspoken desires of the lover in bed, "Come back; come back!" Strangely, Thorpe interprets this poem as a poem of betrayal and stealth (1966, 45–46), though the lover in bed is completely cognizant of the other's leaving, and the thrush's message to return presents no reason why we should suspect betrayal. Rather, the poem seems to present precautions necessary to keep a homosexual alliance hidden from an unsympathetic society. The stealthy movements through the night and passing quietly through the back gate to avoid detection are made doubly hard when both souls long to be united.

"Parted" is a companion poem to "The Dark House," and perhaps the "I" of the poem is simply the lover who reclines sleeplessly in bed as his stealthful visitor makes his way back to his dwelling place. The scene is a dreary winter's eve (the time Sassoon first met Gabriel); the speaker's restlessness is evident from the opening stanza:

> Sleepless I listen to the surge and drone
> And drifting roar of the town's undertone;
> Till through quiet falling rain I hear the bells
> Tolling and chiming their brief tune that tells
> Day's midnight end. And from the day that's over
> No flashes of delight I can recover;
> But only dreary winter streets, and faces
> Of people moving in loud clanging places:
> And I in my loneliness, longing for you . . .

In the second stanza, the lover claims that his day-to-day activities are nothing more than "a beating down of suspense / Which holds me from your arms." The word "suspense" carries two denotations: first, the lover is full of uncertainty about when they will be able to meet again; and second, he is suspended from his lover in the legal sense of the word because of the illegality of their relationship. The sexual double entendres continue into the third stanza:

> I am alive
> Only that I may *find you at the end*
> Of these slow-striking hours I toil *to spend,*
> *Putting each one behind me,* knowing but this—
> That all my days are turning toward your kiss;
> That all expectancy awaits the deep
> Consoling passion of your eyes, that keep
> Their radiance *for my coming,* and their peace
> For when I find in *you my love's release.*

> (My emphasis)

Sassoon was trying to express his emotions with straightforwardness that would match the bluntness of his war poetry, but fear of exposure restricted his freedom. The poem is quite clearly an evocative homoerotic fantasy about lovemaking with the departed lover, but its conventional guise would have safely secured Sassoon's reputation in fox-hunting society.

Sassoon's frustration at having to hide the consummation of his "fever" for Gabriel was sublimated into verse which is almost devotional in its lyrics. "Lovers" and "Slumber Song" are asexual, traditional, romantic love songs to the departed lover—a medieval theme that seems to have obsessed Sassoon. In "Slumber Song," Sassoon describes the return to his angelic lover: "The folding of tired wings; and peace will dwell / Throned in your silence." In "Lovers" the cadence of a child's nighttime prayer is heard in the speaker's concern for his lover. No one, especially the rather inebriate and weak-willed Gabriel, could possibly live up to the romantic, idealistic visions that Sassoon had created for his lover. "The Imperfect Lover," perhaps Sassoon's most biographically explicit examination of his affair with Gabriel, suggests that all was not well with their relationship.

"The Imperfect Lover" is a dramatic monologue which recounts the tail end of a lover's quarrel. Thorpe feels that the poem has the directness of Donne's verse (1966, 44), and indeed, he is correct that a sense of skeptical sarcasm can be heard in the lover's tone. But more than of Donne, the poem is reminiscent of Browning's dramatic monologues; the speaker progressively reveals more and more about his relationship with his lover until, by the conclusion, the reader can judge the social and personal dynamics of the affair quite easily.

The speaker is evidently the dominant figure of the pair. He tells his lover that he cannot expect perfection or sainthood from him, but that he has noted an important change in their relationship since the outset, when they had fallen into "wild and secret happiness."

> But I've grown thoughtful now. And you have lost
> Your early-morning freshness of surprise
> At being so utterly mine: you've learned to fear
> The gloomy, stricken places in my soul,
> And the occasional ghosts that haunt my gaze.

Now the mutual attraction has moved to a more mundane and banal phase; the glitter and romantic trappings of the early days have been replaced by the onset of habit and clashes of personality. The final two lines of the stanza suggest that the speaker's war neurosis is partly responsible for the dark moods which cause tensions between them. He goes on to claim that although his lover is still the "haven of his lonely pride," he must be made to realize the seriousness of their homosexual bond and recognize its implications on a social plane.

> Since, if we loved like beasts, the thing is done,
> And I'll not hide it, though our heavens be hell.

The blunt statement of the speaker's position is elaborated in the final two stanzas, where he requests the same frankness from his lover and makes a plea for honesty and straightforwardness between them:

> Then I should know, at least, that truth endured,
> Though love had died of wounds.

By the conclusion of the poem, the speaker has revealed that his expectations of a love affair—even in one as clandestine as theirs—include truth, honesty, and devotion. The romantic and unrealistic musings of his delicate lover must not obscure the essential "hard" values that are vital to a meaningful experience. The reference to "died of wounds" suggests that the speaker would prefer the nobility and trust that are expected on the battlefield to be carried over to his relationship.

In "Vision," the last of the love poems in the *Picture Show* volume, there is the suggestion that beauty is appreciated primarily because of its transient nature. In fact, the poem appears to be a rationalization on Sassoon's part for not being able to keep alive his passion for Gabriel. The Keatsian lament for the fleetingness of the moment is captured in the concluding lines: "A moment's passion, closing on the cry— / O Beauty, born of lovely things that die."

Sassoon's initial hopes for his relationship with Gabriel Atkin and the dwindling away of love through the period between 1919 and 1920 can be followed in various letters to Ottoline Morrell and Roderick Meiklejohn. Strangely enough, little mention of Sassoon's romantic inclinations appears in his letters to Graves, and the later entries in the *Diaries* have been thoroughly edited of more than passing allusions to the love affair. (In fact, there has been as yet no explanation as to why these important transitional journal entries from 1919 to 1920 have not been edited by Hart-Davis.) By mid-1920, Atkin had slipped so much in Sassoon's estimation that during a visit to New York the poet began what was to become a disastrous love affair with Glen Hunter (*Diaries 1920–1922*, 276); indeed, he admits that he was "craving to be stimulated by a new adventure" as early as the second entry of the new year (*Diaries 1920–1922*, 30).

Perhaps the disillusionment with and furtiveness of his homosexual experiences turned Sassoon away from writing more love poetry until he learned to internalize and sublimate these longings into a more sanitized spiritual poetry such as that of *The Heart's Journey*. Also, one cannot discount Thorpe's discreetly made observation that "Sassoon's natural reticence cause[d] him (perhaps unconsciously) to falsify the intensely private emotion by expressing it in conventional terms" (45). The restrictions placed upon him by society because of the nature of his relationships may have led Sassoon to feel that the effort of writing poetry under such constraints was not worthwhile.

Where then, by the end of 1919, was Sassoon to find his inspiration? In "Falling Asleep," he apparently found a temporary answer. Written in late October of 1919 and omitted from the English edition of *Picture Show*, the poem was included with "Limitations" (a poetical musing about writing what one knows and feels) and "Early Chronology" (a realistic poem describing an eminent anthropologist lecturing about his subject at Cambridge) in an American edition of the same book in 1920. The speaker of the poem, musing alone in his bed, listens to the peaceful and familiar sounds around him and feels comforted by them.

> Out in the night there is autumn-smelling gloom
> Crowded with whispering trees; across the park
> A hollow cry of hounds like lonely bells:
> And I know that the clouds are moving across the moon;
> The low, red, rising moon. Now herons call
> And wrangle by their pool; and hooting owls
> Sail from the wood above pale stooks of oats.

The healing and restorative powers of nature, combined with the power of music (in the third stanza), have the potential to distill the poet's odious reminiscences of the war into something more palatable. Together these powers "can make such radiance in my dream / That I can watch the marching of my soldiers, / And count their faces; sunlit faces." The vision of marching soldiers trampling past in the sunlight soon lulls the speaker into a tranquil frame of mind, and images of the pleasant past come floating by:

> . . . the herons, and the hounds. . . .
> September in the darkness; and the world
> I've known; all fading past me into peace.

In "Falling Asleep," Sassoon had found his poetic renewal in the familiar themes he had once nurtured in his lyrical poetry of ten years earlier: nature and music. But these two youthful concerns were to be tested by disillusionment in love, frustration with the socialist experiment, and the problem of finding some subject worth his attention. In fact, the poems of the next five years are a sad testament of his inability to find anything but his prewar past to write about.

10

Satirical Poems:
The Search for Purpose

The next two volumes of poetry that Sassoon produced, *Recreations* (1923) and *Lingual Exercises* (1925), were both printed privately, a fact that not only suggests the poet's desire to retreat from public attention, but also reveals his insecurity about the quality and direction of his verse. Eventually, a large number of the poems from these volumes were incorporated into a single volume published by Heinemann in 1926— *Satirical Poems*—but only after Sassoon had published most of them in various magazines under bizarre pseudonyms such as Elim Urge and Solly Sizzum.

The thirty-two poems in *Satirical Poems* represent the new voice of the urbane, ironic, and controlled poet that Sassoon aspired to become after the war. He was sensitive enough to recognize that in these poems the "cut and dried issues of the War were no more" (Thorpe 1966, 51), but that consequently his poetry lacked any real antipathy toward what he was satirizing. Referring to the subject matter of his *Lingual Exercises,* Sassoon wrote to Ottoline Morrell that he regretted that "the big thoughts still elude[d his] condensing pen, but they [were] there all right—large uncapturable cloud-scapes shot with the glory of human striving" (Sassoon to Ottoline Morrell, 31 January 1925). The "big thoughts" that Sassoon was contemplating in this letter might have been the materialism and growing philistinism of his age; and he was correct in feeling that in his poetry he had somehow missed the essential spirit of the era.

Almost all the poems of *Recreations* and *Lingual Exercises* were written while Sassoon was living in London with the Australian poet and music critic W. J. Turner and his wife. In his small but comfortable room at 54 Tufton Street, he nurtured his private self and sought "to discover and develop such talents as were his, and to understand and express the finer elements of his being" (*Diaries 1920–1922,* 18). The most curious

aspect of Sassoon's writing during this period is the marked contrast
between the private self, revealed in the diary entries, and the public self
that emerges in the two volumes of poetry.

When Sassoon returned from his American tour in August of 1920,
he felt certain that he had reached the conclusion of one part of his life:
"In a moment of clairvoyance he [Sassoon] realized that he had come to
the end of a journey on which he had set out when he enlisted in the
army six years before. And, though he wasn't clearly conscious of it, time
has since proved that there was nothing for him to do but begin all over
again" (*Siegfried's Journey*, 224). One of his first actions on returning to
England was to turn the literary editorship of the *Daily Herald* over to
Turner; he was then able to dedicate himself wholeheartedly to the
cultural life of London. In a letter to Graves, Sassoon describes his
artistic dilemma as follows:

> In a way I seem to have too many friends and I never get a quiet day. But
> it doesn't matter, as I am quite incapable of writing anything, and I don't
> want to in view of the amount which other people are producing. Perhaps
> I'm past the age for getting enthusiastic about producing poetry. The whole
> business bores me at present. And I don't know enough about human beings
> to be able to write plays or stories of their follies. (Sassoon to Graves, 3
> September 1920)

For the remaining months of 1920, Sassoon lived his inconsistent
double life—attending highbrow cultural events and hobnobbing with
literati and philosophers in between visiting his fox-hunting friends in the
country in an attempt to purge himself of the war or of his intellectual
flirtation with socialism. He made a concerted effort to enjoy intellectual
matters and physical activity, but made little attempt to take up his new
poetic stance. His diary entry for 23 January 1921 succinctly, if rather
crudely, sums up Sassoon's poetic condition at the time: "I am costive,
but conscious of internal improvement" (*Diaries 1920–1922*, 35–36).

The first poem of 1921 to be mentioned in Sassoon's diary—
"Phoenix"—later became the "Preface" in his *Satirical Poems*. According
to his diary (*Diaries 1920–1922*, 39), the poem is based on a "loose
paraphrase" of an extract of Sir Thomas Browne's *Pseudodoxia*. It
exhorts individuals to overcome their preconceived notions of the nature
of truth; they must renew their search at the beginning of their experiences and discard all the false stories, prejudices, and preconceptions that
have obscured truth in the past. The investigation of life must constantly

be renewed and life must be examined from differing perspectives until the truth is discerned. Sassoon's placement of this poem at the front of *Satirical Poems* seems rather strange until one considers that by 1926, when the volume was released, he was deeply involved with his own search for truth. The result of this experiment was *The Heart's Journey*.

Writing "Phoenix" seems to have unplugged the poetic springs of Sassoon's system. A few days after its completion, J. C. Squire, the editor of *The Mercury*, who had recently agreed to print four of his poems, chided him about the negative tone of his verse, and as a result of this conversation, Sassoon wrote twenty-four irritable lines of poetry entitled "Things I Have No Objection To." As poetry, it is stiff and disjointed, but the catalog of Sassoon's likes is rather illuminating. As might be expected, the largest number of pleasant things in life are closely allied to nature:

> Almonds and cherry and apple blossomings
> Dazzle me with delight; the wanderings
> Of bees in April sunshine; and the rings
> That pebbles make dropped in a weedless lake
> Can give me satisfaction.

Along with such natural delights as these, Sassoon enjoys his horse, dog, piano, the old poetry books on his shelf, vintage wines, and "nobly-cadenced prose." The catalog is interesting not so much for what it contains, but for what it omits; there is no mention of friendship, love, family, justice, democracy, socialism, or even fox-hunting. The list of Sassoon's likes are all solitary pursuits that he can enjoy without other people, without social concerns. And while Sassoon had always shown signs of meditative, solitary reflection in his poetry, this poem does suggest the reclusive nature of one who prefers the joys of introspection to any type of social intercourse.

One of the poems written for Squire was a reflective attempt to catch the nuances of Sassoon's American experiences. "Storm on Fifth Avenue" opens with the speaker sitting in a New York restaurant watching a summer storm beginning to gather. As the sheet lightning begins to flash and "an oyster-coloured atmospheric rumpus / Beats up to blot the sunken daylight's gildings," the early evening takes on a sinister aspect. Eventually, rain begins to fall on the American metropolis. In the third stanza, the growing force and intensity of the rain is deftly etched:

Out on the pattering side-walk, people hurry
For shelter, while the tempest swoops to scurry
Across the Brooklyn. Bellying figures clutch
At wide-brimmed hats and bend to meet the weather,
Alarmed for fresh-worn silks and flurried feather.
Then hissing deluge splashes down to beat
The darkly glistening flatness of the street.
Only the cars nose on through rain-lashed twilight:
Only the Sherman Statue, angel-guided,
Maintains its mock-heroic martial gesture.

In stark contrast to the raging elements, the concluding stanza focuses on the speaker continuing his meal in the comfort of the restaurant. After this course will follow an ice cream dessert—and the speaker is content. This materialistic contentment amid the raging of the storm is given further emphasis by the use of apostrophe in the final line: "O Babylon! O Carthage! O New York!" The inclusion of New York with the once great but now destroyed cities of the past suggests that the sybaritic behavior of its citizens bodes ill for its survival. But Sassoon's speaker is not unrelated to Sassoon himself at the time, and he might well have added "O London!" to the final line.

Sassoon, too, had been indulging himself with the fruits of luxury while the great causes were passing him by. He lamented to Lady Ottoline that politics were "too depressing to be mentioned" (Sassoon to Morrell, 2 January 1921). He planned to escape to Venice with Gabriel Atkin in the early spring, but the trip was interrupted by the miners' strike of 1921.

In his diary entries of April 1921, Sassoon wrote with great fervor in support of the miners' strike that was raging at the time. He saw the miners' cause as representative of the struggle for existence of organized labor, but he was uncertain as to what he could do to advance this cause. The supposed injustice to the miners had awakened in him "those inward stirrings of unappeased nobility and self-sacrifice on which [he] nourished [his] self-conceit during the war. The old gesture-craving is still alive, and refreshed after its thirty-two-months' sleep" (*Diaries 1920–1922*, 57). In an effort to do his part for his disadvantaged fellows, Sassoon arranged with the editor of *Nation*, H. W. Massingham, to travel to South Wales and send back dispatches on the strike for the magazine. However much the interviewing and scouting around for a story worthy of his ideals sapped his energy, Sassoon was still stimulated by the prospect of performing a valuable human service, and he wrote on 16 April after hearing that the strike had been called off: "A week since I left London; very much alive the last seven days!" (*Diaries 1920–1922*, 60). But before long, the realization began to haunt him that he was merely a superfluous participant in the event; just two days after writing in his diary how exhilarated he felt by his journalistic experience, he wrote:

> I'd been persuading myself that I was busy, and doing something useful. Now a feeling of futility attacks me, and I draw back from gestures of intellectual sympathy for the miners, like a speaker advancing toward his audience primed with glowing phrases, and then retiring in confused realisation of his own inadequacy for the occasion. (*Diaries 1920–1922*, 61)

A few days later, back in London at a matinee performance by Isadora Duncan, Sassoon admitted that he "scarcely troubled to look at the papers to see how the Coal situation goes on" (*Diaries 1920–1922*, 62).

There was something of the ambulance-chaser mentality in Sassoon. He seemed to crave excitement for its own sake, and the basic human issues underlying the event were not as important to him as the thrill they generated. This rather superficial approach to events is reflected in his poem, "The Case for the Miners." The first stanza opens with an opulent dinner party, where the speaker's fellow diners are "peeling their plover eggs or lifting glasses / Of mellowed Chateau Rentier," and where the atmosphere is redolent of bourgeois attitudes and self-interest. The superficiality of the argument against granting the miners a living wage is manifested in the words of one of the diners just after he has downed his plover's egg with a glass of Chateau Rentier:

> "Why should a miner earn six pounds a week?
> Leisure! They'd only spend it in a bar!
> Standard of life! You'll never teach them Greek,
> Or make them more contented than they are!"

In the clipped speech of the privileged speaker, the poet gives us a forceful but opinionated explanation of working-class mentality and motivations. The finality and certainty of these superficial observations—emphasized with the exclamation point—expose the inanity of the argument and give the reader a clear insight into the speaker's psychology.

The poet admits in the second stanza, though, that he is unable to penetrate the complacency and prejudiced attitudes of his fellow diners; in fact, he finds it difficult to state the miners' case succinctly:

> Indistinctly
> I mumble about World-Emancipation,
> Standards of Living, Nationalization
> Of industry; until they get me tangled
> In superficial details; goad me on
> To unconvincing vagueness.

The final stanza is a childish surrender to petulance when one fails to get one's way. The speaker excuses his own inability to put forth a cogent argument for the miners' strike (which should not have been too difficult for the former literary editor of the *Daily Herald*) and says his listeners have entrenched themselves behind stereotyped rationales for keeping the working man down. However, his immature response in wishing them in the miners' place as punishment for not sympathizing politically is neither effective satire nor convincing argument. Other small considerations weaken the tenor of the poem. What is the speaker doing at such a party at such a time? And if the speaker is committed to the miners' cause, why is he so ill-prepared for the inevitable argument? The answers may be that, like the poet himself, the speaker sees the strike as an opportunity to engage the "enemy" afresh, but by this time the ideals of social equality and justice had become tarnished, and only token gestures remained.

For Sassoon, then, the springboards for poetic inspiration were gradually becoming fewer. Unlike Graves, who at this time was undertaking an eclectic study of psychology while working on his degree at Oxford, Sassoon chose to remain intellectually inactive throughout this period. His diary entries and letters for most of 1921 record that his concerns were escaping to the countryside with Gabriel or to Italy with the Canadian poet "Toronto" Prewett, or attending various musical performances. Only occasionally does Sassoon reveal the direction of his artistic impulse; one particular diary entry for 30 June is extremely indicative of his state of mind.

> I've given up thinking about the War. I am clear of it all, steadily settling down into a new state of mind, craving only for development in the tech-

nique of expression in verse and prose; trying to analyse love; learning more and more to appreciate and understand music. (*Diaries 1920–1922,* 73)

A few days later, after writing eight poems at Garsington, Sassoon noted, "My work lately convinces me that I've nothing to say" (*Diaries 1920–1922,* 74). Perhaps the problem was not that Sassoon did not have anything to say, but rather that he lacked the courage and impartiality to write what was most on his mind at the time: "another *Madame Bovary* dealing with sexual inversion" (*Diaries 1920–1922,* 53).

In the summer of 1921, Sassoon did begin writing a romantic short story centered on his fascination with a fellow soldier, Jim Linthwaite, whom he characterized as "the wild rose of my heart" (*Diaries 1920– 1922,* 68). The story ended as ashes in the fireplace, but the fever of Sassoon's repressed homosexuality became the main theme of his diary throughout this period. And more than any other single factor, this self-torment, along with the necessity of keeping his "secret life" from his mother and fox-hunting friends, kept Sassoon from producing any memorable poetry in 1921. In October, Sassoon decided to visit Rome with his poet-friend "Toronto" Prewett. The results of the visit were a definite release from sexual frustration and an awakening of creative energy. Initially, the journal entries capture very succinctly the nature of Sassoon's depression on his arrival in Rome:

> Rome doesn't disappoint me. It is myself that fails. Why am I so dreary and unreceptive, incapable of imaginative enthusiasm and romantic youthfulness? . . . Is it my own fault that I am under this cursed obsession of sex-cravings? . . .

> Keats came here with death at his elbow. I come here dull-witted and disillusioned, craving for love, craving for imaginative eloquence. Spiritual sickness overshadows me. My mind is somehow diseased and distorted. I live in myself—seek freedom in myself—self-poisoned, self-imprisoned. I write this in a Rome that cannot awake me. (*Diaries 1920–1922,* 86)

Sassoon's irritability continued throughout his first week in Rome. He found that St. Peter's reminded him of a "worldly-minded prelate," and the continuously appearing religious processions winding through the city offended his Anglican sensibility (*Diaries 1920–1922,* 87). Surprisingly, the diary breaks off after just three days of entries, but the important events that occurred can be ascertained from letters and later journal entries. Not long after the 2 October entry, Prewett entered a nursing home suffering from a gastric ulcer. While he was recovering, Sassoon met the man who was to shake him out of the sexual doldrums and whose companionship would fill the pages of the 1922 diary. The man, ironically a German, is referred to only as P.

A letter to Ottoline Morrell on 11 October reveals that Sassoon's attitude toward life in Rome had altered significantly. Not only was he frequently the opera nightly, but he now described Rome as the "dearest city ever known." He wrote to Graves in a similar vein, but added that he had written a line of poetry that impressed him particularly; that line, "Fountains like the ghosts of cypresses" was to become a key phrase in his poem "Villa d'Este Gardens" (Sassoon to Graves, 17 October 1921).

"Villa d'Este Gardens," according to Sassoon, was an inspired, passionate memory of his affair with P. (*Diaries 1920–1922,* 97); but the intellectual impulse inherent in its construction was the problem of how to express the memory of such delightful impressions. Should the poet attempt to recreate the romantic Italy of Shelley and Browning and place himself firmly in the past tradition, or should he "psycho-analyze the present and himself in particular against . . . [the] beautiful elegaic [*sic*] background?" (*Diaries 1920–1922,* 97–98). The writing of the poem forced Sassoon to question the various modern approaches to poetry in order to find a solution. His final choice of Landor-flavored prose and light Byronic satire, with a dash of Browningesque description, became the general poetic direction that he followed for the next four years. He repeated the formula throughout the pages of *Satirical Poems,* changing only the object of the satire as he spotted new targets; and targets for satire did not prove difficult to find in the twenties.

Edmund Blunden singles out "Villa" for special praise in his study of Sassoon's poetry. What Blunden says figuratively pertains to the method Sassoon would adopt for most of his poetry during this period:

> While he walks in his quietly expectant and cheerfully inquiring easiness about the nooks and corners of civilization, Mr. Sassoon receives very vividly the impression of event, character, environment, and changefulness. He perceives atmosphere revealing itself in images, in living personations of the past, the present, and time to come. He often tells us his story with a beguiling ambiguity, an inimitable private gesture which explains that he is only guessing, and is happy in his pastime. He whistles while he sets up his colonnades and invents his masks of history. (Blunden 1950, 317–18)

Blunden's criticism is as ambiguous as the poem itself, but "Villa" would seem primarily to be a satire on the modern poet struggling to find the "proper" response to the "intramural twilight" of the historic gardens.

> "Of course you saw the Villa d'Este Gardens,"
> Writes one of my Italianistic friends.
> Of course; of course; I saw them in October,
> Spired with pinaccous ornamental gloom
> Of that arboreal elegy the cypress.
> . . . .
> While roaming in the Villa d'Este Gardens
> I felt like that . . . and fumbled for my notebook.

Sassoon deftly deflates his own poetic pretensions and perhaps those of his contemporaries. More importantly, with the writing of this poem he had found both release from a dispiriting poetic dry spell and an affirmation of his poetic calling as a satirist.

Sassoon's satiric poems attempt to batter the shallowness and complacency that he observed around him throughout the twenties. Generally, his satire is bent on exposing the superficial values which the newly made entrepreneurial class had foisted on postwar society and the failure of the leisured class to appreciate the cultural and intellectual wasteland left by the erosion of prewar standards. Sassoon felt that popular admiration of art forms such as classical music and painting was filled with hypocrisy, false learning, and cant; but surprisingly, he had even less time for the aesthetic vision represented by Harold Acton and Brian Howard who, according to Martin Green's analysis in *Children of the Sun*, valued art and the artificial over life. Sassoon attacked the nouveau riche for their selfishness and callousness; he claimed they earned their money at the expense of good taste and standards. Consistently throughout the *Satirical Poems*, the reader can detect the poet's growing sympathy with the past amid his general deflation at the standards of the present. A poem like "A Post-Elizabethan Tragedy" satirizes not only the imbecility of critics who impose a Freudian interpretation on late Elizabethan drama, but also the pomposity of the modern audience. Sassoon exhibits a preference for the simplicity of Ford's archaic vision of sibling love between brother and sister over a modern analysis of "expiated incest."

Through both the second and third volumes of his diaries, Sassoon clearly displays an indefatigable appreciation of classical music. The number of concerts he attended both in and outside London points to his compulsion for musical performances. He was even able to utilize his love of music as subject matter in the five satiric poems that he wrote during this period.

In "Evensong in Westminster Abbey," a common man casually saunters into the overpowering abbey in order to cast off "gross thoughts and sabbatize the intemperate husk." Once inside, all hope of achieving spiritual communion is impeded by an awareness of England's "illustrious Dead" who surround him. As the choir sings and the organ booms, all things seem commensurate with the gravity and wonder of the moment: "Spirits aspire on solemn-tongued antiphony, / And from their urns immortal garlands bloom." But in the penultimate stanza, the mood is suddenly transformed when "a clergyman ascends / The pulpit steps" in order to deliver his sermon. First he "smoothes with one hand his hair, / And with the other hands begins to fumble / At manuscript of sermon." The intrusion and emptiness of the sermon exorcise the great ghosts that hover about the abbey: his "diction has turned their monuments to stone; / Dogma has sent Antiquity to sleep." The contrast between the current spiritual vacuity and shallowness of Anglican dogma and its glorious antecedents is clear. But all is not lost: "Out on the organ's fugue-triumphal tone / When hosannatic Handel liberates us at last," the blast of eighteenth-century music with its spiritual upliftedness is what saves the service from being an empty ceremony; music itself becomes a redemptive force.

The satirical "Afterthoughts on the Opening of the British Empire Exhibition" also marks a contrast, in this case between the solemnity and grandeur of the proceedings and the mundane purpose behind the production. The speaker has just returned from the opening of Wembley Stadium—"one face in a stabilized flock"—and reflects on the meaning of all the pomp and circumstance attendant upon the ceremony; his attitude, as he recounts the images of the day's happenings, is one of bemusement. Sassoon cleverly exposes the combination of mass hysteria and blind folly by his overuse of assonance and alliteration: "Ebullitions of Empire exulted" and "Patriotic paradings with pygmy preciseness" followed by "The band bashed out bandmaster music" cannot help but raise a smile and deflate the inspired moment into a bathetic anticlimax. Sassoon also finds opportunity in the poem to take a swipe at the newspaper writers and at the monarchy; the press is busy "collecting its clichés," and the king's speech is described as "hollow" because "he was there to be grave and august and say the right thing." The commercial origin of this masquerade is revealed only when Sassoon introduces his prelate making obeisances "with prayer / To the God of Commercial Resources and Arts"; the purpose of this inauguration is simply to encourage domestic markets for the export trade. (Robert Graves, in *The Long Week-End,* also exposes the commercial crassness of the exhibition [177].)

Predictably, all the associations of capitalism and trade are forgotten in the final stanza when the massed choir conducted by Elgar sings Blake's "New Jerusalem." The music inspires "something inward" and raises the audience's consciousness to an awareness of spiritual freedom and equality instead of contemplation of the crass materialism on display at the exhibition. The power of the music and its ensuing rapture are what make the dreams of building a new Jerusalem "in England's green and pleasant land" a possibility.

In his "Hommage à Mendelssohn," Sassoon defends the composer's Prelude in A-Flat against the accusation of sentimentality by modern music critics who find the "universal yearnings" voiced in his music as psychologically untenable. In the composer's defense, Sassoon praises the elegance of Mendelssohn's style and the capacity of his music to whisk the listener back to an age where heartfelt sentiment was not scorned. Such an age provides a sharp contrast with the hardened, frank, and analytic modern age.

Sassoon's attack on the intellectual pretensions of contemporary philosophy is also evident in "Concert Interpretation," a poem that Thorpe claims to be the most "sustained piece of ridicule" in *Satirical Poems*—"a broadside against modish intellectualism" (1966, 50). Sassoon's barbs here are leveled particularly at the "sophisticated" music audiences who have blindly accepted the dictates of music critics as to what is acceptable with regard to musical taste. In particular, he attacks those audiences who rejected Stravinsky's harrowing dissonances in *Le Sacre du Printemps* "with hisses—hoots—guffaws—" because he "jumped their Wagner palisade / With modes that seemed cacophonous and queer." But now that Stravinsky's works have been accepted by the critical establishment, the very same music is praised with imitative acclaim by the patrons. The poem, however, is more than just an attack on the blind following of musical fashion, for Sassoon realizes that the listeners are unmoved by the dissonance and savagery behind the notes; they have mindlessly and emotionally "adjusted their tastes to this gallantry of goats [and] they have surrendered what little life they possessed" (Thorpe 1966, 50).

The poet's metrical virtuosity in "Concert-Interpretation" also gives adroit emphasis to this attack on the modern intellectuals' indiscriminate following of fashion. Here, the deep musicality of the bassoons is echoed by the *o* and *a* vowels used in the third stanza:

> Bassoons begin . . . Sonority envelops
> Our auditory innocence; and brings
> To me, I must admit, some drift of things
> Omnific, seminal, and adolescent.

Like the concert itself, where the rich, melodic tones of the bassoon eventually give way to discord, the ensuing lines stand in marked contrast to the earlier lines. The rasping hardness of the *c* and *d* vying with the plosive *p* imitate the cacophony in Stravinsky's symphony:

> Polyphony through dissonance develops
> A serpent-conscious Eden, crude but pleasant;
> While vibro-atmospheric copulations
> With mezzo-forte mysteries of noise
> Prelude Stravinsky's statement of the joys
> That unify the monkeydom of nations.

Finally, in the amusing "Sheldonian Soliloquy," which E. M. Forster pertly characterized as both "gluey" and "on the adagio side of andante" (*Diaries 1923–1925*, 70), Sassoon once again deflates the motley "intellectual bee-hive" that in this case has filled the "overheated" Sheldonian to hear Bach's Mass in B Minor. The purport of the satire is carried largely through situational irony; the audience concentrates on the choir's rendition of the "Gloria," which labors to be heard beside the cacophonous roaring of a motorcycle outside the theater. In the college gardens, the birds rhapsodize with their own form of chirped thanksgiving while inside the sweltering Sheldonian, the self-important academics sit "perched" (a witty connection with the birds) and perspiring in their uncomfortable places. But somehow the noble strains of Bach transcend the ludicrousness of the situation and touch something completely beyond the intellectual pretensions of the listeners in the neoclassical surroundings:

> Hosanna in excelsis chants the choir
> In pious contrapuntal jubilee.
> Hosanna shrill the birds in sunset fire.
> And Benedictus sings my heart to Me.

The music has touched the poet's heart; it has lent this thanksgiving a true sense of blessedness that was initially lacking in the stultifying atmosphere, and transformed the entire service.

For Sassoon, classical music became a symbol of something pure and uncorrupted created by the pioneers of the modern age. He used music as a weapon to expose the shallowness of the new cultural values, the sham intellectual pretensions of the middle class, the ineffectual inaccuracies of psychological probings into the secrets of the heart, and the hopeless situation of those people who blindly followed fashion instead of instinct in life. Moreover, the five "musical" poems suggest that Sassoon used music as an anodyne for the encroaching philistinism that he felt pervaded all aspects of English life; music became an escape to a period, such as the early Victorian period in "Hommage à Mendelssohn," where he imagined harmony and balance were more likely to be found. This longing for a quieter, more serene vision of life was eventually to lead to a sympathy with the bucolic and spiritual poetic world of Vaughan and Crashaw.

For Sassoon, like T. S. Eliot, the crassness of the twentieth century was closely aligned with middle-class values based primarily on the efficiency of the machine. Perhaps his brief flirtation with socialism made him sensitive to the affectations and misapplications of power and wealth by this rising class, but he offered no solutions to these problems in his poems. The transcendence of music may have acted as a temporary escape from the hypocrisy and vulgarity of the modern age, but the poet was forced to return to Tufton Street after every concert and face the eroding of his old landmarks and values.

"Monody on the Demolition of Devonshire House" bemoans the obliteration of one of England's treasured houses in order to erect yet another monument to Mammon. The speaker laments the destruction of the stately ducal estate, where once Lord Byron "rang the bell and limped upstairs," in order that the life-style of those who "must loll and glide in yacht and limousine" could be maintained. The poem intimates that this new order of monied people (made out of war profits, no doubt) could demolish a mansion with as "complete / Efficiency of its mammoniac air—" as any heavy artillery during the war. The destruction is complete:

> And not one nook survived to screen a mouse
> In what was Devonshire (God rest it) House.

"The Grand Hotel" was written while Sassoon was staying at Villa d'Este near Lake Como with Frank Schuster, the wealthy music connoisseur, in March of 1924. It is in part an attempt to clear his own mind of the pampered and idle life-style he had been leading. The poem is not so much a satire as a description of the shoddy externals one observes at a deluxe hotel. Ironically, the hotel itself has been superimposed upon a vanished villa and offers to resurrect for its patrons "an austere degree of social status." The hotel houses both the gentry and the businessmen ("noodles and crooks"); all it requires of its patrons is that they pay for its services in cash. The final stanza describes the boredom and superficiality rampant in this costly paradise. The desire and effort to obtain this glitter and wealth have effectively killed anything fresh or spontaneous in the character of its inhabitants; material goods are all the patrons have as proof of their existence. As the speaker concludes after silent observation: "Well, my impression / Is that these folk are poisoned by possession."

The spiritual malaise manifest in Sassoon's journals and the poetry of the period (see especially the journey to France and Italy from 7 March to 7 April 1924) is particularly evident in "Breach of Decorum," which Felicitas Corrigan convincingly claims is based on an incident at the home of Lady Cunard (Corrigan 1973, 106), perhaps during Sassoon's visit on 13 June 1924. (The diary entry for this date has apparently been torn out after the words "Lady Cunard" appear.) The poem is a satire on the frivolity of the rich when they are confronted with a person with a serious moral vision of life. The aptly named hostess, Lady Lucre, has invited a guest to luncheon who unsuccessfully attempts to engage her in earnest conversation about art and spiritual philosophy. Lady Lucre is surprised by such learned discussion and cannot find anything in reply to his remarks: "And while his intellectual gloom encroached / Upon the scintillance of champagne chatter, / In impotent embarrassment she broached / Gold, Goodwood Races, and the Cowes Regatta." Shocked by such "insensitive" treatment at the hands of a social pariah, the nonplussed Lady Lucre can only damn him as a blasphemer with socialist tendencies. Her inability to grasp or even dimly perceive the nature of his arguments demonstrates an inability to see beyond her own closed and insular social world of luncheons and nightclubs.

The same kind of criticism appears in "On Reading the War Diary of a Defunct Ambassador," a biting satire on the self-importance of the privileged class during the Great War. On reading the war diary, the speaker is astounded at the contrast between the leisurely life at the embassy "among the guns," and the actual "guns" that confronted the fighting man. This distinction is made clear in the effective alliteration of the final stanza:

> I can imagine you among the guns,
> Urbanely peppering partridge, grouse, or pheasant—
> Guest of those infinitely privileged ones
> Whose lives are padded, petrified, and pleasant.

Sassoon's attitude toward the privileged class had been well stated in his war poems, but "War Diary" is further indictment of the visionlessness and officialized fatuity that the establishment perpetrated on the soldier.

"On Some Portraits by Sargent" is a poignant satire on the social affectations of the wealthy and their uncanny physical similarities to one another when they appear on the canvas of a portrait painter. Sassoon's target here is not only the public's lack of discriminating powers; it is also the painter himself, whose boredom with his subjects has suffocated all artistic inspiration, but who pursues a wealthy clientele in order to make money. The suggestion in this poem, then, is that money and power in themselves create a sense of ennui which infects all who come into contact with them, including the artist.

Finally, in "Lines Written in Anticipation of a London Paper Attaining a Guaranteed Circulation of Ten Million Daily," Sassoon satirizes Lord Rothermere's subscription drive to raise the *Daily Mail*'s circulation. With Byronic lightness, the speaker traces the noble press lord's lineage back to the Pleistocene Age, when his ancestors "began the upward biological struggle." Stymied by the existence of only oral communication until the Bible "woke things up," the press lord had to pass up writing banner headlines such as "'The Fall. Exclusive Story from Eve's Lips.' / Then 'Public Barred from Eden.' 'Cain Sheds Blood.'" Sassoon's narrator mockingly celebrates the paper's methods for capturing public attention until his voice seems almost strident when he "congratulates" the paper for making a penny out of every piece of news that comes to light. In the last four lines, however, the speaker cannot withhold his rancor for what he really sees as a debasing enterprise. Reluctant to rely on the force of his satire to make this point, Sassoon unnecessarily intrudes into the poem; and his intrusion significantly detracts from an otherwise witty and tightly constructed poem. The interference also suggests that perhaps satire was losing its flavor for Sassoon by the time this poem appeared in September 1925.

The last five poems of *Satirical Poems* to be examined here largely failed as effective vehicles for satire, because in the writing of these verses, Sassoon placed more emphasis on his philosophic notions about life than on the social follies he was attacking. He was often so carried away by his new reflections that the purport of the satire would dissolve and suddenly reappear clinging clumsily to the conclusion of the poem. "The London Museum" and "In the Turner Rooms" are two examples of this tendency.

"The London Museum" sets out to question the role of the monarchy and its attendant institutions in the modern world, but becomes sidetracked and dwells on the question of the value of firsthand experience in life over that of scholarly contemplation. With the seemingly detailed knowledge of a museum curator, the speaker of the poem roams through an exhibition with studied indifference, dismissing the various artifacts and curios displayed:

> This museum is a mortuary for departed passions:
> And I'd barter all the brocaded farthingales in
>   Conservation
> For a single scolding word from great Eliza's lips.

The message, which is reiterated at every display case, is that the dusty displays are unable to retain the vitality of the event, because their creators have turned their back on the present. This failure to perceive the present and conceive "the flowing vistas of the Future" dooms these "antiquarians" to an existence as shallow as their dust-covered displays. The rhetorical question set up in the final line of the last stanza becomes unpurposely ambiguous because the poem has lost its way:

> It is four o'clock; and the London Museum is closing.
> Outside, in the courtyard, a group of patriots lingers
> To watch the young Heir to the Throne step into his
>   hushed Rolls-Royce.
> And I wonder, are they wiser than the Antiquarians?

The anticipated answer is "No!" The reader is expected to see the correlation between the outdatedness of the modern monarchy (all the exhibits described in the poem are of rulers) and its dead relics gathering dust. The "patriots" (the word carries a negative connotation for the ex-war poet) are just as blind as the antiquarians. But the spirit of the poem belies the thrust of the satire, for the poem stresses the importance of using the senses to experience events. The patriots lingering near the steps of the London Museum may be watching a representative of an antiquated class stepping out of an antiquarian institution into a nearly antiquated automobile, but they are wiser than the museum employees because they are alive and looking to the future. They have gathered to witness an event that has significance and meaning for them.

This same theme is reiterated with greater force and clarity in "In the Turner Rooms," a powerful poem that functions better to affirm life's urges than to satirize the romantic poet trying to find inspiration in the Tate Gallery. The artist-speaker sits in the Turner room of the Tate with pencil in hand, waiting for the surroundings to inspire him "to fabricate iambics," but the powerful effect of Turner's brush strokes paralyzes the budding poet; words fail him. He is rudely brought back to reality by having his toes trodden upon by a fellow enthusiast, and once again contemplates Turner to try to discover some inspiration from the canvas. Suddenly his attention is diverted:

> . . . Now my heart
> Leaps toward Romance and knows it, standing there
> In that calm student with the red-brown hair,
> Copying the "Death of Chatterton" with care
> And missing all the magic. That young head
> Is life, the unending challenge . . . Turner's dead.

Here, then, resides the home of poetic inspiration: not in the gloomy overheated rooms of the Tate, but in the contemplation of the vital and the animate. Unlike Chatterton who, Sassoon felt, died before his potential as a human being had even been tested (*Diaries 1923–1925*, 81–82), Sassoon wanted to experience poetic rapture from the wellsprings of the human heart.

These two poems reveal a desire to break away from the clogged and artificial world that Sassoon inhabited. Throughout his diaries, he makes constant references to the artistic pretensions of his friends; he feared that like Lord Berners or Frank Schuster his sensitivity would also become fossilized by aesthetic contemplation of art. Sassoon was longing for some kind of affirmation in life that would engage his need for self-fulfillment and lend him outward excitement; but the problems inherent in his homosexuality and retiring nature propelled him more and more into contemplation of the past, not only back to the war, but further back

into his Edwardian youth and Victorian childhood. The extended diary
entry for 15 September 1924 is indicative of this reflectiveness.

Through the journals, Sassoon refers to his habit of making "Enoch
Arden" visits or feeling "Enoch Ardenish"; this love of secluded places,
especially places that had particular meaning for him through literature
or living, was what set him on the road to Edingthorpe in Norfolk.
Sassoon ventured there to recapture the memory of his eight-week
summer holiday of 1897, when his family lived at the local rectory. The
voyage into the past is recounted with loving detail in his journal, and the
following entry demonstrates the pleasure that the poet felt in being able
to confirm his recollections:

> I could remember that the Rectory stood among some trees; and that the
> church was about a quarter of a mile away from it, on some rising ground.
> I remembered a nut-orchard in the Rectory garden, and the parson's blue
> sermon-paper in a cupboard, which I used for my childish scrawlings. . . .
> But the landscape was strangely unrecoverable in the light of memory; sad
> and remote, it looked now, in the grey end of an autumn afternoon, but the
> place had a rustic charm, like a poem by John Clare or a woodcut by Birket
> Foster. (*Diaries 1923–25,* 201)

A visit to Edingthorpe Church proved to be a further pleasant voyage of
discovery. Admitting that he had forgotten the thatched roof, Sassoon
paused reflectively in front of the lych-gate which was recently erected
in memory of a local lance-corporal who had died during the war.
Stepping, almost symbolically, through the barrier of unpleasant
memories, he passed into the church and heard echoes from the sermon
of twenty-seven years before. The entire walk back through the churchyard and fields opened the floodgates of reminiscence, and Sassoon found
himself in the past: "Mistily I memorised an elongated old shandrydan of
a vehicle with an elderly horse, in which we used to drive to North
Walsham" (*Diaries 1923–1925,* 202). The contemplation of this particular
incident gave him such pleasure that he would turn to it again in 1937
when he was seeking "mental release from Hitler and Mussolini" (Thorpe
1976, 20) in chapter 8 of *The Old Century.*

"Fantasia on a Wittelsbach Atmosphere" is one of Sassoon's earliest
poems to suggest a sympathy with the evanescent prewar way of life.
Like "The London Museum" and "In the Turner Rooms," however, the
poem was not intended as such; it was written, instead, while the love-
smitten Sassoon was in Munich waiting for his overdue reunion with P.

The poem is a recounting of his excursion into the stately Residenz Palace of the dukes of Wittelsbach. The intention here is to mock the opulence of the palace and the character of the ducal family who lived in such surroundings. Initially, the speaker in the poem strolls through the palace feeling appalled by the affluence of the place, but gradually his "spirit shares with monarchismal Tories / The fairy-tale of Flunkeydom, displayed / In feudal relicry of centuries styles." This spiritual sympathy grows stronger, and eventually the speaker is touched and enticed "by super-lavish / Expense; half-cultured coxcomb Kings commanding / In palacefuls the trappings of Autocracy, / With all their country's coffers ripe to ravish." Despite the militant socialist jargon and clichés used here, the concluding stanza deflates the satiric intent of the poem. Once outside the palace and melancholically gazing at the empty shell that once housed gaiety and vitality, the voice of nature speaks in defense of the exiled dukes: "Take them for what they were, they weren't so bad." This obvious empathy with the aristocratic values prompted Edmund Blunden to gloss over this seeming political volte-face and conclude that in the poem Sassoon "is anxious to make all allowances, and look the other way at least [on] the first occasion" (1950, 317). But Blunden is understating things here; in this poem, Sassoon shows a definite preference for the opulent. He has lost much faith in the socialist direction, and his Prufrockian line "Dare one deplore the dullness of Democracy?" is not entirely rhetorical.

At work here are forces that are not dissimilar to those which led Eliot to write *The Waste Land*. Both Sassoon and Eliot were much concerned with the loss of the sense of order in social and cultural life after the war, but where Eliot found in his contemplation of the past a literary affinity with the classics, a royalist political stance, and an Anglo-Catholic religious adherence, Sassoon looked in vain for a cause or direction to lead him out from the ennui which had plagued him since the end of the war. The promises of socialism and of a new democratic society where injustices would be eliminated never really engaged his sympathies; instead, he continued to find relief for his discontent in ever-increasing idealized vision of his own past.

In "A Stately Exterior," a poem inspired by the sighting of a deserted Queen Anne–style house while fox-hunting near Cirencester, the speaker discreetly wanders around the outside of a deserted country hall and praises its well-apportioned approach and muted rose-brickwork "backed by dense arboreal green." The overall effect is breathtaking, but the speaker reminds the reader that this edifice was created in the period "of

pre-taxation Rent-roll-stability / Planned for an impermutable nobility."
Here one would expect the satiric blast of the poet to be felt: "What good
is all this wasted space when thousands of Londoners are homeless"
might be a direction for the poet to take: the reader anticipates, at least,
a chilling diatribe on absentee landlords. Instead, though, the poem tails
off with a mellow lament on the sadness of empty houses and a delicate
hint of Victorian manners as "some Tennysonian ring-dove calmly coos."

"In the National Gallery" sets out to satirize the faceless and
insensitive modern crowds that pour aimlessly into the National Gallery.
Once again, however, the force of the satire dissipates until by the last
stanza the intent of the poem has changed into a paean to an idealized
past as visualized by the great painters. The speaker explains his feelings
about the art work he is viewing in juxtaposition with the mindless mobs
cruising "past each patient victory of technique":

> Here blooms, recedes, and glows before their eyes
> A quintessential world preserved in paint,
> Calm vistas of long-vanished Paradise
> And ripe remembrances of sage and saint;
> The immortality of changeless skies,
> And all bright legendries of Time's creation . . .

The final lines return once again to attack the crassness of the audiences
who "patronize / The Art Collection of the English Nation," but the
evocation of the past and longing for a return to the long-vanished paradise when great men performed great deeds of courage is certainly the
overriding consideration in the poem. In fact, this poem (along with "An
Old World Effect," with its preference for rusticity over Cubist experimentation in art) clearly shows Sassoon's artistic taste as favoring the
tradition of the Old Masters.

In summary, the energy of *Satirical Poems* comes largely from the
contradictions between the promises made to the common man during
and after the war and the resultant actualities of the modern world.
Strangely, the motivation for most of these poems is not caustic satire,
because Sassoon, unlike Auden, did not feel the guilt of one who belongs
to an unjustly privileged class, but rather a frustration with the bourgeoi-
sie for its inability to address the inequality apparent in the social system.
He appears to take a stand somewhere between the reactionary status quo
of the upper class and the seething radicalism of those clamoring for
major change; the satirical verse reflects this middle-of-the-road stance.

His poetry of the mid-1920s is that of an outside observer, armed with pen, paper, and inquiring mind, who is slightly amused by the fantastic indulgences and sober abstemiousness found side by side in contemporary society. His findings (observations), which do derive directly from everyday experiences, are mused on until they yield a particular emotional point of view such as disgust, laughter, or absurdity which colors the framework of the poem. The point of view and the event are then hammered into poetic form in an attempt to capture authentically the impulse and impression with candor and honesty.

Sassoon is to be commended on the acuity of his wit in a number of the satires. In "On Reading the War Diary of a Defunct Ambassador" and "On Some Portraits by Sargent," he not only recovers the passion of his war poetry as he lays bare the "visionless officialized fatuity" that mindlessly sentenced soldiers to death, or the social affectation at being painted by "the hireling of the Rich" and immortalized forever "by the brilliant boredom of his brush," but he also delivers the message with lively and piercing precision. David Perkins points out that throughout the early 1920s Sassoon's style tended to become "less purposefully focused and effectively unrestrained," and that the poet even deflates his own person in his poetry (1976, 278). In "Villa d'Este Gardens," for example, Sassoon even pokes fun at his poetic self gathering impressions while his mundane self fumbles for his notebook to capture the moment.

One of the virtues of Sassoon's ironic verse, then, is the complex and unsettled attitude he has toward his subjects, including himself. There is the constant play of one point of view against another; just about any person, institution, activity, or belief can be made to seem facile or futile at one time and acceptable at another (see, for example, "Fantasia on a Wittelsbach Atmosphere": "My sympathy for the Soviets notwithstanding— / [Dare one deplore the dullness of Democracy?]). This unsettled attitude argues against a firm commitment to any particular viewpoint, but the gentle, urbane nature of most of Sassoon's Horatian satire, unlike his Juvenalian war poetry, looks sympathetically on human failings and is content with pointing out man's incongruities.

Admittedly, *Satirical Poems* represented an experimentation with a poetic form that was not natural to Sassoon. In fact, he stated in a letter to Michael Thorpe that the volume was "an exercise in learning to use words with accuracy (the *content* was only playing a mental game without deep seriousness)" (Thorpe 1976, 13). One method employed in *Satirical Poems* to capture this sense of "accuracy" is his use of colloquial speech, whether it reflects the praise of an educated cricket observer, "Good shot, sir! O good shot" ("The Blues at Lord's") or the peculiarities of the American metaphor, "Gee, what a peach / Of a climate!" ("Storm on Fifth Avenue").

Sassoon stated to Michael Thorpe that the years during which he wrote *Satirical Poems* "were a process of getting the war out of my system" (Thorpe 1976, 13), but the content of these poems certainly reveals how uncertain and inconsistent were his various moods and stances during this period. Sassoon appeared to flit with little mental perturbation between the persona of the hard-nosed socialist and that of the reactionary Tory—between an impeccably clad diner at Lord Berners's table or Frank Schuster's summer house near Bray and a solitary wanderer dining at a quiet inn in a secluded village. This spiritual malaise continued to plague him throughout the years he was writing the satirical poetry; indeed, his diary entries from 1923 until October 1925, when he met the young actor Glen Byam Shaw, are characterized by his casual wandering through England in his Gwynne Eight looking for meaning and inspiration, both poetic and philosophical. But the travel and countless concerts kept him amused, and his lover, Gabriel, despite his alcoholic indulgences and unpredictable behavior, helped to mitigate the rage of the sexual fever inside him. In an unusually revealing self-analysis written to Graves, Sassoon succinctly summed up his situation at this time:

> I have been trying to do some versifying, and I have produced a certain amount, but I have no confidence in the stuff—Either it is elaborate and artificial and mildly ironical—which doesn't satisfy my craving for the ideally beautiful—or else it is "moonwashed madrigals" etc. full of imageless abstractions such as you abhor.

> Nevertheless, I feel more and more strongly, that one can serve the world and oneself in no other way than by toiling to produce something in the "art line." Chaos of futility and bungling and successful vulgarity seems to predominate everywhere. It is difficult to feel hopeful. (Sassoon to Graves, 19 November 1923)

11

The Heart's Journey:
Toward Self-Discovery

As early as 5 October 1923, Sassoon mentioned his need to move away from the unfulfilling satiric verse that he had been writing. He claimed in the journal entry of this date that his next book was to be made up of "love and lyrical poems," and that it would be called *The Heart's Journey* (*Diaries 1923–1925*, 56). The satiric poems had never fully engaged his attention; in a candid letter to Graves in early 1924, Sassoon anatomized his poetic problems:

> You can't think how I resent the smart polished Blenheim style of [the] pieces,—though I enjoy writing them. They give me no emotional satisfaction, and I always end by sniffing at them as being "only exercises." But I suppose they are good practice. (Sassoon to Graves, 13 February 1924)

At this time, Graves and Sassoon were engaged in an ongoing discussion about Graves's most recent volume of poems, *Mock Beggar Hall*. Predictably, Sassoon had had trouble with the philosophical musings in the collection, but the main gist of the controversy turned on the importance of thematic coherence between the poems within a given volume of poetry. Sassoon felt that *Whipperginny* was too loosely constructed and found *Mock Beggar Hall* much tighter in its thematic unity. In his letter to Graves of 9 February 1924, he elaborated his thoughts on coherence and looked ahead to the sequential form of *The Heart's Journey*.

> I am pleased that you are convinced about coherence in books of poems. I believe that it is the solution of the long-poem difficulty. A book of poems should be really one long poem; each one should do its bit toward the cumulative effect of the sequence, and any poem, however effective in itself, which doesn't fit into the scheme should be laid aside.

The Heart's Journey, published in August of 1928, contains thirty-five poems harvested from as far back as 1922 ("IX") and from as late as October 1927 ("XXVII"). The majority of the poems were written in late 1924 and 1925 when Sassoon's self-probings became almost obsessive. The poems are arranged to be read as an introspective sequence charting the growth and development of the emotional and spiritual consciousness. The journey toward spiritual self-awareness is primarily Sassoon's, but the poet's struggle is closely aligned with mankind's struggle to make sense out of the postwar world in which traditional values and certainties have been obliterated.

The first three poems deal with Sassoon's idealistic visions of childhood and of early youth; the next six, with self-satisfying adolescent visions of love. The third group deals with what might be called young adulthood, where the forging of a personal set of values amid the flurry of ideas and theories becomes synonymous with self-discovery; once one has achieved self-discovery, one must choose a direction in life. The next eight poems in the sequence examine the various methods available to achieve self-actualization; they ask where can one find joy in the modern age. Three poems act as a musical coda to the preceding section: the recollection of the Great War blunts all youthful anticipation of happiness. The next four poems continue the heart's journey; in them the soul discovers that earthly considerations are not enough for the realization of one's quest in life. The concluding eight poems might be called "faith poems," for they are concerned with the acceptance of the perfectible and transcendental nature of man, as proposed in a work like Emerson's *Representative Men* (1850).

The opening poem of Sassoon's sequence, written in October of 1923 and described in his journal as an "idyllic poem," can be read as an invocation to his muse to return him to childhood, where his soul can wander through the gardens at Weirleigh and gather memories for his poetry. In the second stanza, his soul returns from the garden "arrayed in white," a recurring image that is reminiscent of the ecclesiastical symbol of purity and innocence. The soul, now laden with images of "summer dawns that banished night" and other recollections, conjures up revelations of childhood that have been "laid waste so long." Armed with these images, the poet is ready to begin his search for self-identity and understanding.

The second poem in the sequence calls on his heart to respond to the memories of all that he "has known long since." The poem is not so much a quest for a new beginning as Thorpe suggests (1966, 209), but rather a plea for the speaker's heart to examine what lies within the nature of his own being. The poem celebrates the patient discovery of the mysterious impulses which direct us to look inside ourselves and seek self-knowledge through self-examination. Once this process of self-examination has begun, the full wonder of man's nature is exposed:

> O life within my life, flame within flame,
> Who mak'st me one with song that has no end,
> And with that stillness whence my spirit came.

Sassoon's journey toward self-discovery is well under way by the third poem, in which the speaker wanders through the garden of his childhood on an early spring day. He likens his current state of mind to those first days of spring when the cold breezes and barren trees hold dominion, but when one senses that the warmth and vivacity of spring are about to burst forth and shatter the wintry stillness.

> Spring touched the glooms with green, stole over me
> A sense of wakening leaves that filled the air
> With boding of Elysian days to be.
>
> Cold was the music of the birds; and cold
> The sunlight, shadowless with misty gold:
> It seemed I stood with Youth on the calm verge
> Of some annunciation that should bring
> With flocks of silver angels, ultimate Spring
> Whence all that life had longed for might emerge.

This, the poet urges, is the best of times because the examination of the life is still ahead and lovingly anticipated, while the burden of unawareness is left gratefully behind.

The next six poems, those dealing with the adolescent awareness of sexual love, are the least artistically adequate in the sequence; indeed, "VI" was found to be so weak that it was one of the two poems omitted from the *Collected Poems* (the other was his "Elegy" to Robbie Ross ["XVII"] which he may have felt did not do justice to his friend). The six poems are all love poems in the broadest sense and attempt to examine the multidimensional nature of love. At first glance these poems, with the possible exception of "VIII," appear trite and simplistic. Poem "IV" states that the nature of love can cause confusion in the lover's perceptions, while "V" suggests that the romantic ardor of the narrator can be fired by contemplation of the beauty of his lover. Poems "VI" and "VII" discuss the pain of separation and the joy of reunion, respectively.

Poem "VIII," entitled "Apocalyptical Indiscretions" when it was published in the *Observer,* is an introspective searching of the grand and violent nature of the lover. All parts of the lover's personality meet: "In me, past, present, and future meet / To hold long chiding conference." Clearly, they decide that he is a product of his own nature; that his lusts are more powerful than his reasoning faculty; and that his imaginative fantasies of future conquests are as yet unencumbered by his realizations of life experiences. The poem expatiates on the potency of the primitive and pleasure-loving id, whose influence in youth often outweighs any considerations of the logical or rational. Here, the impetuous Romeo-like lover seizes the rose of love with little provocation; in this, he is simply affirming his kinship with all mankind:

> In me the cave-man clasps the seer,
> And garlanded Apollo goes
> Chanting to Abraham's deaf ear.
> In me the tiger sniffs the rose.
>> Look in my heart, kind friends, and tremble,
>> Since there your elements assemble.

Poem "IX," called "Martyrdom" when it appeared in *Nation* on 30 December 1922, is the earliest written poem in the sequence and was composed when Sassoon was experiencing his own late-blooming adolescence in Rome with his German lover, P. His diary entry for 28 October 1922 explains the background of the poem and the creation of a key line.

> As it was raining hard we [Sassoon and P.] went into Alinari's photo-shop and sat looking at albums until 4.15. . . . I went all through four volumes of the Louvre, two of Dresden Pinakothek and two pictures at Naples. As a result I purchased two photos of the martyrdom of San Lorenzo by G. Santacroce. . . . The picture is the same with slight variations, and has no interest except in its morbidly sexual appeal to my sexually morbid mind. I "glory with Lorenzo on his grid." (*Diaries 1920–1922,* 280)

The poem has little artistic merit, but it continues the theme of the heart's journey. In youth, love is often seen as a wholly passionate experience, and martyrdom for a loved one or for a cause is a glorious penance. The poem celebrates the pain inherent in this martyrdom, although the

alliteration used to describe the victim's punishments weakens the impact
of the poem significantly.

> And likewise with all the victims, bruised by boulders,
> Stabbed by sadistic swords, on pikes impaled,
> Who propped their Paradise on bleeding shoulders
> And bred tumultuous pomps when princes failed.

In the final stanza, the poet attempts to affirm that the sacrifice of the
martyrs was rewarded in heaven with a spiritual kiss, but the stanza lacks
both depth and conviction.

Adolescence is a difficult period for reflective self-discovery because
the intrusion of sexuality prevents a more balanced view of situations. As
the youth matures in the early adult period, the hormonal imbalance and
fascination with sexual mysteries are less dominant and there is a more
rational questioning of the world around him. During this period of
intellectual growth, the individual begins to sort out those tenets and
activities that have special meaning for him; he begins to find his
uniqueness and personal identity in a conscious process of assimilating
and questioning.

The next three poems in the sequence can be described as the quest
for self-knowledge with regard to one's place in the universal structure
of life. Poem "X" opens by asking what Stonehenge is. In the rather
nebulous answer, Sassoon claims it was built as a monument to man's
seeking to discover his place in an eternity of time. Man is represented
as a shadow passing over the face of the timeless monoliths, and with this
knowledge of his infinitesimal significance in the vastness of the
universe, man should learn to practice humility. "Farewell to a Room,"
the first of the titled poems in the collection, was written just before
Sassoon gave up his room in London after five years of boarding there.
The poems contends that in this room he was a single-minded poet (his
private self), and in the "confederate silences" he sought to discover and
develop such talents as were his: to understand and express the finer
elements of his being (*Diaries 1920–1922*, 18). For Sassoon, this inner
probing of his poetic nature is separate from and independent of his outer
nature; this discovery is not surprising in a man whose entire existence
was a duality.

Poem "XII" aptly concludes the section on self-knowledge. In
Corrigan's book, the critic quotes Sassoon as saying, "[The poem] has
been one of my most successful poems. I value it because it was the first

of the post-war poems in which I discovered my mature mode of utterance" (Corrigan 1973, 103). The cello-voiced verse resounds with the hollowness of a deserted house, the awareness of being alone:

> I thought of age, and loneliness, and change,
> I thought how strange we grow when we're alone,
> And how unlike the selves that meet, and talk,
> And blow the candles out, and say good-night.
> Alone . . . The word is life endured and known.
> It is the stillness where our spirits walk
> And all but inmost faith is overthrown.

Here again, the poet captures a sense of the inner depths beyond man's consciousness. The speaker acknowledges the puzzling duality between that inner self that we can only penetrate in the solitude of our mind and the social, outward self that changes like the reflections of pieces of colored glass in a kaleidoscope. The focus of the poem is the difficulty in converting the revelations of solitary meditations into self-knowledge that can assist one's psychological and spiritual evolution. One premise is especially emphasized in the poem: that the inquiry into what human beings are and what they may become can be answered only within the silent walls of themselves.

The next eight poems in the sequence provide an inquiry into the motivations of man's external actions. If the inner probings into the wellsprings of the unconscious are to generate an awareness and understanding of one's life, then, unless the individual is catatonic or autistic, this enhanced perception must be combined with the ontological realities of the outside world. Ideally, the observations of the outside world should affirm the truths discovered by the inner self; one should find harmony and humility as the operative urges in the development of a society based on cooperation and mutual love. But, of course, the world which Sassoon found himself entering after the protective and insular world of his youth was certainly not spiritually harmonious; instead, he found himself adrift in a modern wasteland. This group of eight poems, then, might be said to attempt to find an answer to the voyager's impassioned plea after enduring the muddle of the modern world: "Where does one find spiritual comfort and direction amidst this chaos?"

Poem "XIII" was written in June 1927 to offer Ottoline Morrell spiritual comfort during one of her various crises. The sympathetic speaker claims that the inviolate memories of youth assist one to find philosophical direction and solace. In "Strangeness of Heart" ("XIV"), the poet reminds the reader that man's bond with nature is essential to his spiritual growth. Implicit in both of these poems is the idea that the unthinking, instinctual nexus between mankind and nature is an unerring arbiter in times of confusion or need. Furthermore, Poem "XIV" intimates that the continuous nurturing of this symbiotic relationship between man and nature can somewhat compensate for the loss of innocence during the process of maturation.

The next three poems proclaim the importance of music, literature, and friendship in an ever-changing world. The "timeless, eternally true" music of Bach and Mozart, the words of Shelley and Blake that act as "lamps for gloom," and the "loyal love" of friendship, such as Sassoon experienced with Robbie Ross—all offer consolation for the poet. Amid the turbulence and upheaval of contemporary life, these three refuges act as "rivers of peace that run beyond the setting sun" (Poem "XV").

Initially, Poem "XVIII"—written at Garsington over Christmas of 1924—seems strangely out of sequence, for it returns to the contemplation of childhood and nature that was the essence of "Strangeness of Heart." Sassoon wrote to Ottoline Morrell shortly after its composition that an unnamed work by Gorki influenced him when he wrote it (probably *Reminiscences from My Youth*); in the same letter he claims that individual freedom can occur "only after intense striving [and] experience," and that he worries considerably about "diffuseness and dilution of emotion" as he grows older (Sassoon to Ottoline Morrell, 6 April 1925). When one takes into account this additional biographical background, the purport of the poem becomes clear. The speaker is alone in his room on a stormy night in the city; the "rain burdened" warmish wind outside is figuratively blowing reminiscences of the past into his mind. The pleasant reveries of his youth relieve his numbed, "town-taxed brain" and reopen his psyche to the once richly felt and emotionally charged experiences:

> Wind from familiar fields and star-tossed trees,
> You send me walking lonely through dark and rain
> Before I'd lost my earliest ecstasies.

But the glare of the city lamplight disperses the vision of the past, and the speaker finds himself wandering "into this homelessness / Where all's uncertain." He laments the exclusion of the past from his day-to-day struggles, but realizes the very nature of freedom requires the severing of the bonds with the past: "Wind from the past, you bring me the last flower / From gardens where I'll nevermore return." Here, then, is the budding existentialist standing on the verge of life contemplating his confrontation with life and the conundrum of freedom. On a personal level for Sassoon, freedom from the past was to offer very little comfort, and his withdrawal "wombward" to Heytesbury, to seclusion, to the Catholic Church, all point to a failure to sever the tie and confront the future head-on.

"To an Eighteenth Century Poet" ("XIX"), too, seems initially out of place in the sequence. Logically, it would have been better placed next to "Grandeur of Ghosts" ("XVI"), in which the poet pays tribute to great writers like Shelley and Blake. The point here, however, is that Cowper is not being praised for his impassioned cries of prophetic utterances, but rather for his "tranquillities" and "quiet-toned persistence." The speaker finds comfort in the realization that the dead poet's words can somehow defy time and touch the sensibilities of a twentieth-century reader; with the barriers of time overthrown, the poet has the potential of reaching the human heart even from beyond the grave:

> This is the power, the privilege, the pride
> And the rich morality of those who write
> That hearts may be their highway. They shall ride
> Conquering uncharted countries with the bright
> Rewards of what they wrought in living light . . .
> Who then shall dare to say that they have died?

Thus, the poetry itself provides a type of immortality for its writer; and Sassoon obviously found comfort in the prospect of touching the life of the yet-unborn with his verse.

The rather disappointing final poem in this section was written in response to the death of Philip Morrell's mother, whom Sassoon barely knew (*Diaries 1923–1925,* 246). Rather than offering another source of comfort or direction in the modern world, Sassoon tells the reader where spiritual direction will *not* be found: in the "afternoon politeness" of "social Academe, good talk, and taste," for all this frivolity pales in the face of the "great stairway" to eternity. In "To An Old Lady Dead," then, comfort is to be gained from the underlying meaning of the emptiness surrounding the old lady's death. The poet is forced into a contemplation of death ("These moments are 'experience' for me"), which leads to insightful appreciation of simple earthly joys:

> When Oxford Belfries chime you do not hear,
> Nor in this mellow-toned autumnal brightness
> Observe an English-School-like atmosphere.

The next three poems remind the sojourner that spiritual development and self-fulfillment are in many ways dependent on the external circumstances surrounding the individual. In 1914, Sassoon's rather languid philosophizing had been abruptly terminated with the onset of the Great War, and the ramifications of the war had colored his interpretation of what was essential in life. For Sassoon, then, the memories of the war and all they entailed had to be confronted and overcome before he could continue his heart's journey.

"To One in Prison" ("XXI") may be the oddest poem in the group. (Even Michael Thorpe passes over it without mention.) The speaker, who has been to an Armistice Day observance, visits a young man in prison for theft. The prisoner has evidently led a very arduous life: he has labored his youth away; his father was killed in the war, and his mother is also in prison for theft. The young convict is quite distraught about the two minute silence observed earlier; the speaker looks compassionately at him, "so woebegone and weary" and feels remorse for the young lad's lot, but the poem concludes with the speaker asking what good comes of feeling pity for the unfortunate, and then of walking away.

> And now—what use, the pity that I am heaping
> Upon your head? What use—to wish you well
> And slam the door? Who knows? . . . My heart, not
>   yours can tell.

The poem appears to be a rather clumsy allegory of the attitude of the unthinking masses towards the Remembrance Day activities. These people pass through the outward motions of sorrow and remorse for those killed and wounded (both physically and mentally) by the war, but then return to their everyday existences without comprehending the true significance of their sacrifice. For Sassoon, the war and its attendant horrors must be realized and fully digested; they cannot be treated superficially and forgotten.

This theme is carried over into the poem "To One Who Was With Me in the War," inspired by a conversation with fellow soldier Ralph Greaves (the Wilmot in *Infantry Officer*). Here Sassoon warns against forgetting the worst elements of the monstrous war because one's memory is necessarily selective. The true horrors and senseless violence unleashed in battle must never be lost to oblivion.

The final poem of this coda is by far the most moving and sincere of the three and proved to be the last poetic words Sassoon wrote about a war which eight years previously had been the center of his existence. "On Passing the New Menin Gate" (Poem "XXIII") resounds with vituperation and distaste for officialdom and cant (and no doubt the War Graves Commission). The speaker in this poem is appalled at the "pile of peace-complacent stone" which will supposedly compensate the dead for the injustice done to them. The dichotomy here between the unheroic simplicity of the unthinking common soldiers, who were little more than cannon fodder, and the massive monument to their achievement is blatantly ironic. The further irony of the grandiose inscription, "Their name liveth for ever," is contrasted with the speaker's knowledge that the majority of names carved in the arch have already been forgotten. To sacrifice all for a space on a monolithic piece of stone is a crime against humanity; the heart must never forget the individual to whom the name belonged.

Sassoon's meditations on the expendable nature of life on the western front led him in the following four poems to question the design of existence. Here, he appears to have concluded that the materialistic comforts and transient joys offered in this world are only reflections of the transcendent harmony and radiance that await the triumphant perpetrator of the divine plan. The weakness of these consciously metaphysical verses and of most of the remaining poems in this volume, however, is that while Sassoon's vision was bound up with achieving a sense of spiritual tranquility and gnosis, the mode of actualization remained tantalizingly obscure.

The Heart's Journey is a far more restrained book than its predecessors, and perhaps the earnest study of the musical techniques of his favorite classical composers (Bach and Mozart) contributed to Sassoon's modified style. The tributes to Bach's fugues and the "timeless" and "eternally true" music of Mozart ("XV") supplant the often jarring disharmony of his antiwar and satirical verse. Here, Sassoon's metrical regularity and verbal harmony are more formal and certain than in his earlier works, for he had developed through the study of classical music what de Sola Pinto calls "the music in language to express the vision of ineffable beauty which . . . haunted him throughout his life" (1951, 222–23). And the poet's fusing of mature musical appreciation with spiritual awareness was fortunate, for intangible concepts like music often act as a metaphor for the wonder that hovers just beyond the physical, as in these lines in "From a Fugue by Bach":

> Praying I know not to whom in this musicless room
> Where my soul like a flame of a candle in ecstasy
>   stood,
> I gaze at my life in a mirror, desirous of good.
> And my solitude girds me with ghosts, with invisible
>   words:
> In the mirror I see but the face that is me, that is
>   mine;
> And the notes of the fugue that were voices from
>   vastness divine.

The opening stanza of "From a Fugue by Bach" ("XXIV") recounts familiarly how Bach's music conjures up visions of heaven and joyfulness, and how music alone can satisfy the poet: "If this in itself were enough, I am crowned with the best." When the music stops, the spell is broken. The music is an example of man's capability through art to glimpse the divine order, but the poet recognizes that he is "barred out from abodes of the blest" at this time, for he has much to learn about the nature of living:

> . . . I know but my need
> To be clearing my lofts of their lumber, to build with
>   my breath
> The litany leading me onward, the intimate creed
> That must hold me enhumbled.

The path to transcendence of the self requires much metaphysical meditation and self-awareness; the poet senses this and realizes that he is not ready for such a journey as yet.

Sassoon's poetic meditations of this period were often reflections of his past, but by 1925 his Romantic musings had been replaced by affinities with the serene Metaphysical poets, especially Vaughan and Herbert, although as Thorpe points out, "he [Sassoon] never rises to the gleaming heights of the one or the more complex imagery of the other" (1966, 208). Like these two poets, Sassoon derived his poetic images from an awareness of simple, everyday reality. The direct, passive style of "At the Grave of Henry Vaughan" is more than just an imitation of Vaughan's work; here, Sassoon, using his own familiar image of daybreak and merging it artistically with Vaughan's vision of the purity

of light, creates a modern sonnet while at the same time paying homage
to the Metaphysical tradition, as the concluding sestet clearly demonstrates:

> The skull that housed white angels and had vision
> Of daybreak through the gateways of the mind.
>> Here faith and mercy, wisdom and humility
>> (Whose influence shall prevail for evermore)
>> Shine. And this lowly grave tells Heaven's
>>> tranquillity.
>> And here stand I, a suppliant at the door.

"At the Grave of Henry Vaughan" ("XXV") originated from a motor
tour of Wales in August of 1924; the resultant sonnet is a poetic
reconstruction of Sassoon's meditations at the simple grave site of the
Silurist. The peaceful nature of the churchyard becomes an emblem of the
afterlife that Sassoon imagines: Vaughan's earthly remains lie "above the
voiceful windings of a river . . . overshadowed by a yew." Vaughan, who
reportedly saw Eternity and described it in his poem "The World," is now
a part of the vision of purest light that he glimpsed when he was alive.
For Sassoon, the meditations at Vaughan's grave remind him that the
practice of Christian virtues such as "faith and mercy, wisdom and
humility" can teach him a great deal about the purpose of existence. By
performing virtuous acts in the service of others and by remaining
humble, he may come to know a taste of "Heaven's tranquillity" here on
earth.

A glimpse of eternity is, in fact, achieved by the speaker in "A
Midnight Interior" ("XXVI"). He is granted a vision of "spiritual significance" when he investigates a circle of brightness cast on the ceiling by
his reading lamp. Within this light he "discovered an arctic snowstorm."
The phenomenon of "pure seeing" continues in the second stanza:

> White flowers were in a bowl beside my book;
> In midnight's miracle of light they glowed,
> And every petal there in silence showed
> My life the way to wonder with a look.

This transcendent glimpse into a further dimension is the poet's confirmation of an existence beyond our senses. In the final stanza, the speaker
prays for release of his earthbound soul in order to comprehend the world
as it should be understood: free from the prejudices and preconceptions

imposed by our reasoning faculties. The poem is an entreaty for man to be open to the wonder within the commonplace and to engender a simplicity of vision in order to understand life.

Finally, in "One who Watches," probably inspired by an emotionally charged evening with Edmund Gosse in October 1927, Sassoon explores the difficulty of accepting the loss of friends through death. The speaker, in an almost Poe-like personification of Death, stands patiently and objectively outside the process of life awaiting the inevitable decease of his friends. In even the happiest moments of laughter, the speaker can think only of how the moment must be preserved and kept vital for the future. The poem concludes Sassoon's personal revelations on a solemn note; the very act of knowing life and grasping its varied significances is at best bittersweet. Sassoon is comforted by knowing that the memories of his friends will live on through him, but this awareness is not enough. Like the evanescence of Bach's music, the state of his meditative life, his glimpse of eternity, and the posthumous memories of his friends all offer comfort and direction, but the universal application of such awareness still eludes the poet.

The last eight poems in the sequence might be called "faith poems"; that is, they all reinforce an almost Emersonian belief in the perfectibility of the nature of man and the importance of some kind of afterlife for the soul, an afterlife that can be confirmed by self-communing. These poems are fraught with religious images and thought, and while Sassoon's conversion to Catholicism was still thirty years away when he wrote them, Michael Thorpe concludes that in the last poems "the religious strain is evident; it is already clear that the paramountcy of the spiritual is forming" (Thorpe to Quinn, 10 March 1986). The "religious strain" at this stage consists of a sense of spiritual rebirth through self-knowledge and an acceptance of universal love as being promulgated through the world by a force as yet unknown, which is often described in slightly veiled Christian terms as a "white light."

Poem "XXVIII," which examines the duality of man's nature by using the well-worn symbols of night and day, focuses on how man must continually struggle against the forces of gloom and despair in order to find images of peace. Just as Dostoyevsky contends that only through personal suffering comes resurrection, the poet affirms that the struggle against the dark forces in man's nature can be overcome only with meditation, introspection, and faith in the benevolent powers of the universe. This inward strength and faith in man's ability to find affirmation in life is also emphasized in Poem "XXIX." The speaker of this lyric is made aware of the spiritual capabilities of mankind through a dream image; his faith is staunch in what he has seen ("This have I surely seen"), although he realizes that the intellectual and rational "mind may mock" the validity of his visionary insight. The poet has faith in his visions despite the charges of irrationality and skepticism during his waking hours.

"All-Souls' Day" ("XXX") clearly affirms the power of intuition and faith over reason. In a letter to Ottoline Morrell, Sassoon anticipates the negative reaction the poem will provoke among his friends; in fact, he writes that the poem is bound to "incur the sneers of the elaborate intellectuals who only care for brainspun conceits" (Sassoon to Morrell, 9 December 1925). The poem utilizes the now familiar dichotomic method; this time the symbols for reason and faith are the "worldhood's charnel close" and "daybreak's burning rose," respectively. The poet proposes that personal faith in the positive nature of good (existence of a soul) is difficult amidst the "obscene derision" of his faithless companions, but that his belief in the transcendence of his soul and nature "sings out into the morning," and this confidence "quell(s) the obscene derision / Of demon-haunters in our heart." The nascent suggestion here is that spiritual certitude is hindered by the interference of other people; Sassoon's already solitary and reflective nature would find no quarrel with this.

Interestingly, "The Power and the Glory" was written just after Sassoon had departed Tufton Street and met Glen Byam Shaw. The exalted freedom he felt at leaving the claustrophobic influence of W. J. Turner (with whom he had quarreled) and the expansiveness of energy he found in his friendship with Byam Shaw are reflected in the optimistic nature of his journal entries at this time. The lively qualities of this poem are especially alluded to in Blunden's criticism of Sassoon's works: he states that "Sassoon's private hymns and utterances of the undying brightness have their own unborrowed qualities" (1950, 321). The three-stanza poem confidently implies that the poet's thoughts are part of God's unknowable plan for his enlightenment; his poetic work not only gives him purpose, but further serves the purpose of the Creator:

> Let there be God, say I. And what I've done
> Goes onward like the splendour of the sun
> And rises up in rapture and is one
> With the white power of conscience that commands.

With this strength and affirmation of purpose, no thought opposing the divine symmetry of existence can be entertained; the heart and faith stand united in their certain knowledge of God. Indeed, Sassoon's surprisingly positive declaration of belief in God's purpose helps us understand why the abbess of Stanbrooke, in her edition of Sassoon's poetry called *The Path to Peace,* decided to place "The Power and the Glory" as the first of twenty-five poems plotting Sassoon's progress toward fulfillment.

Poem "XXXII" promotes the potency of man's faith to dispel the unimaginative dreariness of his superficial, worldly philosophies, while "Conclusion" ("XXXIII") is reminiscent of a *carpe diem* poem with a twist at the end. Beginning with an image of the "dance of change," the poem suggests the whirling and gyrating movements of life. The poet warns that despite this flurry of activity, we must realize that "soon death the hooded lover / Shall touch [our] house of clay." This awareness should add savor to the piquancy of life's offerings; as Marvell suggests, we should "sport us while we may." The difference between the two poets resides in the final reckoning: Sassoon does not see life as being annihilated by death, but rather as a prevision of the "wonder" that awaits us after death. For him, the conclusion of life is just the beginning of knowledge.

Many of the later poems in *The Heart's Journey* and *Vigils* were written under Vaughan's poetic and spiritual influence. Following his model, Sassoon attempted evanescent imagery that seems almost translucent when read. The final stanza of "Conclusion," in which he depends on the short line and on monosyllabic, simple language to bring this translucent imagery to fruition, indicates how close he came to capturing this elusive state:

> For, though the end be night,
> This wonder and this white
> Astonishment of sight
> Make hours of magic shine;
> And heaven's blaze and bloom
> Of transience and divine
> Inheritance of doom.

Sassoon's conviction that "simplicity of mind" was the way to understand and preserve spiritual integrity would have been clearly comprehensible to Vaughan or Herbert. The pursuit of this spiritual understanding has a dignity and gentle ecstasy which is later found in much of his Catholic poetry of the 1950s, but here he simply attempts to fathom the mystical connectedness of all aspects of nature, both animate and inanimate, through his poetry.

"Nativity" ("XXXIV") was sent to Ottoline Morrell in March of 1927, and in the accompanying letter, Sassoon confirmed that he had spent much time trying to understand the nature of his inner life (Sassoon to Morrell, 31 March 1927). The poem suggests that his meditations yielded some spiritual fruit: he has "realized" inner peace—symbolized by the flower opening in his heart in the first line. The candid admission in the second stanza that he had not grasped the full implications of this "simple, secret thing" is mitigated somewhat by the assurance that inner peace is possible:

> O flower within me wondrous white
> I know you only as my need
> And my unsealed sight.

The simplicity of language and the poet's inspired description of spring flowers blossoming in the heart make this poem function cohesively as a delicate celebration of man's receiving the gift of inward peace. And had Sassoon not realized here that a mere flicker of inner peace was not the same as achieving a true state of serenity, this poem might have made a fitting conclusion to his heart's journey.

The concluding poem in the volume is the austerely titled "A Last Judgment." Its deep, gloomy organ tones and apocalyptic images are clearly intended to suggest the Book of Revelation. The purpose of the prophetic statements in this poem, however, is not to warn its readers "of destruction to come, of death to be rained down from the heavens, of cities to be levelled," as Cohen characterizes Sassoon's later poetry (1957, 177); rather, the poet becomes the personal prophet of the individual's karma, and his function is to demonstrate the potential folly of the individual soul through an object lesson. The poem sets up the two alternatives open to man as he begins his private pilgrimage through life: the way of love and the way of lust. The exemplar of lust chooses "the scarlet and the sceptre and the crown of pride." The customary pattern of degradation and corruption follows, and a suggestion of Sassoon's own guilt for his "fevers" might even be heard in the lines: "Mocked and maimed he knew / For scrawls on dungeon walls his priapismic devils." Like Faust before him, the selfish seeker of pleasure finally has to face judgment and cries out to the angel of love for mercy. Unfortunately, the "angel with eyes inexorable and wings once white / For mercy" is "now by storming judgment backward blown." Repentance and realization have come too late; the poor wretch is whirled away "on roaring gales of gloom." The last line with the ellipses—". . . He heard an angel say . . . " —returns the reader to Revelation, where the last angel who turns over the bowl of plagues calls out that "the end has come" (Revelation 16:17). So, too, the end comes to him who does not overcome his selfishness: his heart will be turned to "unrelenting stone." But for those who choose the path of love, the heart's journey will continue onward toward an unexplained unity with the Godhead.

The whole of *The Heart's Journey* might be described as a sequence of poems which chart the development of Sassoon's self-awareness and self-knowledge: the sensitizing of his conscious self and the discovery of his inner self. The volume lacks the intensity of his war poems, but its tone is consonant with the serene austerity of Sassoon's later style and subject matter. In nearly all of the poems, he shows a sense of discovery and wonder at everyday existence, and his poetry celebrates that awareness, as the closing lines of "A Midnight Interior" clearly demonstrate:

> O inwardness of trust,—intelligence,—
> Release my soul through every door of sense:
> Give me new sight; O grant me strength to find
> From lamp and flower simplicity of mind.

A distinct stylistic pattern is at work here: Sassoon purposely avoids repetitive devices and prolonged measures in the belief that direct utterance with few stylistic adornments corresponds best to the straightforward nature of his inward quest. True, the poems lack the tension of the earlier satire, but *The Heart's Journey* is much better than his romantic verse of the prewar period, when Sassoon's exuberance often led to such embarrassingly trite and inauthentic lines as "Come, gentle breeze, and tarrying on your way, / Whisper my trees what you have seen to-day. / Stand, golden cloud, until my song be done, / (For he's too proud) before the face of the sun" ("Companions").

Sassoon's own exploratory journey was not over by the year the poems were completed (1927), but his wanderings of the immediate postwar years were complemented with a map and a compass. From this point onward, Sassoon was to turn inward for his inspiration, to sift the material from his memory over and over again, constantly refining it. He

used it for the six semi-autobiographical prose works that appeared over
the next eighteen years. And the first step of this internal voyage, the first
product of his investigations—*The Memoirs of a Fox-Hunting Man*—took
him back to his youth.

12

Memoirs of a Fox-Hunting Man:
The Reconstitution of Memory

Sassoon had been contemplating writing fiction throughout the 1920s, so his gracious acknowledgment to Gosse for putting the idea of using his sporting experiences as a springboard for a sustained work to help forget the war is much overstated (*Siegfried's Journey*, 100–101). *Memoirs of a Fox-Hunting Man*, which he began in 1926, is more of a companion piece to *The Heart's Journey* than it is a Surtees clone. The novel is a recounting and investigation of Sassoon's background which begins with a lightly fictionalized childhood and carries his alter ego, George Sherston, to the front line of the Somme battlefield on Easter Sunday 1916. Sassoon finished the book exactly twelve Easters later in 1928 (Sassoon to Blunden, 14 April 1928).

In a retrospective piece in *The Saturday Book Sixth Year* (1946), written while he was working on his study of George Meredith and after the trauma of another world war, Sassoon attempted to recapture the pleasurable feelings he had experienced in writing *Fox-Hunting Man.*

> When . . . I began to write *Memoirs of a Fox-Hunting Man*, I surprised myself by discovering that 1896 felt as though it were much more than thirty years ago. This . . . afforded me much intimate felicity. . . . For the nineties had acquired an idyllic flavour. Recreating them was almost like reading *Cranford* [Mrs. Gaskell's prose idyll of life in a Cheshire village (1851)] or the "Barchester" novels. They were as far away as the boyhood of Richard Feverel [hero of Meredith's 1859 novel *The Ordeal of Richard Feverel*]. Stabilized and detached, the past had become a charming perspective late-Victorian picture. How happily humdrum, how exquisitely unperturbed by innovations it all seemed when reflected in the mirror of memory. Time went as slowly as the carrier's van that brought the parcels from the station, and international events were comfortably epitomised in the weekly cartoons of "Punch." France was a lady in a short skirt, Russia a

261

bear, and the performances of the county cricket team more important than either of them. (Thorpe 1966, 70–71)

What Sassoon fails to mention in his article is the motivation behind his exploration of the period, and perhaps his natural reticence to reveal his internal promptings to the reading public is behind this omission. As my previous chapter on *The Heart's Journey* attempted to establish, Sassoon was looking at this time for some kind of purpose and direction for his aimless life; fictional autobiography was a further means to examine his younger self and to try to discover what forces were at work in his development. His exploratory journey into the past yielded much of interest, but as Bergonzi points out: "Sassoon did not feel ready to present his experiences to the world without some attempt at fictional concealment" (Bergonzi 1980, 159).

There were many reasons for this concealment, but the most important of these was a very practical consideration: his mother's sensitivities. Sassoon's mother was very ill during all of 1927. As explained in *The Old Century* (written after his mother's death), the notion of causing her added pain by dredging up the painful experiences of her marital breakup and its emotional aftermath, was unthinkable. So Sassoon simply "killed off" his fictional parents in *Fox-Hunting Man* and created the figure of Aunt Evelyn.

Graves, Bergonzi, Fussell, and other commentators on the novel have all noted that these fictional memoirs are somewhat hampered by Sassoon's decision to make Sherston a simplified version of himself (see Graves's caustic review in the *Clarion*); that is, he fails to take into account his poetic self. But in his first prose work, Sassoon was understandably not overly ambitious, so he decided to eliminate the poetic side of his character in order to concentrate on the external forces that gave value to his prewar existence, which consisted largely of self-education as a sportsman.

In a letter to Blunden written upon completion of the novel, Sassoon exclaimed that he had kept the narration "clear and unencumbered," that the work was intended to "unroll like a scroll"; but he also reminded Blunden that the book was a "recreative exercise [and] nothing more" (Sassoon to Blunden, 14 April 1928). Furthermore, the concept of the novel as a "recreative exercise," the author's desire for anonymity, and the private publication all suggest that desire for popular success did not play a large part in Sassoon's writing of the novel. And yet the book was a commercial and critical success when it was released; it won the

Hawthornden Prize for 1928, as well as the James Tait Black Memorial Prize—much to Graves's chagrin (O'Prey 1982, 203).

The reasons for the novel's critical success were many, but certainly one was Sassoon's recreation of the prewar past. The General Strike of 1926 and the unfathomable demands of the workers and trade unions, as well as the international collapse of faith in the League of Nations and the declining cultural and moral values, gave the leisurely, ordered rustic life depicted in the book an aureate glow for many readers, who were largely of the middle class. The book caught the crest of the nostalgia wave much in the same way that Aldington's *Death of a Hero* and Graves's *Good-bye* would catch the war-novel nostalgia in the following years.

The novel is clearly a period piece; it captures the serenity and insularity of Victorian and Edwardian West Sussex in what Thorpe appropriately calls "an evocation of a vanished way of life" (1966, 78). In some respects it is a collection of Edwardian squirearchical recollections similar to others that appeared throughout the 1920s, but Sassoon's *Fox-Hunting Man* is also much more. It is a careful study of the growth of a sensitive self-consciousness—or what Pascal calls in his study of autobiographical writing "the engagement with the world" (1960, 135). Indeed, the fact that Sassoon had saved the discussion of poetic awakening for his more traditional autobiographical works does not mean that Sherston had been deprived of many of Sassoon's sensitivities.

Paul Fussell, in a chapter called "The Binary Vision of Siegfried Sassoon" (1983, 90–105), finds the key to the novel in Sassoon's impulse to contrast the war with the vision of life before the conflict. Agreeing with Arthur E. Lane's contention that Sassoon's early years were so leisured and pleasant that he was particularly sensitive to the contrasts provided by life at the front, Fussell points out that polarities "determine[d] his whole lifetime mental set and bec[a]me the matrices of his memory" (1983, 92). What Fussell fails to mention, however, is that this polarizing had already been used in many of the poems in *The Heart's Journey*. In "On Passing the New Menin Gate," for example, the unheroic simplicity of the common soldier's response was set against the ostentatious memorial. In Poem "XXVIII" man's dual nature was symbolized by night and day. Still, Fussell's theory of polarity does get to the heart of Sassoon's self-exploration.

The first noticeable polarity established in the novel is between its two completely fictional characters: Aunt Evelyn and Tom Dixon. Aunt Evelyn, with her protectiveness and limited social aspirations for herself and George, is in direct opposition to Dixon, who desires to make a sportsman out of his young master. Through clever maneuvering of his unworldly mistress, Dixon manages to untie George from the matriarchal apron strings and introduce him to the hunting world of Dumborough. These two fictional characters are representative of George's developing personality traits. In one sense, he is the shy and retiring boy of whom his aunt approves, but he also has a strong instinct to be the daring sportsman that Dixon encourages him to become. The early sections of the novel are an investigation into which direction he will choose.

In part 1, Dixon manages to dupe Aunt Evelyn by taking George to a meet at Heron Gate; there George hopes to see once again Denis Milden, the first of several "perfect" role models that come along in his life. Having watched Milden ride with "unhesitating self-reliance," Sherston feels a certain envy at his hero's accomplishments. When Milden deigns to make conversation with the overawed Sherston, a fox darts out and gazes at the boys "with human alertness"; Milden naturally raises the alarm, but George suddenly and passionately exclaims: "Don't do that; they'll catch him" (*Memoirs,* 44). The recognition of having made a fool of himself by showing concern for the fox is mortifying, and George tries to compensate for his social gaffe by some hard riding, but the action cannot be undone. Clearly, the two sides of the man—single-minded sportsmanship and sensitivity to nature—have already been firmly established.

In his article "Neither Worthy Nor Capable," John Hildebidle demonstrates that in "The Flower Show Match" chapter of *Fox-Hunting Man,* Sassoon sets up a fundamental paradigm of accidental heroism that will pattern the structure of the complete *Memoirs.* Hildebidle sees George largely as a passive character whose "unwitting involvement" in events brings him undeserved "heroic" stature. The weakness of this theory, however, is that it overlooks Sherston's positive actions. The drift of the article seems to be that Sherston was "lucky" to have punched home the winning run or to have stayed on the saddle when Cockbird hit the final fence, whereas in reality, Sherston's victories, no matter how they are played down by the mature narrative voice of the older Sherston, were generated by something more than accident. Sassoon's description of the scoring of the final run shows clearly that Sherston "calmly resolves to look lively and defeat his [the bowler's] destructive aim." He hits the ball and aggressively shouts for Peter to "come on," and when he scores the final run his gallantry is rewarded. The young hero gains repute as a sportsman as well as insights into adult life.

The lesson of the flower show episode for young Sherston is the discrepancy between appearance and reality. Aunt Evelyn cautiously awards the prize for vegetables to Mr. Bathwick, only to discover that his tomatoes and cucumbers have been purchased. George realizes that the Butley umpire is partial to the Butley team, and Parson Yelden, who cares more for cricket and pheasants than for his parishioners, fails to show Christian forbearance when he looks up at the scorer with an "unevangelical expression on his face" (*Memoirs*, 60), having failed to make a run for his team. The octogenarian Mrs. Maskall, whose biting, uncharitable comments about her neighbors cease only when she can vilify the Roman Catholic church, offers Sherston a model of hypocrisy. Evidently, the rural Eden has its rough edges, and George's perambulations around the showgrounds offer much material for reflection.

In *Fox-Hunting Man,* Sassoon offers the reader a portrait not only of a young fox-hunting man in the making, but also of a developing nature lover. In the often quoted description of the early summer morning at Butley, when George watches the scarlet disc of the sun climb an inch above the hills (*Memoirs*, 48), an intuitive perception of natural beauty and harmony suggests more depth in George's character than we might expect. The close attention to auditory and olfactory natural detail makes him closer in character to Lawrence's Paul Morel than to the hard-riding "Boots" Brownrigg. The evidence here suggests that the semi-autobiographical figure of George Sherston is endowed with an artistic consciousness, and if Sassoon distilled the poetic out of his character, he still left traces of his sensitivity intact.

Sassoon examines some of Sherston's less desirable attributes in the next chapter. Leaving London by train, Sherston comments dismissively:

> Raindrops tricked down the windows as we steamed out of the station, and I was glad to avert my gaze from the dingy and dilapidated tenements and warehouses which we were passing. Poverty was a thing I hated to look in the face; it was like the thought of illness and bad smells, and I resented the notion of all those squalid slums spreading out into the uninfected green country. (*Memoirs*, 73)

Reading his *Golf Illustrated* (another acceptable pursuit of the sportsman) and surreptitiously observing his refined fellow travelers, George is conscious of keeping up appearances of his class. His Aunt Evelyn in her "countrified tweed coat and skirt and her dowdy little hat seemed only just presentable" (*Memoirs*, 74). When his exhausted aunt brings an apparatus for making tea out of a "plebeian looking basket," George is mortified by the impression she must be making on the refined couple close by and simply ignores the whole procedure. George knows he has behaved badly, but the social implications override his duty to "make amends" for his thoughtless actions and feelings. His distancing himself from London's poverty and from his aunt's simplicity of character suggest that the values of the leisure class are taking hold and that George is losing his natural empathy with the real and the essential. Indeed, his philosophy of life is summed up quite clearly when he drops out of Cambridge: "I was content to take it easy until something happened." This rather idle, cavalier attitude involves him in book collecting (not for what is inside, but for the attractiveness of the covers), but eventually leads him back to the comfortable mindlessness of riding and fox-hunting.

In the chapter entitled "A Day with the Potford," the reader is treated to a further revelation of Sherston's character. George has gone into town to purchase new clothes for the coming season, and the joy of being pampered and spoken to like a fox-hunting man by the sycophantic salesman brings him a feeling of smug satisfaction. The same afternoon, George attends a violin recital by Fritz Kreisler, and the incipient huntsman is transported by the serene eloquence of the Handel sonata to a short-lived realization that "such music was more satisfying than the huntsman's horn" (*Memoirs,* 107). Again, Sassoon explores himself through the polarities of the fox-hunting mentality (the adherents of which he will come to call "conventional, grown-up children" [*Diaries 1920–1922,* 110]) and the sensitivity of the artist.

The next three chapters chronicle George's apprenticeship and eventual success as a fox-hunting man. His meeting Stephen Colwood and winning the Colonel's Cup both contribute to his eventual friendship with Denis Milden (now hunt master); their ideal winter of hunting with the Packlestone is described with loving fondness. In these chapters, though, very little internal development of character occurs; Sherston is locked in a world where, despite financial extravagance (inherent in the words "fox-hunting man" is a very solid private income and plenty of leisure time), the only important concerns are an ample number of jumpable fences and an abundance of foxes. Sherston's development as a fox-hunter is in direct proportion to his decline as a feeling human being. With the blinkered vision of "upper middle class stupidity" (*Diaries 1920–1922,* 111), Sherston describes Packlestone country:

Its character was varied—cow-pastures and collieries being the extremes of good and bad. In some districts there were too many villages, and there were three or four biggish industrial towns. This abundance of population seemed to me an intrusion, and I wished I could clear every mean modern dwelling out of the hunt. (*Memoirs,* 203)

The lack of concern for, or awareness of, activities going on around the fox-hunters is so encompassing that even as late as 1913, Sherston can partake of this life-style "with a comfortable feeling that here was something that no political upheaval could interrupt" (204). The only discordant element he perceives in a Midlands that has recently been rent asunder by long coal strikes and industrial unrest is "those damned socialists who want to stop us hunting" (204). The irony here is that the socialist credo is reduced to a direct threat not to the class structure, but to one of the recreational activities of its elite.

Sherston as the "happy hunter," like his later manifestation as "happy warrior" in *Infantry Officer,* is so completely immune to intellectual effort and is "so completely identified with what [he] was doing and so oblivious to anything else" (214) that human awareness dwindles to a minute portion of what it should have been. Indeed, when the hunting season comes to an end, Sherston imagines a summer in fashionable Mayfair where acceptance into "the well-oiled ingredients of affluence and social smartness" (216) becomes an end in itself.

A corrective to this vision is voiced by the reflective narrator who admits to now having heard "the hollow echoes in that social apparatus" (216). The narrator is full of tolerance for his younger self, and the gulf between the two selves is made somewhat understandable by the experiences George has in the last two chapters of the book. Sherston will be jerked violently out of his complacent dream world and exposed to the harsh realities of death in his role as infantry officer. The unobtrusive, tasteful death of faithful Miriam at the conclusion of chapter 8 contrasts poignantly with the deaths that lie ahead.

Chapter 9 is primarily a chapter of change and preparation. Sassoon lovingly recreates the halcyon days of innocence before he was sent to the front. The discipline of the yeomanry is reminiscent to that of the school, but Sherston bears the ordeal because he has serious aspirations toward heroism; he wants to learn everything he can about soldiering. Through the training process, his body is strengthened to the point that he feels confidence in his role as a soldier. But Sassoon begins to expose the superficiality of military life almost as soon as his alter ego has taken his commission in the Royal Flintshire Fusiliers. When Sherston makes a trip to Craven and Sons to purchase new clothes before joining his regiment, the scene is reminiscent of his earlier trip to purchase hunting boots. (The name of Sherston's tailor suggests that Sassoon's rancor for those who made money out of the war could not be suppressed even ten years later.) But here, Mr. Stoving chats "his way courageously through the War; 'business as usual' was his watchword" (233). The irony is that clothes do make a difference, for when Sherston reports for duty with a less elegantly dressed Yorkshireman named Mansfield who gave up an £800 a year position to serve his country, poor Mansfield is badly maligned by the haughty adjutant, while Sherston's "reception was in accordance with the cut of [his] clothes . . . " (234).

Clitherland Camp is the antithesis of the rural peasantry of West Sussex. Its purpose is to train killers, and the grotesque description is in keeping with its grisly intentions:

> The district was industrial. Half a mile away were the chimneys of Bryant's Match Factory. Considerably closer was a hissing and throbbing inferno, which incessantly concocted the form of high explosive known as T.N.T.; when the wind was in the east the Camp got the benefit of the fumes, which caused everyone to cough. Adjoining the Camp, on the other side, was a large Roman Catholic cemetery. Frequent funeral processions cheered up the troops. The surrounding country, with its stunted dwelling-houses, dingy trees, disconsolate canal, and flat root-fields, was correspondingly unlikeable. (235)

The descriptive passage not only mirrors on a small scale what awaits Sherston on the battlefield in France, but also places him in a completely alien environment. His early days at Clitherland are extremely difficult until a role model appears in the unassuming, fair-haired and fine-featured figure of Dick Tiltwood.

Reminiscent of Stephen Colwood and Dennis Milden, Tiltwood is the "shining epitome of his unbittered generation" (241). He guides the awkward Sherston through the training period with patience and sincerity. Their relationship grows closer as the days go by, although Sassoon chooses to avoid any hint of eroticism in the novel. Instead, he concentrates on Dick's role as a comforter; when Sherston receives the news of Stephen Colwood's death, Dick is present to share the grief and to justify for George the purposeful death. Most importantly, Dick is with him when the two officers sail for France and the western front.

The death of Colwood effectively concludes Sherston's extended youth, and at this point the sobered Sherston realizes that he is leaving everything of importance behind in England. His developing maturity can be seen in the empathy he is able to show as he and Dick pull out of Victoria Station on their way to the front:

> Victoria Station: Aunt Evelyn's last, desperately forced smile; and Dick's father, Canon Tiltwood, proud and burly, pacing the platform beside his slender son and wearing cheeriness like a light unclerical overcoat, which couldn't conceal the gravity of a heart heavy as lead. What did they say to one another, he and Aunt Evelyn, when the train had snorted away and left an empty space in front of them? (244)

Sherston shows here the first inkling of sensitivity since his pre-fox-hunting days as the war, and the growing knowledge of his potential extinction, jolts his dormant sympathies for life and his loved ones.

Having the good fortune to be quartered behind the line on arrival allows Sherston to experience the brutality of the war in small doses, and his appointment as a transport officer keeps him away from the trenches for long periods. To escape the unpleasantries, he falls back into reminiscences of past fox-hunting days. When he learns that his old groom, Dixon, is nearby, he pulls a few strings to get him assigned to his battalion as transport sergeant. Having "him near me," he says, "would make all the difference" (265). The news of Dixon's unexpected death from pneumonia, however, destroys all thoughts of recovering the past, a feeling that is confirmed on an unexpected leave to England.

In Butley, Sherston feels out of place and edgy. He even avoids visiting Stephen Colwood's father at the rectory because his note suggesting that "obedience and self-sacrifice for right and truth in spite of suffering and death is Christianity" (269) no longer rings true to him. Realizing that "his past was wearing a bit thin," George feels an almost romantic desire to get back to France in order to serve some kind of worthwhile purpose. But if the past world offers little respite, the future offers even less. On the evening that Sherston returns to the trenches, Dick is killed while out on a wiring patrol. And that night, as Dick is buried, Sherston is initiated into the grim reality of war: "A sack was lowered into a hole in the ground. The sack was Dick. I knew Death then" (274).

Sherston's sudden awareness of death effectively obliterates any hopes of recapturing the pleasant memories of Butley; the conversion from fox-hunter to Boche-hunter is complete. Sherston, with revenge in his heart, dedicates himself to "getting a bit of [his] own back" (275). The next two volumes aptly demonstrate that this attitude is as empty as that of the fox-hunting man, but at this point, on Easter Sunday of 1916, as Sherston waits for the sun to rise over the ruined villages and leafless trees, his mind can only drift back to the recent visit home and the loss of his friends. He realizes on this Easter Sunday that no resurrection awaits his friends killed in the war, and that the sweet memories of Butley no longer offer a safe haven for escape. His past life is over; the future lies "somewhere out of sight beyond the splintered tree-tops of Hidden Wood" (282).

Sassoon, then, had taken himself back to the moment in his life when the past had been obliterated, when he stood facing an uncertain future as an infantry officer. Through the writing of this fictional memoir, he had continued the inward delvings begun in *The Heart's Journey;* furthermore, the recognition of his dual-faceted personality—the introverted lover of nature in conflict with the unthinking, extroverted fox-hunter—offered a wealth of material for the next two volumes of fictional memoirs and three volumes of autobiography. Indeed, the next seventeen years of Sassoon's life were to be spent repeatedly refining these same memoirs. The resultant journey inward was to become just as real an exile from the violent memories of war and the distasteful future of commercialism as Graves's escape to Majorca. The poet's decision to scrutinize his "impercipient past" (*Siegfried's Journey,* 224) allowed him the luxury of recollecting his younger self "with all the rich emptiness of immaturity [and with] all [its] gaps and impetuosities [and] intolerance [and] omniscient misapprehensions" (Sassoon to Tomlinson, 17 November 1941). For Sassoon then, this examination of his past became a "recreation" that filled the middle years of his life, offered him a successful method of giving "the modern world the slip" (*Old Century,* 140), and initiated an understanding of his physical and spiritual self.

The final result of this introspection appeared exactly thirty years later in Sassoon's *Lenten Illuminations,* in which the newly received member of the Roman Catholic faith met his "unilluminated self" with its "outcast and unprotected contours of the soul." By this time, too, the poet had finally achieved a sense of inner harmony and peace in what he predictably called "a child-minded calm." But admittedly, the road to this peace had been long and taxing:

> There had been many byways for the frustrate brain,
> All leading to illusions lost and shrines forsaken . . .

Now, though, the path was clear; the mist had blown away over Hidden Wood and victory was in sight:

> One road before us now—one guidance for our gain—
> One morning light—whatever the world's weather—
>   wherein
>   wide-eyed to waken.

The heart's journey of Siegfried Sassoon had finally ended in "that all-answering Heart" of Christ.

13

Graves and Sassoon:
From Poetry to Prose

In retrospect, one could say that the decision for both Graves and Sassoon to move from poetic expression to prose memoirs in the late 1920s was only to be expected. By then, each writer had realized that his poetry was no longer a medium capable of communicating what he wished to articulate, and the relative obscurity of both writers' postwar verse, compared to the commercial and literary success of their prose writings, stands as a clear testimonial to the foresight of these decisions. And yet, as I have attempted to demonstrate, some of their poetry written during the 1920s deserves greater recognition than it has hitherto received. As it happened, most of their poetic work in the latter part of the decade was to be eclipsed by the appearance in the early 1930s of innovative poetry by Auden, Day-Lewis, and Spender. With the appearance of *New Signatures* in 1932, much critical attention shifted to the political and social concerns aired in that anthology, while Sassoon, interred in Wiltshire with his introverted reflections, and Graves, writing eclectic poems in self-imposed exile in Majorca, were left behind in a backwash of poetic obscurity.

Sassoon never again achieved the poetic success of his war poems. The essential movement in his poetry through the 1920s was away from the concerns of war and its political aftermath—a gradual disengagement that is monitored first by the bitter invective of *Counter-Attack* and the sardonic, satirical visions of *Picture Show,* and then by the wry and lightly ironic societal criticisms of postwar society in *Satirical Poems.* But by 1925, Sassoon had become weary of the satire that had dominated his poetry since the experience of the war, and his vituperative political poetry had given way largely to an occasional potshot at the failure of promised social reforms; the emotional emphasis of his writing had moved from a passionate, antiwar stance to a mordant observation of the twenties' social scene.

By the time he came to write *The Heart's Journey,* his gradual disengagement from the concerns of postwar society had placed him snugly back in the "solitary minded" contemplative world of art which, as de Sola Pinto points out, was "the region in which he [was] most entirely himself" (1951, 222). His deeper poetic responses drifted towards the introspective themes that he nurtured before the Great War: the appreciation of music, the celebration of nature, and the joy of solitary meditation. In fact, Sassoon defended his return to traditional Georgian subject matter in the age of Eliot and Pound some years later in a lecture at Bristol University, when he called for a return to the "language of the heart" as opposed to logical dehumanization. He praised directness and simplicity as opposed to Modernist complex obliquity, and expressed a Wordsworthian belief in the function of poetry to convey emotion. Thorpe sums up the essence of Sassoon's lecture as follows:

> *On Poetry* is a personal defence of the Wordsworthian tradition of "simplicity." It is a plea for the primacy of a poetry which will arouse "immediate pleasure" in dealing with the undying themes of love, friendship, mortality and all that can "touch the heart." Concomitant with these themes should be the passionate observation of natural scenes and objects. Nature is *the* source of imagery since it is with what Wordsworth calls "the beautiful and permanent forms of nature" that man has his most vital relationship outside those of the human world. (Thorpe 1966, 182)

But Sassoon's vision of what "made" poetry and gave it a place in the modern world was personal and subjective in the extreme. His rejection of the political writings of the 1930s, his suspicion of the complex ambiguity of imagery, his dislike of verbal audacity, and his distrust of intellectual pretensions were all elements that would place his poetry out of fashion. His poetry seemed old-fashioned in a world where younger poets were using the latest scientific and psychological advances afforded by the contemporary world to discover poignant new images and, in some cases, to support the call for a new social order. Modernist experimentations with new verse forms, such as Auden's jazz lyrics in two-four time or Eliot's explorations in free verse made Sassoon's return to the traditional sonnet and lyric forms with their conservative rhyme schemes appear anachronic.

In *On Poetry,* Sassoon firmly rejected modern didactic poetry as local and transient; but instead of pursuing this rejection by voicing it in his own poetry, he retreated even further into his unique style and subject matter. The poetic fabric of *The Heart's Journey,* which, after all, was a comparatively short volume of lyrics, forced Sassoon to reevaluate the fundamental essentials of his own existence: to reaffirm what elements gave his life special poignancy and meaning. And when the discoveries that his inner explorations had yielded became too intense and sprawling to be distilled into verse form, he turned to the fictional memoir, which gave him greater scope to reexamine the past. It allowed him dreamy reminiscences of the pleasures of his sporting youth, spent in the prelapsarian days of Edwardian privilege, with its "summer evenings after cricket-matches, and sunset above the tall trees, and village streets in the dusk, and the clatter of a brake driving home" (*Diaries 1915–1918,* 94).

For what is *Memoirs of a Fox-Hunting Man* but, like *The Old Century and Seven Years More* (written a decade later), an evocation of the hearty fox-hunting life and parochial values of the privileged classes before the war? While Sassoon admits in several letters to Blunden that he knew this retrospective approach was indulgent and romanticized, the prose form nevertheless offered him the scope to examine his past and purge the memories of the war with greater precision and coherence than he was ever able to achieve in his poetry.

After the war, Graves's poetry, like Sassoon's, passed through many different stages. He labored unsuccessfully with nursery rhymes, folk songs, lullabies, and nonsense verse: the typical Georgian formulas which filled blithe pages with simplicity and charm. The difficulty for him after his rejection of the Georgian mode was to find a form in which to express his experiences of the war and the psychological manifestations that lingered through the 1920s.

The resulting poetry was uneven and experimental. Graves examined the aberrations of an abnormal mind in the complex imagery and blank verse of "Pier Glass" or in the very simple meter and rhyme scheme of "Haunted House." He moved with apparent ease from a study of psychological states to a philosophic phase in which his poetry became so abstract that a poem like "In Broken Images" became little more than an argument "elaborated for the sake of a pattern of opposites that meet and mount like the vertical and horizontal surfaces of a staircase" (Hayman 1955, 32). At this juncture, Graves seemed more interested in the pattern of his work than in its content, and by 1926 the promising war poet's new verse was largely unread.

The *Poems: 1914–1926* collection reveals, amid a number of arresting and innovative poems, a sense of directionlessness. Strangely, perhaps, Graves did not seem to find much to praise or emulate in his contemporaries (see "The Marmosite's Miscellany" and *Contemporary Techniques of Poetry*), and clearly he drew little solace from reflection of the past or the transcendental nature of experience as in Sassoon's "A Midnight Interior." Instead, Graves chose what might be called an austerely intellectual approach to poetry and reduced his material to what he calls in his *Survey of Modernist Poetry* the "hard, matter of fact skeleton of poetic logic" (35). This rejection of traditional and metaphysical answers to complex poetic and philosophical inquiries left Graves wide open to the influence of the self-confident Laura Riding. Under the strict tutelage of Riding, Graves's poetry passed under the scrutiny of a skilled surgeon: his experimentation with ballads and nonsense verse was purged; the sentimental love poetry and verses of amatory escape were sobered; the relativistic notions were tightened and toughened. The resultant poetry, which appeared in *Poems: 1926–1930*, introduced a new severity in his poetic voice as well as a shrewdly penetrating insight into the blind, foolish, and corrupt nature of mankind. Riding's ability to take him outside "his kind" and to make him "invisible" (to overcome his past) culminated in his rather elitist attitude and virulent attacks on friends; it led Graves to break completely with English society.

By the time Graves and Riding left for Majorca, his poetic reputation was in eclipse and his poetry was largely ignored. His personal purging of earlier works at this time (for Graves was an acute critic even of his own writings) clearly demonstrated that he had said good-bye not only to English society, but also to the kind of poetry he had been writing before Riding's appearance. Henceforth, his poetry would concern itself with capturing in verse only those essentials of truth which lay shrouded in the deceptiveness of language ("Hell," "In Broken Images"), love ("Pure Death"), superficial cleverness ("Warning to Children," "Tow Path"), and religion ("Lift-Boy"). The early poems of his apprenticeship with Riding were almost all analytical explorations of the foolishness of modern conceptions of life, and show their writer to be not only detached from, but also frustrated with, its idiocy.

For Graves, then, the apprehension of immediate experience without the buffers of the deceptive language of social convention, without the masks of English prejudices and upper-class conventions, became a hallmark of his poetry during this period. To clear his mind of its former emotional and social commitments required a complete break with the past and a promise of a fuller and more honest existence in the future; life with Laura Riding offered such an opportunity.

The contempt that Graves held for the old worldview is clearly manifested in his poetry of the late 1920s. But Graves realized that the lyric form was not the most expedient method by which to exorcise once and for all his memories of the war or to vent the feelings of acrimony accumulated during the period between the final disintegration of his marriage and Riding's recovery from her failed suicide attempt. Realistically, he was also aware that money would be needed in order to settle Nancy and their children in England and for his own move abroad with Riding. The prose form could reach a much larger audience than his poetry and therefore would prove more profitable (see "Postscript to *Good-bye To All That*" in *But It Still Goes On,* 13). After three feverish months of writing his autobiography, Graves departed into the self-imposed exile in Majorca which would last for nearly ten years and out of which he was to emerge a more experienced, wiser poet and lover.

By the late 1920s, both Graves and Sassoon had deviated from the contemporary direction of Modernist poetry and decided to write prose memoirs examining their past, both for the purpose of extirpating war memories and to reflect on how they had developed into what they had become. It proved to be an enlightened choice for both writers. The Sherston memoirs and Graves's *Good-bye* have achieved the status of virtual classics in the sixty-five or so years since their publication, whereas their poetry of the years after the war has languished in forgotten volumes. The timeliness of publication and quality of the prose works guaranteed a much wider and more sympathetic readership than their postwar poetry and secured both writers a position in the history of English literature.

Appendix

The following is a transcription of the verse letter sent to Graves by Sassoon on 24 July 1918, while Sassoon was recuperating from a head wound at the American Red Cross Hospital in Lancaster Gate in London:

I'd timed my death in action to the minute—
(*The Nation* wish my deathly verses in it)—
The day told off –13– (the month July)—
The picture planned—O Threshold of the dark!
And then, the quivering songster failed to die
Because the bloody Bullet missed its mark.

Viva I am: They would send me back
Kind M.O. at Base; Sassoon's morale grown slack;
Swallowed all his proud high thoughts and acquiesced . . .
O Gate of Lancaster, O Blightyland the Blessed . . .

No visitors allowed
Since Friends arrived in crowd. . . .
Jabber–Gesture Jabber–Gesture—Nerves went fut and
    failed
After the first afternoon when
MarshMoonStreetMeiklejohnArdoursand
enduranSitwellitis prevailed,
Caused complications and set my brain a-hop:
SleeplesssexasperuicideO Jesu make it stop.

But yesterday afternoon my reasoning Rivers ran
solemnly in   Wish peace in the pools of his
spectacled eyes and a wisely omnipotent grin;
And I fished in that steady grey stream and
Decided that I After all am no longer

The Worm that refuses to die. But,
    A gallant and glorious lyrical soldier;
    Bolder and bolder; as he gets older;
    Shouting Back to the Front
    For a scrimmaging Stunt. . . .
    (I wish the weather wouldn't keep on getting
      colder.)

Yes, you can touch my Banker when you need him;
Why keep a Jewish friend unless you bleed him.

O yes, he's doing very well and sleeps from Two till
    Four.
And there was Jolly Otterleen a-knocking at the Door—
But Matron says she mustn't, not however loud she
    knocks,
(Though she's bags of golden Daisies and some
    Raspberries
    in a Box,)
Be admitted to the wonderful and wild and wobbly-witted
Sarcastic soldier poet with a Plaster on his crown
Who pretends he doesn't know it—(he's the Topic of the
    Town)

My god my god I'm so excited; I've just had a letter
From Stable whose commanding the 25th Battalion
And my company he tells me, doing better and better,
Pinched six Saxons after lunch and bagged
Machine guns by the bunch—
But I . . . wasn't there . . .
O blast, it isn't fair . . .
Because they'll all wonder why
Dotty Captain wasn't standing by
When they came marching home.

But I don't care; I made them love me although
They didn't want to do it, and I've sent them a
Glorious Gramophone and god send you back to me
Over the green eviscerating sea—And I'm
Ill and afraid to go back to them because those
Five-niners are so damned awful
When you think of them all bursting and you're

Lying on your bed with the books you loved and
Longed for on the table; and your head all
Crammed with village verses about Daffodils and
Geese . . . O Jesu make it cease—

O Rivers please take me and make me
Go back to the war till it break me.
Someday my brain will go BANG
And they'll say what faces wer'
The soldier-lads he sang!

Does this break your heart . . . What do I care?

Works Cited

Works of Robert Graves

POETRY

Collected Poems. London: Cassell, 1938.
Collected Poems. London: Cassell, 1975.
Collected Poems: 1914–1947. London: Cassell, 1948.
Country Sentiment. London: Secker, 1920.
Fairies and Fusiliers. London: Heinemann, 1917.
The Feather Bed. Richmond: The Hogarth Press, 1925.
Goliath and David. London: The Chiswick Press, 1916.
The Marmosite's Miscellany. London: The Hogarth Press, 1925.
Mock Beggar Hall. London: The Hogarth Press, 1924.
Over the Brazier. London: The Poetry Bookshop, 1916.
The Pier Glass. London: Secker, 1921.
Poems: 1914–1926. London: Heinemann, 1927.
Poems: 1914–1927. London: Heinemann, 1927.
Poems 1929. London: The Seizin Press, 1929.
Poems: 1926–1930. London: Heinemann, 1931.
Poems: 1930–1933. London: Barker, 1933.
Ten Poems More. Paris: Hours Press, 1930.
Treasure Box. London: The Chiswick Press, 1919.
Welchman's Hose. London: The Fleuron, 1925.
Whipperginny. London: Heinemann, 1923.

PROSE WORKS

Another Future of Poetry. London: The Hogarth Press, 1926.
But It Still Goes On: An Accumulation. London: Cape, 1930.

The Common Asphodel: Collected Essays on Poetry, 1922–1949. London: Hamish Hamilton, 1949.

Contemporary Techniques of Poetry. London: The Hogarth Press, 1925.

The Crane Bag. London: Cassell, 1969.

The Crowning Privilege: The Clark Lectures, 1954–1955. London: Cassell, 1955.

Difficult Questions, Easy Answers. London: Cassell, 1972.

The English Ballad. London: Benn, 1927.

Five Pens in Hand. New York: Doubleday, 1960.

Food for Centaurs. New York: Doubleday, 1960.

Good-bye To All That: An Autobiography. London: Cape, 1929.

Good-bye To All That: An Autobiography. Harmondsworth: Penguin, 1960.

Lars Porsena; or, The Future of Swearing. London: Kegan Paul, 1927.

Mammon and the Black Goddess. London: Cassell, 1965.

The Meaning of Dreams. London: Cecil Palmer, 1922.

Mrs. Fisher; or, The Future of Humour. London: Kegan Paul, 1927.

My Head! My Head! London: Secker, 1925.

Occupation: Writer. London: Cassell, 1951.

On English Poetry: Being an Irregular Approach to the Psychology of this Art, from Evidence Mainly Subjective. London: Heinemann, 1922.

Oxford Address on Poetry. London: Cassell, 1961.

Poetic Craft and Principle. London: Cassell, 1967.

The Poetic Unreason and Other Studies. London: Cecil Palmer, 1925.

Review of *Memoirs of an Infantry Officer,* by Siegfried Sassoon. *The Clarion* 2 (1930): 287.

Steps: Stories, Talks, Essays, Poems, Studies in History. London: Cassell, 1958.

The White Goddess. London: Faber and Faber, 1948.

COLLABORATIVE AUTHORSHIP

Graves, Robert, and Alan Hodge. *The Long Week-End: A Social History of Great Britain, 1918–1939.* London: Faber and Faber, 1940.

Graves, Robert, and Laura Riding. *A Pamphlet Against Anthologies.* London: Cape, 1928.

Graves, Robert, and Laura Riding. *A Survey of Modernist Poetry.* London: Heinemann, 1928.

UNPUBLISHED LETTERS FROM ROBERT GRAVES

Letters to Gertrude Stein. Beinecke Rare Book and Manuscript Library, Yale University, New Haven, Connecticut.

Letters to Herbert E. Palmer (39 letters). Harry Ransom Humanities Research Center, University of Texas, Austin, Texas.

Letters to L. A. G. Strong (23 letters). Harry Ransom Humanities Research Center, University of Texas, Austin, Texas.

Letters to (and from) Laura Riding. Beinecke Rare Book and Manuscript Library, Yale University, New Haven, Connecticut.

SECONDARY SOURCES ABOUT ROBERT GRAVES

Auden, Wystan Hugh. 1962. "A Poet of Honor." *Shenandoah* 13.2:5–12.

Blackburn, Thomas. 1961. *The Price of an Eye.* London: Longman.

Bullough, Geoffrey. 1959. *The Trend of Modern Poetry.* London: Oliver and Boyd.

Burns, Albert W. 1969. *Robert Graves and Laura Riding: A Literary Partnership.* Diss., Boston University. (Ann Arbor: UMI 1986, 6918742.)

Canary, Robert H. 1980. *Robert Graves.* Twayne English Authors Series 279. Boston: Twayne Publishers.

Carter, D. N. G. *Robert Graves: The Lasting Achievement.* 1989. Totowa, N.J.: Barnes and Noble.

Cohen, J. M. 1949. *Robert Graves.* Writers and Critics Series 3. Edinburgh: Oliver and Boyd.

Creely, Robert. 1959. "Her Service is Perfect Freedom." *Poetry* 43:395–98.

Davie, Donald. 1962. "Impersonal and Emblematic." *Shenandoah* 13.2:38–44.

———. 1959. "The Toneless Voice of Robert Graves. *The Listener* (2 July): 11–13.

Day, Douglas. 1963. "Swifter Than Reason: The Poetry and Criticism of Robert Graves." Chapel Hill: University of North Carolina Press.

De Bell, Diane. 1976. "Strategies of Survival: David Jones, *In Parenthesis,* and Robert Graves, *Good-bye To All That.*" In *The First World War in Fiction,* edited by Holger Klein. London: Macmillan.

Enright, D. J. 1961. "Robert Graves and the Decline of Modernism." *Essays in Criticism* 11:319–37.

Forster, J. P. 1979. "The Gravesian Poem or Language Ill-Treated." *English Studies* 60:471–83.

Frank, Frederick. 1976. "The Cool Web of Memory: An Iniatory Reading of Robert Graves's *Good-bye To All That.*" *Focus on Robert Graves* 5:74–85.

Fraser, George Sutherland. 1962. "The Reputation of Robert Graves." *Shenandoah* 13.2:56–59.

———. 1959. *Vision and Rhetoric: Studies in Modern Poetry.* London: Faber and Faber.

Fuller, Roy. 1958. "Some Vintages of Graves." *London Magazine* (February):56–59.

Garnett, David, ed. 1939. *The Letters of T. E. Lawrence.* New York: Doubleday, Doran, and Co.

Gaskell, Robert. 1961. "The Poetry of Robert Graves." *Critical Quarterly* 3:213–22.

Graalman, Robert. 1977. "One Story Only: Robert Graves and the Poetry of Transfiguration." Diss., University of Tulsa.

Graves, Richard Perceval. Letter to the author, 15 January 1987.

———. Letter to the author, 11 August 1987.

———. 1986. *Robert Graves: The Assault Heroic 1895–1926*. London: Weidenfeld and Nicholson.

———. 1990. *Robert Graves: The Years with Laura, 1926–1940*.

Haller, John. 1957. "Conversations with Robert Graves." *Southwest Review* 42:237–41.

Hayman, Ronald. 1955. "Robert Graves." *Essays in Criticism* 5:32–43.

Higginson, Fred H. 1966. *A Bibliography of the Works of Robert Graves*. London: Nicholas Vane.

Hoffman, Daniel. 1967. *Barbarous Knowledge: Myth in the Poetry of Yeats, Graves, and Muir*. New York: Oxford University Press.

———. 1960. "Significant Wounds: The Early Poetry of Robert Graves." *Shenandoah* 17.2:21–40.

Hoffpauir, Richard. 1988. "The Love Poetry of Robert Graves." *University of Toronto Quarterly* 57:422–38.

Kirkham, Michael. 1969. *The Poetry of Robert Graves*. London: Athlone Press.

———. 1973. "Robert Graves's Debt to Laura Riding." *Focus on Robert Graves* 3:33–44.

Kohli, Devindra. 1975. "Dream Drums: Child as Image of Conflict and Liberation." *Malahat Review* 35 (July):75–100.

McKinley, James. 1974. "Subject: Robert Graves: Random Notes of a Biographer." *New Letters* 40.4:37–60.

Mason, Ellsworth. Letter to the author, 16 September 1987.

Matthews, T. S. 1977. *Under the Influence: Recollections of Robert Graves, Laura Riding, and Friends*. London: Cassell.

Mehoke, James. 1975. *Robert Graves: Peace Weaver*. The Hague: Mouton.

Moran, James. 1963. "The Seizen Press of Laura Riding and Robert Graves." *The Black Art* 2:34–39.

Muir, Edwin. 1926. *Transition: Essays on Contemporary Literature*. New York: Folcroft.

Musgrove, Sydney. 1962. *The Ancestry of the White Goddess*. Bulletin 62. Auckland: University of Auckland.

O'Connor, Frank. 1968. *My Father's Son*. London: Macmillan.

O'Prey, Paul, ed. 1984. *Between Moon and Moon: Selected Letters of Robert Graves, 1946–1972*. London: Hutchinson.

———, ed. 1982. *In Broken Images: Selected Letters of Robert Graves, 1914–1946*. London: Hutchinson.

Pettet, E. C. 1941. "The Poetry of Robert Graves." *English* 3:216–20.

Plimpton, George. 1977. *Writers at Work*. The *Paris Review* interviews 4. London: Secker and Warburg.

Richman, Robert. 1988. "The Poetry of Robert Graves." *The New Criterion* 7:66–73.

Rivers, W. H. R. 1923. *Conflict and Dream.* Edited by G. Elliot Smith. London: Kegan, Paul, Trench, Trubner, and Co.

———. 1920. *Instinct and the Unconscious: A Contribution to a Biological Theory of the Psycho-neurosis.* Cambridge: The University Press.

Seymour-Smith, Martin. 1956. *Robert Graves.* Writers and Their Work 78. London: British Council.

———. 1982. *Robert Graves: His Life and Works.* London: Hutchinson.

Simon, Myron. 1974. "The Georgian Infancy of Robert Graves." *Focus on Robert Graves* 4:49–70.

Snipes, Katherine. 1979. *Robert Graves.* New York: Frederick Ungar.

Spender, Stephen. 1946. "Poetry for Poetry's Sake and Beyond Poetry." *Horizon* 76:221–38.

Stade, George. 1967. *Robert Graves.* Columbia Essays on Modern Writers 25. New York: Columbia University Press.

———. 1965. "Robert Graves on Poetry, 1916–1929." Diss., Columbia University. (Ann Arbor: UMI, 1986, 6512368.)

Steiner, George. 1960. "The Genius of Robert Graves." *Kenyon Review* 22:340–65.

Thomas, William David. 1975. "The Impact of World War I on the Early Poetry of Robert Graves." *Mahalat Review* 35 (July):113–29.

Thwaite, Anthony. 1961. *Contemporary English Poetry.* London: Heinemann.

Underhill, Hugh. 1983. "From a Georgian Poetic to the 'Romantic Primitivism' of D. H. Lawrence and Robert Graves." *Studies in Romanticism* 22:517–50.

Weinzinger, Anita. 1982. *Graves as a Critic.* Salzburg: Institut für Anglistik u. Amerikanistik, Salzburg Universität.

Wexler, Joyce P. 1979. *Laura Riding's Pursuit of Truth.* Athens: Ohio University Press.

Williams, Charles. 1930. *Poetry at Present.* Oxford: Clarendon.

Works of Siegfried Sassoon

POETRY

Collected Poems. London: Faber and Faber, 1947.

The Heart's Journey. London: Heinemann, 1928.

Rhymed Ruminations. London: Faber and Faber, 1940.

The Road to Ruin. London: Faber and Faber, 1933.

Satirical Poems. London: Heinemann, 1926.

Selected Poems. London: Faber and Faber, 1968.

The War Poems of Siegfried Sassoon. London: Heinemann, 1919.

PROSE WORKS

The Complete Memoirs of George Sherston. London: World Books, 1940.

Counter-Attack and Other Poems. London: Heinemann, 1918.

Diaries 1915–1918. Edited by Ruperbt Hart-Davis. London: Faber and Faber, 1983.

Diaries 1920–1922. Edited by Rupbert Hart-Davis. London: Faber and Faber, 1981.

Diaries 1923–1925. Edited by Rupert Hart-Davis. London: Faber and Faber, 1985.

Memoirs of a Fox-Hunting Man. London: Heinemann, 1928.

Memoirs of an Infantry Officer. London: Heinemann, 1930.

The Old Century and Seven More Years. London: Faber and Faber, 1938.

Picture Show. London: Heinemann, 1919.

Sherston's Progress. London: Heinemann, 1936.

Siegfried's Journey. London: Heinemann, 1945 .

The Weald of Youth. London: Faber and Faber, 1942.

SECONDARY SOURCES ABOUT SIEGFRIED SASSOON

Blunden, Edmund. 1950. *Edmund Blunden: A Selection of His Poetry and Prose*. London: Hart-Davis.

Cohen, Joseph. 1957. "The Three Roles of Siegfried Sassoon." *Tulane Studies in English* 7:169–85.

Corrigan, Felicitas. 1973. *Siegfried Sassoon: Poet's Pilgrimage*. London: Gollancz.

Farmer, David. 1969. *Siegfried Sassoon: A Memorial Exhibition Catalogue*. Harry Ransom Humanities Research Center. Austin: University of Texas.

Fussell, Paul, ed. 1983. *Sassoon's Long Journey*. London: Faber and Faber.

Keynes, Geoffrey. 1962. *A Bibliography of Siegfried Sassoon*. London: Hart-Davis.

Lane, Arthur E. 1972. *An Adequate Response: The War Poetry of Wilfred Owen and Siegfried Sassoon*. Detroit: Wayne State University Press.

Mallon, Thomas. 1983. "The Great War and Sassoon's Memory." In *Modernism Reconsidered*, ed. Robert Kiely. Cambridge: Harvard University Press.

Martin, W. R. 1979. "Bugles, Trumpets, and Drums: English Poetry and the Wars." *Mosaic* 13.1:31–48.

Moore, L. Hugh, Jr. 1969. "Siegfried Sassoon and Georgian Realism." *Twentieth Century Literature* 14:199–209.

Morrell, Lady Ottoline. 1975. *Ottoline at Garsington: Memoirs of Lady Ottoline Morrell, 1915–1918*. Edited by Robert Gathorne-Hardy. New York: Knopf.

Pinto, Vivian de Sola. 1951. *Crisis in English Poetry*. London: Hutchinson.

———. 1939. "Siegfried Sassoon." *English* 2.10:215–24.

Silk, Dennis. 1975. *Siegfried Sassoon: Guinness Lecture at the Salisbury Festival of Arts, July 1974*. London: Compton Russell.

Silkin, Jon. 1972. *Out of Battle: The Poetry of the Great War.* London: Oxford University Press.

Stewart, James Floyd. 1972. "A Descriptive Account of Unpublished Letters of Siegfried Sassoon in the University of Texas Collection." Diss., University of Texas at Austin. (Ann Arbor: UMI, 1986, 737649.)

Swinnerton, Frank. 1935. *The Georgian Literary Scene.* London: Hutchinson.

Thorpe, Michael. Letter to the author, 10 March 1986.

———. 1966. *Siegfried Sassoon: A Critical Study.* Leiden: Universitaire Pers.

———, ed. 1976. *Siegfried Sassoon: Letters to a Critic.* London: John Roberts Press.

UNPUBLISHED LETTERS OF SIEGFRIED SASSOON

Letters to Edmund Blunden from 1926 to 1966 (164 letters). The Harry Ransom Humanities Research Center, University of Texas, Austin, Texas.

Letters from Sir Sydney Carlyle Cockerell from 1922 to 1955 (85 letters). The Harry Ransom Humanities Research Center, University of Texas, Austin, Texas.

Letters to Robert Graves from 1917 to 1926 (125 letters). Citation collections, Morris Library, Southern Illinois University, Carbondale, Illinois.

Letters to Sir Henry Head from 1921 to 1938 (115 letters). The Harry Ransom Humanities Research Center, University of Texas, Austin, Texas.

Letters to Roderick Meiklejohn from 1916 to 1950 (79 letters). The Harry Ransom Humanities Research Center, University of Texas, Austin, Texas.

Letters to Lady Ottoline Morrell from 1916 to 1936 (275 letters). The Harry Ransom Humanities Research Center, University of Texas, Austin, Texas.

Letters to Dame Edith Sitwell from 1921 to 1957 (104 letters). Washington State University Libraries, Pullman, Washington.

Letters to H. M. Tomlinson from 1926 to 1958 (137 letters). The Harry Ransom Humanities Research Center, University of Texas, Austin, Texas.

GENERAL REFERENCE WORKS ON THE WRITERS AND THE PERIOD

Bergonzi, Bernard. 1980. *Heroes' Twilight: A Study of the Literatur of the Great War.* 2d ed. London: Macmillan Press.

Buckley, Jerome Hamilton. 1984. *The Turning Key: Autobiography and the Subjective Impulse Since 1800.* London: Harvard University Press.

Cockshut, A. O. J. 1984. *The Art of Autobiography in 19th and 20th Century England.* New Haven: Yale University Press.

Crawford, Fred D. 1988. *British Poets of the Great War.* Selingsgrove, Pa.: Susquehanna University Press.

Fairchild, H. N. 1962. *Religious Trends in English Poetry (1880–1920).* Vol. 5. New York: Columbia University Press.

Ford, D. H. Letter to the author, 10 June 1992.

Fussell, Paul. 1975. *The Great War and Modern Memory.* London: Oxford University Press.

Green, Martin. 1980. *Children of the Sun: A Narrative of "Decadence" in England after 1918.* New York: Wideview Books.

Hassall, Christopher V. 1949. *Edward Marsh.* New York: Harcourt.

Hildebidle, John. 1983. "Neither Worthy Nor Capable: The War Memories of Graves, Blunden, and Sassoon." In *Modernism Reconsidered,* ed. R. Kiely. Cambridge: Harvard University Press.

Johnston, John H. 1964. *English Poetry of the First World War.* Princeton: Princeton University Press.

Liddell Hart, Basil. 1972. *History of the First World War.* London: Pan Books.

Parsons, I. M., ed. 1978. *Men Who March Away: Poems of the First World War.* London: Chatto and Windus.

Pascal, Roy. 1960. *Design and Truth in Autobiography.* London: Routledge and Kegan Paul.

Perkins, David. 1976. *A History of Modern Poetry: From the 1890s to Pound, Eliot, and Yeats.* Cambridge, Mass.: Belknap Press.

Pilling, John. 1981. *Autobiography and Imagination: Studies in Self-Scrutiny.* London: routledge and Kegan Paul.

Ross, Robert H. 1967. *The Georgian Revolt: Rise and Fal of a Poetical Ideal, 1910–1922.* London: Faber and Faber.

Silkin, Jon, ed. 1986. *The Penguin Book of First World War Poetry.* 2d ed. Harmondsworth: Penguin.

Sossaman, S. 1976. "Sassoon and Blunden's Annotation of *Good-bye To All That.*" *Focus on Robert Graves* 5:87–89.

Spender, Stephen. 1955. *The Making of a Poem.* London: Hamish Hamilton.

Taylor, A. J. P. 1982. *The First World War.* Harmondsworth: Penguin.

Thomson, David. 1983. *England in the Twentieth Century: 1914–79.* 2d ed. Harmondsworth: Penguin.

Webb, Barry. 1990. *Edmund Blunden: A Biography.* New Haven: Yale University Press.

Wohl, Robert. 1979. *The Generation of 1914.* Cambridge: Harvard University Press.

Index